Restaurant
Management
Guide

Restaurant

Management
Guide

Robert T. Gordon

Institute for Business Planning
ENGLEWOOD CLIFFS, N. J. 07632

© Copyright 1985
Institute for Business Planning, Inc.
Englewood Cliffs, N.J. 07632

Third Printing, 1985

Library of Congress Cataloging in Publication Data

Gordon, Robert T.
  Restaurant management guide.

  Includes index.
  1. Restaurant management—Handbooks, manuals, etc.
I. Title.
TX911.3.M27G667 1984   647'.95'068   84-19814
ISBN 0-87624-511-4

WHAT THIS GUIDE WILL DO FOR YOU

The goal of this Guide is to furnish you with virtually all the information you will ever need to be outstandingly and increasingly successful in this competitive and exciting industry. The Guide is written for the practical operator in easy-to-understand language. Used properly, it will give you the edge on your competition and bring you the growing satisfaction and financial return that your efforts deserve.

This is a fast-reading Guide, crammed full of effective practices and techniques. It is a storehouse of practical information and proven tips gathered over 35 years of association with highly successful restaurants large and small, their owners and managers. These tips, which have been used so successfully by others, are accompanied by charts and checklists for easy use and implementation. For the seasoned manager, it is a complete review of the steps that must be followed if a business is to realize its full potential. For the newcomer, it is a virtual road map to success. For anyone, its practical advice can be sought and put to instant use whenever a problem arises in any area of restaurant operation.

This Guide will take you step by step through the process of increasing your sales and controlling costs. In these times of changing economic conditions, it is imperative that you prepare adequately for the future, whether that future is tomorrow or five years away. The Guide will show you how to develop an effective organization, and will also furnish you with information and checklists to help you in managing your own time.

The keystone of more profitable restaurant operations is the menu. In this Guide, you will find hundreds of tips that others have used in the development of menus that sell. There are samples of special promotion menus, with charts and concise instructions to tell you how to price for profit. The Guide points up the changes that occur around us, how they can affect your business, how you can stay informed, and how to deal with change before it occurs.

This Guide sets down the right techniques needed to control

food production with accompanying charts, checklists and sample records that are absolutely necessary to the control of costs. You will find checklists and tips for avoiding production problems caused by inadequate equipment and excessive preparation time and service. You will also see easy-to-adapt examples of how others have greatly increased sales and profits by employing the techniques that are outlined and explained in this Guide.

Buying skill is crucial if the restaurant is to earn top money for you. This Guide will show you how you can *make* hundreds of dollars with sound purchasing policies, and how to make sure that you don't *lose* hundreds of dollars with poor storage and handling practices. There are thousands and thousands of dollars wasted in the storerooms, kitchens and refrigerators of restaurants. Using this Guide will help you to prevent, in your restaurant, the waste and losses that are so prevalent in many others.

There is much talk about how hard it is to find good help these days. This Guide furnishes proven tips and techniques that will enhance and improve your entire labor situation. For example:

- Tips on recruiting and selection of quality employees

- Increasing sales and profits through better training of people

- How to measure performance and establish reachable goals

- How to communicate with your employees, and how this will increase your profits

- How to develop fringe benefit packages that your restaurant can afford, and that pay off for you personally

- How to protect yourself in the face of changing laws and regulations that affect your business

- How unions can affect your business, and how best to deal with them when it's necessary

This Guide deals at length with cocktail lounge operations and the merchandising and sale of wine. There are loads of proven money-saving ideas on:

- Purchasing and receiving

- Pricing of liquors and wines

- Cash and inventory controls

- Control of sales and securing of profits

The Guide discusses the kind of accounting you need for adequate control of your money—how to forecast sales and expenses accurately—how to select your accountant, and how to communicate with him for best results after he has been selected—how to analyze your labor requirements and then relate them to a work schedule that will do the job you want.

Remodeling or expansion calls for expertise and deep soul searching. This Guide, with the help of checklists, will help you to make the right decisions. There is information on consultants: who they are, what they do, where to find them, how to evaluate their expertise, and how to be sure you receive the most value for the money you spend.

Whether you are in the business a long time or not, this Guide will provide you with the help you need to run a more profitable restaurant. It has taken the new and the old and blended them into the most practical and useful information source available anywhere at any price today.

—Robert T. Gordon

About The Author

Robert T. Gordon is a veteran of some 35 years of restaurant operations and management experience. Having been involved, at one time or another, with the operation of restaurants, clubs, hotels, fast-food restaurants, commissaries and institutional food service organizations, Mr. Gordon knows just about everything there is to know about the restaurant and food service industry.

Mr. Gordon has held positions as Regional Vice President with ARA Services; General Manager, Rice Hotel; a partner in several successful fast-food restaurants in Dearborn, Michigan; District Manager for Shoney's Big Boy operations in West Virginia; and is currently President of Gordon Associates, Inc., his own consulting firm.

Robert T. Gordon is a member of the Texas Hotel and Motel Association, the Texas Restaurant Association, Food Consultants Society International, Society for the Advancement of Food Service Research, and an active teacher of Hotel and Restaurant Management courses at the Hilton College of Hotel and Restaurant Management, University of Houston, Houston, Texas.

SUMMARY TABLE OF CONTENTS

CHAPTER 1—MAGIC KEYS TO MAKING MORE MONEY IN THE RESTAURANT BUSINESS

How Written Guidelines Can Help You . . . Why You Should Define The Type And Direction Of Your Business . . . How To Set Goals For Maximum Profit . . . Making The Best Use Of Your Time . . . How To Get Better Control Of Your Time: A Checklist . . . How Smart Sales Promotion Pays Off Big—and much more.

See detailed Table of Contents on page 101.

CHAPTER 2—EYE-CATCHING MENUS THAT BRING IN BIGGER DOLLARS

Special Benefits Of A Prepared Menu . . . Menu-Crafting Tips . . . How To Prepare A Well-Written Menu . . . Layout Techniques . . . How "Special" Menus Can Bring in Extra $$$ . . . Make The Menu Your Promise To Your Guests . . . The Importance of Good Service— And Training . . . How To Prevent Costly Mistakes When Adding New Items To The Menu . . . How To Develop A Menu Pattern That Will Sell . . . Pricing Your Menu For Maximum Sales Volume Or Lowest Cost . . . Tracking The Success Of Your Menu . . . How To Boost Profits Through Wine Sales—and much more.

See detailed Table of Contents on page 201.

CHAPTER 3—MONEY-MAKING SECRETS OF FOOD PRODUCTION

How To Use Standard Recipes To Stabilize Your Food Cost . . . Where To Find Standard Recipes—And How To Develop Them For Your Restaurant . . . How To Schedule Production—And Save Money By Doing It Right . . . How To Keep Production Costs Under Control

... Making Meal Planning A Breeze With The Popularity Index ...
How Checklists Can Help You Avoid Problems—and much more.

See detailed Table of Contents on page 301.

CHAPTER 4—HOW TO BUY FOOD RIGHT FOR MAXIMUM PROFITS

The Advantages Of Having Purchase Specifications ... How To Develop Keen Purchasing Skills ... Useful Tips On Purchase Specifications ... Testing The Products You Buy ... Selecting The Best Method Of Cooking Meat ... The Benefits Of Maintaining Good Records ... Should You Use One Supplier For All Items? ... Efficiently Storing Your Food And Supplies ... How To Prepare An Inventory Record System ... How Improper Storage Results In Loss Of Profits ... Inventory Control Methods That Work ... How Best To Calculate Your Inventory Turnover ... Checklists For Purchasing, Receiving, And Storage—and much more.

See detailed Table of Contents on page 401.

CHAPTER 5—HOW TO GET MORE AND BETTER WORK FROM YOUR EMPLOYEES

Five Reasons For High Staff Turnover ... The Key Steps To Hiring Employees That Are Right For The Job ... How To Develop A Better Application Form ... How Best To Interview Prospective Employees ... How To Ask Result-Getting Questions ... How To Put An Applicant At Ease ... How To Develop A Successful Training Program ... Model Training Session For Waiters And Waitresses ... How To Measure Employee Performance ... When And How To Do The Appraisal ... Key Ingredients For Better Communications ... How Well-Groomed and Smartly Attired People Can Increase Sales ... "Training For Profit" Programs ... Developing A Personnel Policy Manual—and much more.

See detailed Table of Contents on page 501.

CHAPTER 6—HOW TO GET SERVICE HELP TO DO SUCH A GREAT JOB THAT REPEAT BUSINESS IS GUARANTEED

How To Make Your Plates More Attractive ... How To Organize An Efficient Service Staff ... How To Get Acceptable Employee Productivity ... Surefire Techniques That Turn Servers Into Sellers: The Approach, Suggestive Selling, The Pre-Meal Briefing, The Tasting

Session, The Bonus Plan . . . Why Good Service Doesn't Stop When Your Meal Does . . . How Best To Present The Check—and much more.

See detailed Table of Contents on page 601.

CHAPTER 7—HIDDEN GOLD IN YOUR COCKTAIL LOUNGE

The Importance Of Internal Control . . . How To Set Up A Cost Control System . . . Key Ways To Keep Track Of Your Inventory: The Physical Inventory, The Operating Statement, Establishing A Par Stock, Automatic Beverage Metering Systems . . . Establishing The Right Prices . . . Easy Ways To Use The Metric System . . . House Rules For Employees And Patrons . . . Controlling Cash And Charge Sales . . . How To Handle Complimentary Drinks . . . How To Take Bar Inventory—and much more.

See detailed Table of Contents on page 701.

CHAPTER 8—INTERNAL CONTROL: HOW TO KEEP TRACK OF ALL YOUR MONEY

The Importance Of Keeping Good Records . . . What Daily Sales Records Can Do For You . . . How To Turn Your Daily Sales Records Into Profits . . . How To Develop An Operating Budget . . . Forecasting Sales and Other Revenue . . . Forecasting Costs And Expenses . . . A Model Statement Of Costs . . . How To Budget Food Costs . . . Analyzing Sales And Costs . . . How To Use Statistical Tables To Compare Your Operating Results . . . How To Do A Labor Analysis—and much more.

See detailed Table of Contents on page 801.

CHAPTER 9—HOW TO INCREASE YOUR PROFITS BY STAYING ON TOP OF CHANGES IN THE MARKETPLACE

How To Turn Negative Changes Into Positive Ones . . . Where To Find Out About Changes That Might Affect You . . . An Example Of How You Can "Lose Your Shirt" By Not Keeping Informed . . . Keeping Track Of Events That Affect Supply And Demand . . . Where To Find Out About Important Legislative Changes . . . How To Cash In On Changes . . . How Best To Deal With Changes That May Occur In Shopping Centers . . . Changes That Might Influence Your Business: A Checklist—and much more.

See detailed Table of Contents on page 901.

CHAPTER 10—HOW TO SIMPLIFY REMODELING OR EXPANSION PLANS

A Pre-Expansion Checklist . . . Developing Financial Data On The Profitability Of A New Restaurant . . . How to Prepare A Pro Forma Statement . . . How To Forecast Costs And Expenses . . . Where To Find Good Management People To Staff An Additional Restaurant . . . How To Succeed And Expand As An Absentee Owner . . . How To Get Started On An Actual Expansion Program . . . Selecting A Site . . . The Advantages Of Consulting Professionals—and much more.

See detailed Table of Contents on page 1001.

CHAPTER 11—HOW TO MAKE ADVERTISING AND PROMOTION DOLLARS PAY OFF FOR YOU

How Much Should You Budget For Advertising? . . . Using An Advertising Agency . . . How To Insure Success From Your Advertising Campaign . . . Advertising Media—And How To Profit From Them . . . How Best To Promote Your Restaurant . . . Reasons For Running Promotions . . . Sales Promotion Techniques . . . How To Measure The Potential Of Your Promotion Plans . . . Additional Promotional Ideas That Pay Off Big—and much more.

See detailed Table of Contents on page 1101.

CHAPTER 12—SURE-FIRE WAYS TO INCREASE PROFITS

How To Stay Ahead Of The Competition . . . How To Make Certain That Your Guests Will Return . . . How To Provide An Atmosphere That Says "Welcome—We Want Your Business" . . . In-House Selling: The Way To Fame And Fortune . . . How To Hold On To Those Hard-Earned Dollars . . . How To Build A Responsible Staff . . . Economic And Social Changes That Can Mean Opportunities For You—and much more.

See detailed Table of Contents on page 1201.

CHAPTER 13—HOW TO GET TOP BENEFIT FROM TAX SAVINGS AND SHELTERS AND BUILD FINANCIAL SECURITY

How Your Restaurant May Be Able To Pay Your Living Expenses—Tax-Free . . . How To Set Things Up So The Restaurant Pays Per-

sonal Medical Bills . . . How You Can Cut Your Family Tax Bill By
Giving Your Child A Share Of The Business . . . What To Do Now To
Keep A Restaurant In The Family—And Pay No Estate Tax . . .
How Putting Your Spouse On The Payroll Can Pay Off In Thou-
sands Of Dollars In Extra Deductions . . . Thirteen Dollar-Saving
Tax Credits Restaurant Owners Commonly Overlook . . . How You
Can Write Off The Cost Of Checking Up On Your Competition . . .
How To Make Sure The Restaurant Gets The Benefits Of A Corpo-
rate Setup—and much more.

See detailed Table of Contents on page 1301.

Magic Keys To Making More Money In The Restaurant Business

Table of Contents

Magic Keys To Making More Money In The Restaurant Business

The basic objective of all business ventures is, of course, to make a profit; and all of the elements of a business venture are in place for that purpose. The capital assets, i.e., building, land, equipment, etc., are only valuable to a restaurant if they can contribute to the earning of profits. Similarly, the staff (cooks, waiters, dishwashers, etc.) and the food and supplies are only valuable if they contribute to sales and profits. And it is the responsibility of management to use and direct these various elements properly in order to enhance the restaurant's profit potential.

Therefore, planning and setting objectives are an essential part of every manager's job. The main objectives are the goals or targets that the business will strive for over short- and long-range periods. *Short-range* planning refers to the sales and profit goals of one year or less. These goals will then become the target or budget figures against which you will measure your performance. *Long-range* planning may include further market penetration, such as opening a second restaurant to be built at some future time. This kind of planning is also known as strategic planning, and usually includes guidelines as to how the goals are to be achieved. Virtually every successful business engages in some form of planning. In fact, trying to run a business without planning is like trying to sail a ship in strange waters without charts.

How Written Guidelines Can Help You

Your new restaurant is more apt to be successful—and you'll be wealthier—if you will first take the time to analyze your overall objective or philosophy of the business. This will make it easier for you to sit down and write it out. Don't gloss over this task, as it is imperative that you and all of your people have a clear understanding about the way you want the business to go—and just how you feel it can best get there.

If you are an action or doer-type of person, you may have a problem with this task, as doers are usually more comfortable with the action or day-to-day battles in a business than with the philosophical or reflective sides. Furthermore, this type of person usually knows instinctively how to get the job done, but cares, either little or not at all why it actually succeeds. However, stating your objective in writing will help you to better understand *why* you are starting the business, *where* you expect it to be some years in the future, and *how* it is to get there.

Once you have decided on your objectives for the business, you can then begin to develop the policies and procedures for attaining them. There are good reasons for developing and formalizing policies and procedures in your restaurant. Although you may know what *you* want your staff to do and how *you* want it done—the staff may not. If you merely tell them what to do and how to perform, without formal written guidelines and directions, you may create trouble for yourself by virtue of people misinterpreting what you say. Remember, it is often true that what we say is not always what we mean. For example:

1. Everyone on the staff will not *hear* the directions in the same way, and they will be "doing" their own thing in their own fashion. And that may not be the way you want things done.

2. Even with written policies and procedures, people won't always follow the rules. But without them, it is next to impossible, since no manager can be in more than one place at any one time.

3. If you don't write down guidelines, you will probably find yourself countermanding your own orders, or being inconsistent in running the daily operations. Very few restaurant managers can remember to handle all of the details that occur on a busy day. If you want to make lots of money, don't even try!

The restaurant business requires that everyone pay strict attention to hundreds of small details every day. That's why formal policy and procedure based on sound and experienced planning is so important. However, just writing down these policies and procedures with no follow-up will not get the job done either. You have to maintain an open and clear communication between the various departments at all times. This applies in all restaurants, large and small.

Sometimes the owners of small restaurants are unable to see how their restaurants can have separate departments, but they do. Every restaurant has a kitchen and some form of service area, whether a formal dining room or a simple take-out counter. All restaurants must buy raw material for preparation and sale. Even though the same person may perform more than one job—for example, buy and cook—there are still other tasks to be accomplished.

In order to understand and practice the principles of management, you must be able to see the divisions of labor and how each task relates to the others. When problems arise in one area, there is usually a chain reaction that carries over into other parts of the organization. For instance, if the cook is upset and takes it out on the waiter by being nasty to him—the waiter then snarls at the bus boy who gets upset and forgets something when he resets the next table. That may cause the customer to be nasty with the waiter who then shouts at the cook, and the whole scenario repeats itself. Management has the job of coordinating these tasks, so that disruptions are minimized and your customers can enjoy your restaurant.

You must maintain a clear and open line of communication with your employees at all times. Further, you should actively promote communications between employees. Encourage the exchange of information, as well as the flow of suggestions, all for the good of the business.

WHAT TYPE OF RESTAURANT IS BEST FOR YOU?

If you are just starting out, you have probably already decided what type of restaurant you want. Since there are a wide array of choices, they can be classified in several different ways, as follows:

- *Kinds of Food*—Steaks and chops, seafood, ethnic foods (Italian, German, Chinese, etc.), short order (coffee shop, diner, etc.), sandwiches, barbecue, or soup and salad to name a few.

- *Cooking Method*—In this classification, you might also find barbecue restaurants as well as table-side cooking. Some years ago, the broasted chicken restaurants made a big splash.

- *Style of Service*—This might also include table-side cooking, cafeterias, dinner houses, buffeterias, or takeout restaurants.

- *Desired Market*—Here we find the restaurants that seek out a certain segment of the market. For example, there are family restaurants where children are welcome, and there are certain kinds of dinner houses that cater to an adult-only market.

- *Fast Food*—This can include almost any kind of food, but generally refers to a standardized and simplified menu—and could rightfully be included in most of the foregoing classifications.

Why You Should Define The Direction Of Your Business

When you consider the diversity of the restaurant industry, you can clearly see why the intended direction of the new business must be carefully defined. To do this:

1. *State the type of restaurant that you intend to present to your market.*
   "The Name Restaurant is to be a fast-food type of restaurant that will combine limited sit-down and take-out service. It will develop a luncheon market from the nearby business firms. In addition, it will strive to build a strong evening family-based business."

2. *Identify the pricing policy.*
   "We will offer an acceptable quality of food that meets our market expectation. It is our policy to maintain moderate prices while offering a high quality of food preparation and service."

3. *State your intention as to expected size of the business.*
   "It is our goal to have three separate restaurants at the end of five years from the opening day of the first one."

Combining each of these paragraphs into one simple statement will produce a "Statement of Objective" that will be the philosophy of your business. Now let's take each one apart and see just what it means. After all, words are cheap and empty objectives won't be worth anything at all.

1. Since you have defined the style of restaurant that you want, you can now begin to get down to details. Number one on the list will be the menu pattern; it should be written now in a broad or general form. A small restaurant that intends to offer a limited menu might have a pattern such as the one in Figure 1-1.

Sample Limited Menu

Entree Possibilities
Beef Ka Bobs
Chicken and Dumplings
Yankee Pot Roast

Sandwiches
Hamburgers
Bacon, Lettuce & Tomato
Ham and Cheese
Tuna Fish
Chicken Salad

Specials
Chili
Salad Bar
Soup

Corn Bread

Desserts
Ice Cream
Pie

Coffee
Tea—Hot & Iced
Beer and Wine

A larger restaurant with a wider variety of items might develop a pattern such as the following:

Meat
Filet Mignon
Sirloin Strip
Veal - Sauteed
Prime Rib

Poultry
Chicken Breast
Fried Chicken

Seafood
Fresh Fish
Shrimp, Deep Fried
Lobster Tail
Crab, Soft Shell
Scallops, Sauteed

Other Items
Salad Bar
Omelettes
Vegetables, Hot
Homemade salad dressings
Soups, Homemade,
   homemade
   rolls/butter

Desserts
Home-Baked Pies & Tarts
Chocolate Mousse
Ice Cream and Sherbet

Coffee Espresso
Coffee, regular
Tea

Cocktail Bar
Full assortment of mixed drinks and liqueurs
Beer (6 varieties)
Wine—Glass/Carafe/Bottles

Figure 1-1

Next will come the decisions related to name, size, location, interior finish and equipment design and layout. (These will be covered later in this Guide.)

2. Identifying a pricing policy in this manner implies that you will exercise great skill in the purchase of food and supplies, so as to maintain moderate pricing. Further, it clearly states that you will not settle for less than outstanding skill in the areas of food preparation and service. (You will find all sorts of techniques and tested ideas in this Guide to help you ac-accomplish these all-important tasks.)

3. Setting a goal for growth will furnish the spur needed to get the job done. At the same time, you will be mindful of the need to monitor closely your present business, as well as the general economic outlook in your community. (Growth implies change, and this Guide deals with the problems that might be encountered.)

How To Set Goals For Maximum Profit

Setting the right goals for your restaurant—and reaching them—will make the difference between profit or loss. Consider the following key areas:

- *Sales Goals*—You should be striving for improvement in sales from one period to the next. But you must be realistic with your goal setting, so that you don't set your targets too high. Proficiency in this area of forecasting requires that you study not only your own business, but also the industry and total economy in general.

- *Cost and Expense Goals*—While you must have sales volume to exist, you must also hold cost and expense at required levels. Failure to do so may also cause financial loss. The way to manage these items is by budgeting and then measuring performance against budget goals.

- *Capital Expenditure Goals*—All restaurants must plan for the day when they will face the need for replacing equipment, or remodeling the present space, or building a second restaurant. To make such a large expenditure, you either need some reserve cash or a successful business track record, plus an accumulation of assets sufficient for bank loan purposes.

Profit from operations (all income before occupation costs) in an average profitable restaurant serving food and beverage will be in the range of 16 to 16.5 percent of total sales. If your restaurant is doing $750,000 per year in sales and yielding 16%, then you will have an operating profit of $120,000. To put it another way, if you had saved one percent of sales in labor cost and one percent of sales in food and beverage cost, that two percent of sales would have dropped down to the operating profit line. In other words, you would have made an extra $15,000 in profit.

MAKING THE BEST USE OF YOUR TIME

In a busy restaurant, it is usually difficult for the manager to find the time to handle all the necessary tasks each day. This is why your time must be jealously guarded and wisely used.

For example, one of the major time-wasters is this: every day salesmen, customers, other merchants, job seekers and fund raisers will want to see you. You'll have to pass at least a pleasantry or two with each, and more time than that with some. You must be able to schedule those kinds of visits—and know when and how to close the conversations. In addition, you will want to know and be friendly with other merchants, since it is important to exchange information with them.

With job seekers, you should know whether or not you are in need of more employees, and if so, what kind and how many. You should be able to move quickly into an interview if warranted, have application forms readily at hand, and have all the information regarding wages, benefits and schedules at your fingertips.

As for customers, you will find that some of them love to visit with you, or they wouldn't be there in the first place. In such cases, you must remember that there are other customers in the restaurant who deserve the same attention. Therefore, you should learn to move graciously from diner to diner—while conveying the impression that each one of them is "the most important person in the house."

A sound organizational plan for your restaurant will help you to distribute your time wisely, and will also aid in relieving you of those duties that can be safely delegated to others. Of course, plans will vary in complexity with the scope and size of the business. The larger and more departmentalized the restaurant, the more complex the organizational plan.

Organizing your restaurant means grouping your people in such a way that they can all strive effectively toward the common goals for everyone, profit for you the owner, and maximum wages for each member of the team. To do this, the lines of authority should be drawn and responsibilities designated. (See Figure 1-2 for

Line Organization Plan

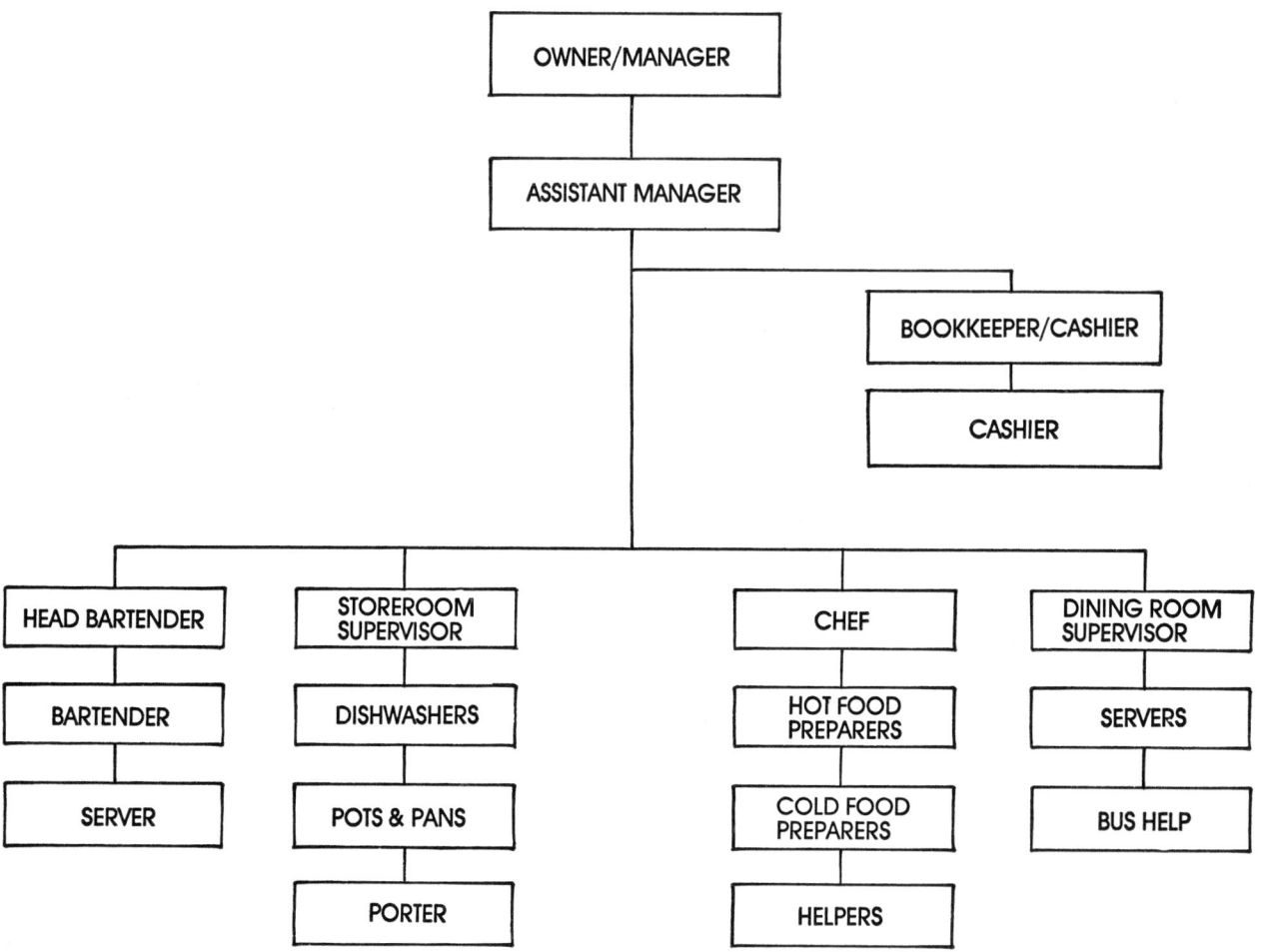

Figure 1-2

a typical line organization plan that might be found in a medium-sized restaurant offering table service and a cocktail lounge.)

This plan depicts the various levels of supervision in the organization, and shows in graphic form the reporting relationships between members. A brief description of each of the blocks could be as follows:

Owner/Manager—This implies that the owner also intends to be the manager. If the owner is to be absentee, then this position would be titled MANAGER only. The placement position on the chart says that this is the person in charge of, and responsible for, the entire organization.

Assistant Manager—This block denotes the presence of an assistant manager who is responsible to the Owner/Manager. All other supervisory positions report to the assistant manager. In reality, the assistant manager is probably the person in charge when the owner/manager is away from the business. When the owner/manager is present, the assistant is the person who helps out in different ways as needed. There are certain duties that should be delegated to the assistant manager such as: taking inventory, ordering and receiving of merchandise, and scheduling of personnel.

Bookkeeper/Cashier—This position is shown as a staff job separate from operations. The dual title requires keeping the records, plus the additional duty of acting as cashier during one or more meal periods daily.

Cashier—As written, this implies that the cashier is just that, with no additional duties. Very likely, this position could be filled by a part-time person who would be responsible to the Bookkeeper/Cashier.

Head Bartender—This person is responsible for the operation of the bar or bars. Bartenders, servers and possibly bar helpers would be responsible to this person. Certain responsibilities such as opening the bar in the morning, checking inventory levels, restocking the bar, and preparation of syrups and mixes could be delegated to this person.

Storeroom Supervisor—This person is responsible for the storage and safeguarding of all food and supplies, and possibly including liquor, wine and beer. In addition, it entails the stewardship function of restaurant sanitation. For this reason, dishwashers, pot and pan washers, and porters report to—and are responsible to—this person.

Chef—As stated, this person is responsible for all phases of food production, the kitchen and those production people vested in this position.

Dining-Room Supervisor—All matters relating to the dining room including opening, seating of patrons, service, and closing are delegated to this person.

How To Get Better Control Of Your Time: A Checklist

In addition to the items given above, preparing checklists that outline the tasks requiring your daily, weekly and monthly attention will help you to make efficient use of your time. These lists should then be translated into a form of schedule for yourself. For example, the following is a checklist for duties that must be done each morning:

- ☐ Visit with chef and check availability of items needed for day's production. Review labor situation, and identify any problem areas in preparation and service.

- ☐ Spot-check entire restaurant for sanitation and security.

- ☐ Review previous day's business. Check cashier's report and examine bank deposit slips.

- ☐ Open and peruse mail; take action as needed.

- ☐ Visit with cashier and/or bookkeeper, noting and correcting problems where necessary.

- ☐ Review dining-room service with hostess, and preview the day's menu.

- ☐ Inspect service staff with hostess, and assist her in briefing the staff on the day's menu.

- ☐ Supervise the taste test of pre-prepared foods appearing on luncheon menu.

- ☐ Prepare to greet guests and oversee the operation of the restaurant.

Undoubtedly, you will have other items that you will want to include on your own checklist. By scheduling what you can, you will be in a much better position to cope with emergencies and unusual events that cannot be planned for.

HOW SMART SALES PROMOTION PAYS OFF BIG

Your overall planning should also include a sales promotion plan to draw customers in for special occasions. While cost control is extremely important in a restaurant, a sales program and the generation of revenue are even more important.

Some restaurants have been known to make the grade with little or no promotion, but those are the exception rather than the rule. Remember, the restaurant industry is highly competitive and consumers do have a wide choice of places in which to spend their food service dollars.

Promotion in your restaurant will be most effective if you plan far enough in advance to insure a real "professional" effort. Too often promotions are the result of last-minute thought, and although they bring some increase in revenue, fail to realize their full potential.

Your best approach will be through the use of a planning calendar. By this, I don't mean some special kind of calendar that you would get at the office supply store, or as a promotional piece from a vendor. Several different kinds of calendars will do, but the important point is the system, rather than the tool. It is a rather simple procedure that requires a minimal amount of research. The benefits will far outweigh the efforts if you put the entire program on a year-long schedule, and allow for sufficient lead time on each promotion for adequate planning and execution.

Before you begin construction of your forecast and budgets for the next year, put together a calendar of events that you want to promote during that year. Suppose, for example, that you want to run one special promotion per month. Procure a desk calendar that lets you see at least one full month at a time, and that has space for writing notes on it each day. Next, go through the coming year and decide on the kind of promotion you want for each month.

For instance, you might wish to promote Valentine's Day in February, and have some sort of Salute to the Newlyweds in June. Mark your calendar accordingly, and then go back at least six weeks from a particular promotion time and signal on the calendar a get-ready time. For example, if Valentine's Day, February 14, was your promotion day, you would indicate a signal at approximately January 1 to begin your preparation. Such a system will allow enough time for design of ads to play up the special occasion, and for the procurement of special props, foods or whatever might be needed for the promotion. Later on in this Guide, you will find ideas to use on advertising and promotion, along with how to construct budgets for control of these expenses.

You will also want to establish some guidelines for how much you can afford to spend for each of these promotions during the year. The guidelines or budget for each event will go hand in hand with your planning calendar. Therefore, when you are thinking about a particular promotion and just how it is to be done, try to set some sort of limit on the total amount of money that you will spend for it. The expenses might include such items as cost of food and beverage, advertising, and promotional handouts. This kind of system is excellent for restaurants because this business lends itself so beautifully to promotions of all kinds.

Eye-Catching Menus That Bring In Bigger Dollars

Table of Contents

Eye-Catching Menus That Bring In Bigger Dollars

The menu is, of course, central to the development of an attractive and successful restaurant. And yet it is amazing how many restaurants are developed without a clear understanding of its importance.

In addition to the fact that it is the basis for everything else that a restaurant does, a menu reflects your ideas as to what *kind* of restaurant you want to have. You should take note that "menu" is used in the broadest sense—for there are many successful restaurants that have no formal printed ones. Some restaurants employ wall blackboards; some, such as the highly successful Al's in St. Louis, Missouri, present the food itself, uncooked, on a large beautifully garnished silver tray which is brought to the customer. There are restaurants that rely on the spoken word only, with the maitre d' reciting the offerings of the day; and there are also those "limited menu" restaurants that offer only one or two specialty items daily. Regardless of what plan you have in mind for your restaurant, that plan is best realized through the preparation of a menu.

Special Benefits Of A Prepared Menu

- The type of menu may affect how the building should be laid out. It may also dictate, along with government codes, how many parking spaces are needed and whether valet parking should be considered. It generally establishes the intended speed or tempo of service to be offered, and in turn gives you a clue as to how many times your seats are apt to turn over during meal times.

- The menu guides the designers and planners. It suggests certain types of interiors and color schemes. It is the road map for the kitchen planners. The menu dictates the quantities, sizes, capacities and types of equipment needed for production and service.

- The menu is the management guide to purchasing food and supplies. It also helps to determine the number of workers needed, along with the skills that may be required to conduct the business.

- The menu is the prime, number-one sales tool in all restaurants. It either whets or diminishes the appetite of the diner.

- The menu is the price list of offerings for sale.

- In a sense, the menu is the restaurant's contract with its customers. It offers items for sale that may be accepted or declined.

MENU-CRAFTING TIPS

Since the menu is essential to your restaurant's success, then planning what will be on it is your most important job. Planning means more than a first writing—it means constantly watching, evaluating and revising the menu as necessary.

Writing interesting, saleable menus is an art that requires some basic writing skills. A menu should be directed to the clientele that you want to attract. In other words, your diners must be able to understand it. While there may be a certain snob appeal to menus with unfathomable titles and descriptions of offerings, the well-constructed, plainly written menu will always be the one most appreciated. This does not mean that menus should not use words other than English. The exclusive use of any one language is impossible, because of the widespread development and acceptance of ethnic foods. Even so, the skillful writer will construct a menu in such a way that it facilitates reading and understanding by the majority.

How To Prepare A Well-Written Menu

The menu should speak to the guests. It should be your "voice," inviting the reader to sample the taste delights that flow smoothly from your kitchen to table. Your menu should reflect all the good qualities sought by your patrons.

Your menus should always be clean and fresh in appearance. And they should be discarded when they become spotted, torn or just plain tired. Dirty, unkempt menus, no matter how well written, suggest poor sanitation and overall inefficient operations.

While adjectives and descriptive phrases are useful, they can be greatly overdone. Take a look at these two examples:

A. Broiled Prime New York Sirloin
   Steak, 12 oz .... $_____

B. A tender, mouth-watering 12 oz. Prime New York Sirloin, broiled to perfection as you like it, 12 ounces of beefeater's delight .... $_____

They both offer the same thing. But all the extra verbiage in "B" is probably wasted. No restaurant has to describe further a 12 oz. Prime New York Sirloin. And there is certainly no need to repeat "12 ounces." Further, any discriminating diner buying a prime steak these days assumes that your broiler cook knows how to prepare it. Telling too much, in fact, might even detract by "hiding" the name of the offering in the middle of the description. As far as I am concerned, if I order an item of that caliber and it is not "as I like it," someone is going to hear about it. I believe most patrons feel that way.

However, this is not to say that I am against the use of certain descriptive adjectives on menus. On the contrary, they are necessary to the art of culinary showmanship. Well-written menus will have a mouth-watering and appetizing appeal to your guests, and will be a major contributor to total sales in your restaurant. But there are many successful restaurants that offer menus with little or no description at all. One example is a popular and famous restaurant in Rockport, Texas. The following are excerpts from that menu:

fresh redfish almondine

broiled rib-eye of beef

beef wellington (for two)

baked potato

onion soup a la Francaise

Is The Size Of A Menu Important?

The size of the menu is also important. Picture this scenario—

A party of four seated at a standard-size table. The setting is lovely with service plate, gleaming flatware, water and wine glasses, ashtray, candle, condiments, etc., and along comes the captain with the menus. Each guest is now presented with a book of five pages, attractively encased in what seems to be leather-covered 3/8" plywood. Each of these documents is 18" high by 10" wide. Add to this scene a dimly lit dining room, and we now have the ultimate in discomfort.

We all know the rest of this story—the guests attempting to find a small ray of light for reading; trying to see the other guests over or around these obstacles; and after deciding what to order, trying to find some place to store the menu until the captain finally returns. This is no way to treat a guest!

A good way to win friends and customers is to size the menu for easy handling. Also, you should maintain an adequate lighting level in the dining room—making it easy to buy. Your customers will appreciate your efforts, and they might even buy more!

Layout Techniques

There are many effective styles of menus you can use. Most of them list the items by category in a similar fashion—starting with appetizers, followed by salads, entrees, desserts and beverages. A restaurant should also spell out the method of pricing. For example:

- If a menu is priced a la carte, it should be plainly stated.

- Combination a la carte and table d'hote menus should also be clearly separated and identified.

- Menus should be specific as to what is included in a meal at the price stipulated.

Remember, buyers should not be surprised with additional charges on their bills. This is not a good way to build good customer relations.

Laying out a menu may call for the help of an expert. There are many companies that specialize in layout and design, type styles, and color coordination. They can also advise you as to the kind of paper to use, and whether or not your menus should be laminated. These firms are listed in the Yellow Pages of your local telephone book, and can be found under "Menus" or "Printers."

Before going to an expert, a good way to enrich your own storehouse of knowledge is by collecting other restaurants' menus. (Most good managers have an extensive file of menus and are constantly searching for new ideas to adapt.) You should study these menus carefully, and work closely with the consultant you retain. In the process you will become quite expert yourself!

The matter of choosing colors for a menu is also an important area in which expert advice can be beneficial. Blending colors that are pleasing to the eye, enhance the food, and complement your restaurant is a job for someone who is artistic—and who also understands the hard world of retailing. There have been many studies done by various research groups on the impact of color and color combinations as related to sales. Some of these studies relate to packaging of foods, laundry items, etc., that are found on the shelves in supermarkets. Studies show that certain colors appeal most to men, while others have greater appeal for women.

Other studies indicate that many people can't read without glasses, and that some of these folks don't wear glasses in public. Consequently, some people can't read labels. Therefore, manufacturers identify their products with arrows or other easily identifiable marking. (This is another idea you can incorporate in your menu.) If you are interested in finding out more about these studies, you can usually obtain additional information from the Psychology and Business Departments of your local college or university. Your city library is another fine source for information of this kind.

HOW "SPECIAL" MENUS CAN BRING IN EXTRA $$$

Special menus can mean extra sales by satisfying certain groups of people's needs. A good example of this is the senior citizen group. These people usually search out moderate prices, and may settle for reduced portion sizes. Many of them have enjoyed fine dining during their working lives, and appreciate restaurant operators who make a special effort to cater to them. Population statistics document the fact that the general population is aging and life expectancy per capita is increasing. In other words, the senior citizen market will continue to grow—and it will certainly have an increasing influence on restaurant sales in the future. Therefore, you may want to take this into consideration when preparing your menu.

Adding special menus to your operation can mean adding dimensions to your market. Actually, almost all restaurants already offer some form of special menus, i.e., children's menus, holiday specials and low-calorie offerings to name just a few. Then there are the special beverage menus: jumbo Margaritas and many others. All of these specials are of course offered as promotions.

Presentation of special menus requires some careful planning. It means additional research into the cost structure of the items, in order to determine the proper selling prices. Also, you must take into consideration the effect on overall sales mix and total volume.

Low-Calorie Specials

When presenting special menus, you should also consider the final result of an offering. Many so-called "specials" do not deliver what they say they do. For example, the following "low calorie" special is offered in a very popular restaurant in one of the midwestern cities:

Broiled Ground Beef Patty
Cottage Cheese
Peach Half
Melba Toast
Iced Tea

Let's say that the Ground Beef Patty is 4 ounces, the Cottage Cheese is 1/2 cup with a Peach half, and there are two slices of Melba Toast, we can then figure that this adds up to approximately 579 calories. People who are serious about dieting, and who are looking for say approximately 300 calories, may not consider this a "local" luncheon. So in this case, what is advertised as low calorie really is not—and anyone who is really counting calories will not be fooled.

Children's Menus

Many times you'll see special menus that are either too brief or lack appeal. A good example of this is in children's menus. Often, just the size of the portion from the standard menu is reduced, and it offers nothing more. Let's face it, children's menus will probably never bring in high-volume sales, but why not please *both* children and parents by having items the kids like, at prices the parents can afford. This is an excellent sales-generating tool which will get parental appreciation, and will undoubtedly bring them back with or without the children.

There is nothing wrong with having your restaurant prepare a special children's menu—with pictures and titles—and featuring foods that have "child appeal." For example, kids like cold cereals, fruit, peanut butter and jelly sandwiches, hamburgers, hot dogs, ice cream, cookies, etc. If you present the menu properly, you can probably get the price you need to sustain the service.

Special Promotions

You should always be alert for situations that prompt special promotions. Examples that come quickly to mind are the observed holidays such as Easter and Thanksgiving. Additionally, there are the festive days such as Mother's and Father's Day, Valentine's Day and St. Patrick's Day. Furthermore, you can start a customer birthday file and send cards out suggesting that the celebration be held at your restaurant. You might even offer something as an enticement, such as a cake or a bottle of wine with the meal. Writing, offering and preparing special menus takes research time, imagination and some effort, all of which can pay off big in profits for you. Not only do these programs increase sales, but they are fun to do. Where else can you make money having fun!

MAKE THE MENU YOUR PROMISE TO YOUR GUESTS

One way to think of your menu is as an offer to sell merchandise of a certain quality at a quoted price. When the diner orders the selection, it's as if a contract has been consummated.

- You have now agreed that certain merchandise, i.e., the food, will be delivered as represented on the menu.

- The guest has agreed to your terms, i.e., the price as stated.

The most recent trend in this regard is the enactment of legislation by some state governments called "Truth in Menu." Although these laws have been hotly disputed by restaurant groups, there is still reason to expect them to become a "fact of life" in most states. What it means is that what you offer on your menu is what you must provide. For example, if you offer "fresh garden vegetables," they must be fresh and not frozen. Or when your menu states "Prime Beef," it must not be Choice or some other grade. Actually, this legislation may be good for the restaurant industry, since credibility is probably the most important quality a restaurant owner can have.

Therefore, when you offer an item for sale, be sure that you can and will deliver what has been promised. For instance, if you offer fresh, hot rolls, don't serve cold, stale ones. More and more of this is seen in our restaurants since the introduction of the microwave ovens. While this equipment is a marvelous aid in today's kitchens, it is only as good as the people using it. In the case of the rolls, the oven will do great things by reconstituting products, but it can't revive the "dead." Neither can it provide heat forever; speed of service is still important.

Also, be sure you have (or can obtain) quality ingredients for the items you are offering—and that your staff has the necessary skill to prepare them. Too often we see plain brown gravy being passed off as an exquisite sauce. As a rule, when this occurs, the guest usually finds the meat to be similarly bogus. At that point, most people make a mental note never to return.

It's to your interest, in other words—whether you're legally required to or not—to provide what your menu promises.

The Importance Of Good Service—And Training

It is important to be sure that your guests receive the good service that you have promised them. This doesn't mean that French-style service should be offered in a moderately priced family restaurant. It does mean, though, that your service style should fit your restaurant—and that *all* service personnel should be trained to provide the same service.

For example, "arm" service should not be used by some servers when trays are provided—and are being used by other servers. Furthermore, insist that they be used, even if it means losing a server or two. When using tray service, make certain that the trays are properly sized and that enough tray stands are furnished—then provide the training for their proper use.

Once you have decided on a particular style of service for your restaurant, you must take the necessary steps to see that the staff— including supervisory personnel—have the proper training. The training should either be done by you directly, or at least be given under your close supervision so as to live up to your expectations.

Often you see the service in a restaurant break down simply because the supervision is vested in some untrained host or hostess. This represents a false economy. If you could determine the cost of lost customers and sales opportunities due to inadequately trained supervisors—and add that to the wages you are paying them—you would soon see how costly untrained supervisors really are. Proper training, then, is essential. (See also Chapter 5.)

Your state restaurant association representative can be of help in selecting a training program that will fit your needs. It may also be able to recommend tapes and movie clips that will be useful to you. In addition, there are a number of books you can obtain that will help you in developing a training program:

        □   *The Dictionary of Occupational Titles*, published by the Federal Government (found in most major libraries).

❑ *The Management of Service for the Restaurant Manager,* Raymond J. Goodman, Wm. C. Brown Co., Publishers, Dubuque, Iowa.

❑ *Training Booklets and Manuals,* from The National Restaurant Association, 311 First St., N.W., Washington, D.C. 20001

How To Prevent Costly Mistakes When Adding New Items To The Menu

The following short story is an example of how checklists, accompanied with careful consideration, can often prevent costly changes that don't pan out.

Sam has a nice restaurant with a menu that is pretty standard for his kind of business. After a trip to a competitor's place, he decides that adding Prime Rib would put him even with the competition. In order to pass that competition, he further decides that carving from a cart in the dining room would really add some "pizazz." (You are probably starting to get the picture.)

Anyway, in comes the new cart—pretty, but it takes up considerable aisle space, and really slows down the rest of the service. Well, that can be solved—take out a table or two; however, seating was "tight" before, and not having those seats means lost sales. Further, coordinating the serving of the accompaniments to the beef meant a further disruption for the service staff.

This scenario has no ending, but the point has been made. Actually, the addition of the Prime Rib may have been good, but the method of service with insufficient planning was disastrous. In all probability, what really happened was that the expensive cart was relegated to the storeroom where it still sits today—even though the storeroom was too small to begin with!

Oftentimes an owner or manager will see a new item somewhere and, without too much thought, add it to the menu. That is like adding a fifth wheel to an automobile, without studying the process and retooling the assembly line. Any time you introduce a change in your menu, you must first be sure that the service staff can handle it. It is also a good idea to use checklists when planning new ventures or changing old ones. Before you change your menu, use the following checks to see if you are on the right track.

Kitchen

☐ Can the present staff handle another change, or must you add another person? Do you have to remove something else from the menu in order to add the item? What?

☐ Will the present equipment stand an extra item? Do you have sufficient and proper storage? Is there a ready supply of these items, or is it the "special order" variety?

Service

☐ Is your china properly sized and shaped for this service? Or must you buy some new type of dish?

☐ Can this item be "held" and still be served fresh and attractively? Can you keep it hot? Cold?

☐ If it is of the "gourmet" variety, can your service staff handle it smoothly and with flair? Do you have the proper cart? Table-side cooking or serving equipment?

☐ *Will it sell*? Or is it out of character with the balance of your menu?

HOW TO DEVELOP A MENU PATTERN THAT WILL SELL

This is where it all begins, and "where you separate the men from the boys." Since the menu is the backbone of the business, developing a good one will take some experience, as already outlined. Here are the important ingredients that go into a winning menu:

- The menu must be attractive and interesting. This requires *flair and imagination* in the writing and the layout. A dull menu won't sell much.

- The menu must have balance. This means it must include a sufficient mix of items, i.e., taste, shape, size, texture, etc. It also must offer an adequate range of prices to satisfy the widest possible market available. For example, when a party of six comes to your restaurant, chances are the group will include those who are able and willing to spend freely, and those who are not. If your menu is constructed so as to offer a variety of items with an acceptable range of prices, the group can solve the problem by asking for separate checks—and everyone in the party is then satisfied. If not, next time that group will go elsewhere.

Many restaurants are aware of this need in menu construction, and offer a wide range of items and prices in the restaurant. However, there are those that, even though they have large menus in terms of items, still offer a very narrow range of prices. A very good example of a well-planned menu in terms of food variety, price differential, and an overall well-designed sales mix and presentation is found in some of the newly formed chain restaurants. A look at these menus will quickly show you that their menus offer a sufficient variety of food items and price ranges to satisfy a high percentage of diners. Further, arrangement of items in the menu seems to cause people to read it all, and that's good merchandising.

Pricing Your Menu For Maximum Sales Volume Or Lowest Cost

You must always be aware of the sales mix and how it relates to the volume you desire. That means keeping good records in order to identify the "strong" and the "slow" sellers. When you keep good sales information, you can then make price adjustments with some measure of expertise. For instance, it may be possible to either raise or lower the price of an item and thereby increase the sale of it. In the matter of lowering the price, you may find a strong surge at which time total volume will overcome the higher unit cost.

How To Save Money By Pre-Costing Your Menu

You must determine the plate cost of every item you sell. Only then can you strike the proper sales mix in menu offerings. This sounds like a simple job, but it can be tedious and time consuming. Although different forms are used for this all-important function, they all do basically the same thing.

Figure 2-1 is an example of one way you can determine the cost of a plate. It is included in the *EZ KEEP SYSTEM* for restaurants, and is reprinted through the courtesy of Edwin K. Williams and Co., 5324 Ekwill Street, Santa Barbara, California 93111.

The next step is to evaluate the entire menu as to the cost of sales target. Each item will not deliver the same cost due to price considerations. For instance, the food cost percentage to sales on a steak item will probably be higher than fish, and coffee will likely be lower than milk. The trick in pricing is to offset the higher cost items (because of resistance to higher prices) with lower cost items (sold at lower prices), and still maintain needed volume:

MENU ITEM:				
INGREDIENTS	UNIT MEASURE	UNIT PRICE	PER ONE SERVING	
			PORTION SOLD	PORTION COST
		SUBTOTAL		

OTHER COSTS:
GARNISH ____
PLACE SETTING ____
OTHER ____
SUBTOTAL ____
PLATE COST Ⓐ ____
SELLING PRICE Ⓑ ____
Ⓐ ÷ Ⓑ PLATE COST % ____ •

Figure 2-1

Steak Plate	$20.00
Total Cost	8.68
% of food cost	43.4%
Fish Plate	$14.00
Total Cost	4.20
% of food cost	30.0%

If you sell 20 Steak Plates and 10 Fish Plates, your cost of sales will be at 39.9%, and total sales of $540. On the other hand, sales of 20 Fish Plates and 10 Steak Plates will yield a total cost of 35.5%, and sales of $480. The question now is: Which is best? There really is no standard answer. In addition to the foregoing, you must also consider the other items on the menu and their relationship to cost. Also, the sales mix must be constructed so as to return the desired dollar volume to insure adequate cash flow.

Sales mix, as used here, can be defined as the presentation of a variety of items that includes certain items offered with some special promotion to the guests. If the mix is "right," then the gross profit from *total* sales will be on target as planned—even though the menu includes items that individually have a different percentage of cost or gross profit.

"Specials" are usually offered in a different manner (spoken word by waiter or waitress, written on chalkboard, colorful menu clip-ons, etc.) than the regular bill of fare. Their intent is to promote the sale of certain low-cost items, while building sales volume. It is always a good idea to quote the price with any special offering, because guests generally think of a special as being a lower-priced item.

Next to consider is the impact of beverage sales. Since these have higher gross profit margins, the effect to the restaurant is a lower total cost of sales. In other words, if pricing has been properly done, then total cost of sales (food and beverage) will rise or fall with sales fluctuations in beverages, when food sales and food costs remain constant.

TRACKING THE SUCCESS OF YOUR MENU

There is no way to evaluate the sales mix of a menu properly without sales records. Instinct plus observation will certainly aid the average manager in determining which items are the "hot" sellers. However, if you want to "fine tune" your operation for profit, you will establish and maintain adequate records that will quickly point out the "winners" and "losers."

There are many systems in use that keep track of individual menu item sales. One operator I know simply uses a stenographer's notebook. In that restaurant, the cashier extracts the items from the guest checks and records the sales by meal and date in the book. There are also various types of mechanical counters that do this. Information on them can be obtained from your restaurant supply house.

How To Pick The Best Cash Register System

The most effective sales-recording devices today are the modern electronic cash registers. But some of these machines—depending on the model—do far more in the way of controlling than others. Therefore, if you decide to invest in one, you should remember that there are big differences. Beware of models with flashing lights and ringing bells—as some of these machines do very little else.

There are three basic types of cash register systems in use right now. Undoubtedly, there will soon be others. These systems control more than just sales records, but that is all that we'll concentrate on for now. The three major types are:

1. *The Back-Room Computer System*
   This system employs a minicomputer that operates as the master processor of information. The cash registers at the points of sale are "dumb"—in that they only receive and

transmit information to the minicomputer. There are certain advantages to this system, including the size of the computer and its information storage capacity. The cost of the individual registers is low, and replacement of an individual register in the system is relatively inexpensive. The major disadvantage of this system is in its size. It is designed for the high-volume multi-register (more than 5) user. In addition, if the computer goes down, then all information-gathering ability is lost.

2. *Master/Slave System*

This system is similar to the back-room computer system in that it has one minicomputer. That computer is located in one of the machines known as the "Master Register." All other registers in the system are slaves to the master in that they only receive and feed information to the master. The greatest advantage to this system is the lower cost as compared to the back-room system. It accomplishes nearly as much as the larger one, and is more readily adaptable when only one, two or three registers are needed. The major disadvantage to this type of equipment is the dependency of the slaves on the master. If it goes down, then the entire system is rendered inoperable.

3. *Stand Alone System*

In this system, each cash register contains its own minicomputer. Each machine stands alone in that it gathers and processes its own data. This system is probably best suited to the smaller organization with only one or two registers. Its major advantage is its lack of dependency on either a master or back-room computer. If one register breaks, the others in the system are still functional. Obviously, the major disadvantage would be the high cost to the larger operations since each individual register is more costly.

If you are in the market for a cash register system, be sure to examine and price the various offerings carefully before you buy. Most cash register companies will be pleased to give you demonstrations. So be sure to ask for one. Then, if you still don't know what to do, seek out professional advice from a neutral source.

Only Ride The Winners

Make sure that you carefully watch your sales records so that you know when to move the slow sellers off the menu. There is no profit in items that don't sell. When to change an item is largely a personal matter. But one way would be by watching inventory turnover by item. If, for instance, you are turning your inventory four times per month or about once each week, but a certain item lays in storage without movement for, say two weeks, then it should be checked for saleability. Here is where a good inventory system really pays off. (See Chapter 4.)

Copying a competitor could be a mistake unless you have a very good idea that the "hot" item down the street will be equally "hot" in your place. Further, copying others will often lead to a "mish mash" of items on a menu. That condition may destroy the theme of a restaurant and make the total environment uncomfortable for the patrons. If you think you need to make a change, exercise caution and research the matter carefully.

One sure way to monitor your menu is to keep clear open lines of communication with your service staff. They know what the patrons are saying about your restaurant. They also know what your patrons say about the competition. This is just one more good reason to hold regular staff meetings during which time—you listen.

Spending time with your patrons and listening to their comments is also very educational. There are too many restaurant managers who don't spend enough time in the dining room. That is a bad habit to fall into, since it isolates management from the point of sale.

Watch Out For Changing Economic Conditions

There will be changing conditions in the economy and in the community that will have an effect on the items you sell and the prices that you charge. Commodity prices will fluctuate with supply and demand. An example of this is the price of beef. If supply is plentiful and demand moderate, then wholesale prices will tend to be down. But what usually happens then is that the producers trim their herds, thereby shortening the supply. In the meantime, consumers have increased their consumption due to the lower prices, and at that time, wholesale prices tend to climb. So you must watch these cycles and know when and how to buy. Sometimes it may pay to carry a heavy inventory on a particular item in order to protect your price. But that will only be true if you do not have to borrow money at high interest rates in order to carry the supply.

Then too, the neighborhood in which your restaurant is located may undergo economic changes. Such change may bring demand for new items on your menu. You must be alert to what goes on around you. Your restaurant must interface with the community and if the community undergoes change, it may be wise for you to make some changes also.

A good way to keep up with the "outside" world is by reading your local newspaper, bulletins and periodicals from trade associations. Both the National Restaurant Association and your own state association publish information that is very important to you. Also, there are many magazines and journals published for the food service industry—and one or more of these may be helpful in identifying changing patterns and trends in the business.

HOW TO BOOST PROFITS THROUGH WINE SALES

All over the U.S. there are thousands of operators, like you, who have increased their profits through wine sales. According to Mr. Joseph Detter, a Wine Sales Manager in Houston, Texas, wine sales in this country have risen by 400% since World War II, and sales of quality champagne have increased by 700%. A well-defined and properly managed wine sales plan in your restaurant will bring you some nice, juicy profits.

Merchandising wines effectively means knowing how to buy and how to sell. In between are such things as storage, service, training and price.

First, you should sell what you can be proud of. However, that doesn't mean that you sell only the most expensive wines. On the contrary, it means that no matter what price structure your restaurant demands, you search for and offer the very best at an affordable price. You should develop your own taste and rely with confidence on your own judgment. Your guests know what they like, and if you pay attention to your business, you will soon know too. *Important*: be sure your wine inventory is properly stored and that you turn it regularly.

Second, be realistic with your pricing formula. You want the wine to sell, but if it is priced too high, your patrons won't buy it. The whole trick in wine sales is volume. You should strive to maximize sales by boosting the individual check average. In addition to increasing your profits, it also increases the potential tips for your service personnel.

Here is a wine pricing formula that seems to work for a number of the restaurants in Houston, Texas. These operators strive for a market mix of sales that yields one-half as wine and beer, and one-half from "hard" liquor. In order to reach their goal, they mark the low-cost wine up from 3 to 4.5 times the cost per glass or bottle. The more expensive wines are marked up 2 to 2.8 times the cost per bottle.

Note: The State of Texas requires a payment of 10% of gross sales from all mixed beverage permit licensees. This tax is not an add-on—which means that the house realizes 90% net of all sales of liquor, wine and beer. The following example accounts for such a tax.

1 glass

Cost — $0.35 × 4 = $1.40
Selling Price (rounded up) — $1.50

Cost — $1.50 — .15 (tax 10%) = $1.35
.35 ÷ 1.35 = 25.9% COS

1 bottle

Cost $6.00 × 2.5 = $15.00
Selling price — $15.00

Cost — $15.00 — 1.50 (tax 10%) = $13.50
$6.00 ÷ 13.50 = 44.4% COS

If you sold 75 glasses of wine

Sales — $112.50 — 10% tax = $101.25 net

and 12 bottles

Sales — $180.00 — 10% = $162.00 net

The yield on wine sales would be—

Sales $101.25 + $162.00 = $263.25
Cost $26.25 + $72.00   = $ 98.25

$98.25 ÷ $263.25   = 37.3% cost of sales on wine

The above example would meet the stated goal of cost of goods on wine at between 35 and 40 percent of net sales. Try this formula, making whatever adjustments are necessary to fit your own particular situation.

Third, make the sale of wines easy by having the source of supply readily accessible to service personnel. Be sure the staff people have corkscrews on hand, and that they know how to open a bottle of wine properly. If you have a large variety of bottled wines on hand, use a number system on the menu, so that the bottles can be easily found.

Fourth, schedule frequent training sessions and bring in a local supplier. There are films available from the Wine Advisory Board that are especially designed for waiter and waitress training sessions. Run your training sessions in a professional manner. Teach your personnel how to sell wine properly, and encourage them to do so. You can create more interest by instituting incentives such as commissions on wine sales, or prizes for most wine sold in a week, month, etc.

Fifth, be sure that your customers know about your fine wines. Doing this is easy. You can use—

- Well-designed wine lists

- Table tents, available from wholesalers

- Reminders on your menu

- Word of mouth (seeing to it that your service personnel suggest wine to your patrons)

Increasing your wine sales will mean instant profits to you. The only cost is the inventory itself. As a consequence, the gross profit on those sales will become net profit to you!

3

Money-Making Secrets Of Food Production

Table of Contents

3 Money-Making Secrets Of Food Production

Do you have sales of $400,000 per year or more in your restaurant? Would you like to make about $20,000 more? You don't even have to increase your sales to do that. If you do the things recommended in this chapter, you can improve the management of your business, and in the process, probably increase your income by at least five percent.

Too many operators leave the detail of planning production to others, and in most cases, sacrifice profits in the process. Expecting a busy working chef or salad person to monitor sales trends, manage inventory levels and guess how many customers will be served on a given day is inviting trouble. Because you are in a business of producing food for sale, controlling production may well be your most important job.

There are certain steps that must be taken to manage production levels of menu items properly in a commercial kitchen. Over-production of food has helped to put more than one restaurant out of business. Also, raw food prices are high, and those cost dollars must all be converted to sales dollars if you are to survive in this business. Under-production is the counter to over-production, since it means that you don't have enough food prepared to satisfy customer demand. Remember, if you don't have it, you can't sell it—and if you don't sell it, you won't be in business very long.

In this chapter, you'll learn the tools and techniques needed to control the amounts of food to be prepared by the kitchen staff. In addition, the value of recipes in stabilizing the quality and cost of food will be covered. In other parts of this Guide, forecasting, purchasing techniques and the need for an awareness to economic changes that might affect the business will be discussed.

How To Use Standard Recipes To Stabilize Your Food Cost

The standard recipe is one of the most useful attention-getters and profit-builders you can use in your restaurant. The largest and most successful food service companies in the world use them—and swear by them. No matter what the size of your operation, you too can benefit from using a standard recipe. For example:

- Consistent use of standard recipes insures that the proper ingredients are used in the correct amounts when preparing a menu item. Control of these factors is a must if you are going to stabilize your food cost.

  Mr. John Farquharson, President, Araserve Sector of ARA Services, operators of commercial restaurants as well as food service installations in colleges, hospitals, ballparks, etc., says standard recipes may be worth 10 percentage points of food cost. If yours are worth as much and you have a yearly food cost of $200,000, then your potential savings could be as high as $20,000 per year. That amount, if saved, will drop right to the bottom line as profit.

- Another plus from the use of standard recipes is the advantage of producing items that are consistent in quality. Customers come to your restaurant because you have certain things they like. Sometimes it is decor, or service, etc., but usually it is a particular food offering.

  The best way for you to insure that customers receive what they want is for you to have control over how the food is prepared. All of us—including your employees—have good days and bad days. Therefore, if you don't use a written guide (recipe), then your food quality will probably vary. If that happens, there may be days when your customers become dissatisfied. And when customers experience inconsistency, they begin to look for different restaurants.

  So if you want to make big profits, be sure you run a consistently good restaurant. If customers can trust the high quality of your food, day after day, they will keep coming back. And when they come back, they will bring others.

WHERE TO FIND STANDARD RECIPES—AND HOW TO DEVELOP THEM FOR YOUR RESTAURANT

Good Standard Recipe Sources: Quantity recipes can be found in various places. For example, one good source is *Food for Fifty* by Fowler, West & Shugart, published by John Wiley & Sons, Inc., New York. In addition, the Educational Department of the National Restaurant Association sells a quantity recipe file, as does the Cornell University School of Hotel Administration. These sources will provide the basis for starting your own file. Furthermore, take advantage of the hundreds of cookbooks that are for sale. These will most likely provide you with a recipe or two. Magazines and newspapers are also good sources.

Test First And Modify: In constructing your own file, you of course need to research and test the recipes before you offer them for sale. Your kitchen at home is every bit as good as any large company research facility for this job.

After you have tried the recipes at home, you can then experiment in the restaurant kitchen. When recipe quantities are changed from small to large, they will require some adjustment in the ingredient ratios. For instance, if you have a recipe for 6 servings and you want to increase it to 24, you first divide 24 by 6 which gives a ratio of 4 to 1. You then multiply the individual ingredients by 4, to increase the total recipe yield to 24. Once that is done, you must experiment with the recipes until you find the proper ingredient balance, since all ingredients will not require increasing in the same proportion.

When you are working with recipes, be sure to keep a good set of notes. In that way, you will be able to add and subtract, adjust and readjust until you have the product you want. Once you have worked out the final adjustments, it can be added to your standard recipe file.

Keep A Recipe File: It is a good idea to spell out all cooking procedures. For example, there are two schools of thought on roasting meat. One recommends a fast initial searing at a high temperature (500°), and dropping the oven temperature immediately to about 325°. The other school recommends a slow roasting at 275° for a longer period of time. Once you have tried both methods to see which you prefer, prepare your recipe and adopt the method as standard for your restaurant.

The form of the recipe file is a matter of personal taste. Some operators have their recipes in loose-leaf notebooks, while others use

5″ x 8″ file cards. I prefer the latter. The recipes can be filed by categories, i.e., soups, entrees, desserts, etc. Such a file is easy to use when scheduling production, and planning food and supply purchases. In order to protect the cards in the kitchen during production, clear plastic shields can be used.

Recipes should never be left lying around. They should only be removed from the file when they are being used and returned when finished. Carelessness will result in lost recipes and a breakdown in the system.

How To Schedule Production—And Save Money By Doing It Right

Production schedules are built on sales forecasts. Once you have projected your sales, you are in a position to forecast the production needed to satisfy your customer demand. Here is how you do it:

Step 1—Enter on your production record the name of the dish to be produced, and the number of portions that will be needed.

Step 2—Go to the recipe file and pull the necessary recipes for production. Check them over and deliver them to the various departments, along with the production schedule that you have prepared. It is a good idea to deliver them personally a day ahead of time, so that you can have a short meeting with the people responsible for the actual production. During the meeting you can discuss the day's menu, and if there are any potential problems, attempt to solve them early.

Step 3—Watch the production process. Be sure that you supervise for compliance with your instructions, and that everyone is working to the standard you have set.

Step 4—Follow through by checking on the number of portions that were yielded by the particular recipe. If production was either short or long, find out why—and make every attempt to see that it doesn't happen again.

The production record form is simple and easy to use. (*See* Figure 3-1 for a sample form that you may find useful in your restaurant.)

These records will refresh your memory on what happened the day you last served a certain item or combination of items, such as:

—Day of the week and month of the year

—What the weather was, i.e., sunny, rainy, etc.

Food Production Record

Menu Item	Recipe Number	Portions To Prepare	Raw Ingredients Needed	Portions Left/Time Ran Out	Comments
DEPARTMENT	DAY	DATE	MEAL	SPECIAL CONDITIONS	
HOT FOOD	ThuRS	4/17/—	Lunch	Holiday – Stores to Close	
Beef Stew	S-14	40	See Rec.	Out 12⁵⁰	Good Seller
					May have needed 20 more portions
Rst Leg of Lamb	L-5	20	1 Leg Approx. 18 lbs	Left 4	Ok Bus
					Slow today
Chix Pot Pie	C-12	10	See Rec.	Left 7	Poor Seller –
					Discontinue

Figure 3-1

—Outside temperature

—Any special happenings on that particular day, i.e., local election, strike at nearby plant

—Total dollar sales per meal

—Total number of customers per meal

—Total portions or items sold by category, e.g., 26 New York sirloin, 14 baked stuffed pork chops

Whether or not your menu changes frequently, these records can still be of great value to you. Watching well-kept sales records will not only show what sold today, but also what is apt to sell on another day in the future.

How To Keep Production Costs Under Control

All costs are best controlled before they are incurred whenever it is possible to do so. The key to that kind of control is called *PLANNING*. The plan to be used in the control of food production cost relates directly to the use of a sales forecast. It is important to have an accurate history of past sales for comparative purposes when forecasting future sales. Actually, the history provides the starting point from which you work on the forecast.

The most basic ingredient in controlling production costs is the sales forecast. Although there is a certain amount of intuition involved with any forecast, the use of good sales records will certainly minimize the guess work.

Different kinds of restaurants have different problems related to menu preparation and production control. If you were to establish broad categories, they might be grouped as follows:

—Restaurants having menus that change daily as in cafeterias and buffets.

—Restaurants having menus that are fixed but offer specials that change periodically. Dinner houses and hotels are examples.

—Restaurants that have menus that infrequently change, e.g., the so-called fast-food group.

The first group relies heavily on sales records and, in many cases, develop cycle menus in their operations. These are menus with items that repeat on a pre-planned cyclical basis. Generally the cycles change with the seasons.

Making Meal Planning A Breeze With The Popularity Index

A popularity index computed for each item on the menu can be a big help in meal planning. Such an index is derived by dividing the number of portions sold by the total number of items in the same category (meat, fish, etc.) that were sold. For example:

Menu Item	Portions Sold	Popularity
Roast Beef	62	.31
Broiled Haddock	49	.25
Knockwurst /Kraut	86	.44
Total Portions Sold	197	100.0

Next, the popularity index is applied to the forecast for the business day in question. The planner will know that last time there were 197 portions sold. The sales record will also show whether that was a good day or a slow day, and why. The planner must then forecast the number of customers he estimates there will be. At that point, he can determine how many entree portions are expected to sell. The next step is, of course, to calculate how many portions of each menu item will be needed using the popularity index. (In actuality, that was probably determined for purchasing beforehand.)

Forecast—225 entree items needed

Menu Item	Popularity Index	To be Prepared
Roast Beef	.31	70
Broiled haddock	.25	56
Knockwurst/Kraut	.44	99

Obviously, there are also other factors that enter into this process. For example, poor sellers should have been eliminated and new items added.

This technique can be useful in any kind of restaurant. If you offer a set menu, except for changing specials, you can still index the special against the balance of the menu. Even if your menu changes infrequently, you will want to forecast your sales based on past history and present trends. All restaurants should forecast for purchasing information. (Too many operators buy from habit and, as a consequence, are either over- or under-stocked.) That same forecast is then applied to production in order to avoid leftovers and "run outs."

HOW CHECKLISTS CAN HELP YOU
AVOID PROBLEMS

You can ease many of your production headaches, help your kitchen run smoothly, and head off potential problems if you use checklists of equipment needs, plating, and food service. Here are some examples:

Checklist To Determine Equipment Needs

FROM THE MENU—

- List those items requiring oven preparation and length of baking time.

_____	_____
_____	_____
_____	_____

- Will the oven capacity accommodate this production?
- Is the broiler capacity sufficient? The grill?
- Are there enough pots and kettles for the soups, sauces and gravies?
- Will the bain-marie, or steam table, hold all the hot items? How many pans are needed for holding purposes? What size?
- Is there any need for special equipment? Saute pans? Skillets? Stock pots?
- How will the food be portioned and dished up? What size ladles? Serving spoons? Tongs? Food scoops?
- Will a scale be necessary for portion control? Do we have one?
- What is general condition of the kitchen equipment? Oven thermostat? Cold spots?
- Is the person on staff who will do the preparation sufficiently skilled to handle new items?

Furthermore, when scheduling production, you must be aware of how the items are going to be served. You will also need to know if the items can be produced with efficiency and served to the customers in the same way.

With few exceptions, owners and managers want to "turn their seats" as often as possible. (For the uninitiated, one turn of a seat means one customer. The more turns, the more customers—and the more customers, the more cash in the till.) Diners, for the most part, don't want to be pushed, but they do want attention. Therefore, in order to make a good profit in your restaurant, you must work every possible angle to deliver smooth, easy and fast service in a comfortable and attentive manner.

Proper Plating And Food Service Checklist

Check the following points in regard to your own restaurant. These all have to do with how well your service staff can procure food from your kitchen.

- ☐ Is the china properly sized in relation to the portions offered?

- ☐ Are the right dishes available for attractive and speedy dishing up in the kitchen?

- ☐ Are the serving trays properly sized to handle the kind of parties that most often frequent the restaurant?

- ☐ Is the kitchen properly equipped to keep dishes either hot or cold as needed?

- ☐ Have you studied the work area to see if the kitchen personnel are accommodated with dishes, supplies, etc., within easy reach? Or must they constantly move out of their stations for equipment?

- ☐ Is the service pickup area adequate in size and layout? Can service personnel quickly pick up and move out?

- ☐ Is the food check control station organized and equipped for fast and accurate checking, to insure against unnecessary time delays in service?

How To Buy Food Right
For Maximum Profits

Table of Contents

4

How To Buy Food Right For Maximum Profits

Every restaurant operation, no matter how large or small, should have purchase specifications. These "specs" represent the plan under which you buy merchandise for preparation and resale. They spell out the quality standards to which you purchase. For instance: beef stew specs will indicate the cut from which the beef cubes are to come, the size of each cube, and possibly the grade of beef from which they are cut.

Every restaurant is vulnerable to such uncontrollable problems as disruptions in supply and skyrocketing wholesale prices. In addition, all owners must cope with pilferage, spoilage and delivery shortages. But there are some things you can control to keep your enterprise profitable. You can take a great step toward better profits by determining what and where you want to buy well in advance of actually placing any orders. Preparing a set of purchase specifications for your restaurant will help you to buy "right"—and buying "right" is the first step toward selling for profit.

THE ADVANTAGES OF HAVING PURCHASE SPECIFICATIONS

One benefit of having purchase specifications is the fact that most of the decisions related to product grades, cuts, yields, etc., have been made in advance—when you were not under pressure to buy. Another benefit is that you'll be able to determine which purveyors are best for your business.

If you are knowledgeable and decisive in your buying, the purveyors will quickly notice the fact. That means that they will supply you with only those goods that you demand. In turn, you will soon find out which dealers you can trust and rely on for the kind of service you want. Keep an eye on things, and supervise your receiving function to be certain that what you ordered is what was actually received.

The "specs" or guide for purchasing is of course developed from your menu. Development requires thorough research into many areas including price, product yield, market conditions, portion control and "proper" quality of merchandise. It is not something to be drawn up and then shoved into a desk drawer, never to be seen again. Rather, it is a very important management tool that should be used daily when contemplating or actually purchasing food, beverage and/or supplies. Further, it must be constantly studied and modified as follows:

- When menu changes are contemplated, the market for new items must be researched for price and availability.

- Once decisions regarding new menu offerings have been made, the purchasing guide must be adjusted to reflect any changes necessary to support the menu modifications.

Since one of the biggest problems encountered by restaurant owners or managers is finding enough time in a day to do all of the many tasks, the job of purchasing is often delegated to someone else. When there are no written policies or guidelines for the delegates to follow, there is little or no control over the activity that requires the highest expenditures. But if adequate control is exercised over purchasing, your gross profits will increase and inventory levels will decrease.

How To Develop Keen Purchasing Skills

The two most important ingredients of good food buying are buyer education and maintaining good records.

Smart purveyors know that the best road to a long-term relationship is through buyer awareness. So don't be afraid to take advantage of the opportunities available to you to learn from them. For example, you should visit the produce terminals, meat processing plants, wholesale grocery warehouses, etc., asking lots of questions and taking notes for future reference.

Another way to better educate yourself is by checking with your local restaurant association for books and articles on the subject of food and beverage procurement. Here you will uncover a wealth of material for your file.

In addition, most trade shows have some exhibits related to food and beverage products. It is a good idea to attend several of these shows in order to stay current on new products and changes that are occurring in the industry. Restaurateurs who go to these shows repeatedly find that they give a far greater return than the money and time spent attending them.

Your best source for information, however, is found right in your own restaurant, as outlined below:

- Your customers are the ultimate critics of your buying, preparing and serving skills. So if you are good, they will let you know by coming back to your restaurant again and again. But if you fall down in any of these areas, they will usually tell you first by offering criticism, and if that fails, by not coming back.

- Your employees can be top-notch assistants if you use them properly. Therefore, take your people into your confidence regarding purchasing decisions. Discuss the merits of various products with them and let them offer advice. Try their ideas when possible, and let them be party to the testing of same. Then follow up by discussing the results.

  Final decisions as to what to use, and how, are of course up to you. However, you can learn a great deal from your staff and, at the same time, make hundreds of points by letting them be team members instead of uninterested workers.

USEFUL TIPS ON PURCHASE SPECIFICATIONS

Simply put, you should know *why* you are buying certain products. Good operators don't just buy "ground beef." They buy according to their needs. Many of the Hamburg Restaurant operators, for example, buy ground chuck over ground round—although it's less expensive—because they find it to be a juicier final product. Then some like a ratio of 80% lean to 20% fat, while others prefer a ratio of 85:15. And there are also operators who prefer beef patties with a small percentage of soy added. Prices will vary, of course. But what you have to do is strike a balance between what will satisfy your customers, and what will provide maximum return to you.

When considering meat items for instance, you should be looking for maximum yields of cooked items, as well as palatability. An example of how this can affect your bottom line would be the difference in grades of a roast beef cut. Generally speaking, the high end of the grade, or "Prime," will have more fat than the lower, or "Good." In between is "Choice." These grades will vary as to quality and yield. And what you should buy will depend on your customer's tastes and pocketbooks, as well as your own particular profit requirement.

Testing The Products You Buy

Selection of the best buys for your own specific needs will be the result of study and diligence on your part. In the case of roast meats, much will be learned if you run yield and taste tests on the products you buy. This is a relatively simple matter of weighing the roast prior to cooking, and weighing it after cooking, to determine the net cooked weight. Further, the number of portions yielded should be counted to determine the amount lost during the slicing process. The same testing procedure is used regardless of whether the roast is boneless or bone-in. Just be sure, however, that when testing, you measure like items one against another.

The following is an example test procedure:

Case 1

1 Top Round Beef Roast
   Raw Weight -   10 lbs.
Roasted at 325°F for
- hrs.
   Cooked Weight   7 lbs.

Yield 25 - 4 oz. portions

Case 2

1 Top Round Beef Roast
   Raw Weight -   10 lbs.
Roasted at 425°F for
- hrs.
   Cooked Weight   6 lbs.

Yield 20 - 4 oz. portions

Using the above example, if the price per portion was a $5.95 luncheon special, you would have lost 5 luncheon sales, or $29.75, cooking the meat at a higher temperature—thus decreasing the number of portions available for sale.

Selecting The Best Method Of Cooking Meat

Most experts agree that the lower the roasting temperature the higher the yield of cooked product. They also tend to agree that the palatability of the final product is enhanced by the lower roasting temperatures.

The cooking of meat, as well as poultry and fish, is a broad subject, however. Understanding the technical changes that take place through cooking requires some study and research. Further, the "best" method for roasting in one restaurant may not be the "best" method for you. All of these factors—yield, palatability, waste, etc.—are further complicated by the recent steep increases in energy costs. In addition, cooking times may vary due to the different kinds and the physical conditions of ovens in use.

As mentioned, it is in your best interest to study this subject further since any increases in yield and quality of product will likely mean higher profits for you. Material on this subject is found in many cookbooks. In addition, there are several textbooks available that address the subject:

> *Food Service in Institutions*
> West, Wood, Harger and Shugart
> John Wiley & Sons, Inc.
> New York

> *Cooking Meat in Quantity*
> National Live Stock and Meat Board
> Chicago, Illinois

What About Canned Fruit?

Another area where money can be spent needlessly is in the selection of canned fruit. Different grades are available, and each of them can of course be used for different menu items. As with most products, the price differs between grades. Therefore, in addition to the price consideration, you must consider the product yield and intended use. The following lists the grades of fruit and when to use them:

> *Grade A or Fancy*—When appearance and flavor is of first importance.

> *Grade B or Choice*—Very good for most uses.

> *Grade C or Standard*—When cooking is necessary for further preparation, or as one of several ingredients in a preparation formula or recipe.

> *Substandard (sometimes called D)*—For the same uses as Grade C or Standard, but when appearance is of still less importance.

"Pie" grades of fruit, usually canned in water, can also be used in these instances, and may or may not be of the same grade, depending upon the particular commodity.[1]

THE BENEFITS OF MAINTAINING GOOD RECORDS

Keeping a good accounting of prices and product yields is a must. With such records at hand, you will be able to explore the markets and search out the very best buys for your restaurant. These records will also help you decide what quantity to buy.

Keep in mind that your suppliers are in business to sell, and they will be pleased to sell you as much as you care to buy. Often restaurant owners and managers forget that they too are in business to sell. Therefore, take a hard look at your inventory. If it is too heavy in relation to your sales, cut it down—and put yourself back in the selling business.

How To Keep Track Of Suppliers' Prices

Since suppliers are in competition with each other, it follows that prices for similar items will probably vary among them. In order to keep track of what they're charging, you can prepare bid sheets for each food category. (See sample below.)

When comparing items, don't be fooled by the lowest price on a bid, as it may not be what you wanted. Anyway, if a low-priced product turns out to be unsuitable, the "real" price you pay will be much higher.

DATE   BID SHEET

CO. NAME —PRICE

Q	ITEM					

[1]Adeline Wood, *Quantity Buying Guides*, Volume II (New York: Ahrens Publishing Co.).

Should You Use One Supplier For All Items?

Some operators prefer to use one vendor to supply all items, if possible. In many areas of the country this is not only logical, but necessary. Because the cost of running and maintaining delivery vehicles today is high, most suppliers are no longer willing to make deliveries with less than full truckloads. Further complicating the overall situation is the fact that suppliers are shrinking in number—with the remainder growing in size and volume. With this volume growth has come centralized warehousing, which utilizes sophisticated inventory control systems and delivery vehicles that carry more tonnage per trip.

All of this means that small and medium-sized restaurant owners are often compelled to buy larger amounts of merchandise. They must do this in order to qualify for delivery from companies that require orders exceeding their established minimum amounts for delivery. These developments have caused inconveniences for operators in major cities too, and some have had to change their buying habits. But it has had a much greater effect on restaurants located in outlying areas and small towns, where many low-volume restaurants are located. Storage also becomes a critical problem for these people, since their facilities are often very limited.

It is wise for today's operator to seek out and deal with suppliers who will deliver the quality and quantity that fits into the operation. That may mean buying like items from one or more sources.

It is also possible to save money by cutting off deliveries when possible. Years ago, restaurant owners went to market themselves and saw what they bought. Some still do. If you are close to a produce market, you can go there as often as you like, buy and carry your own. That cuts out the distributor's profit, and the difference between their delivery charges and your own transportation cost is profit to you. These savings can be substantial. In addition, the education gained through selecting your own produce and negotiating prices will be notably rewarding.

EFFICIENTLY STORING YOUR FOOD AND SUPPLIES

Improper storage of food and supplies is a wasteful practice that will cost any operator big dollars. In order to purchase sensibly, you must first determine your needs. Need can only be determined accurately if you can readily tell what you already have on hand.

There are many restaurants in which taking an inventory is virtually impossible. Their storerooms are in a shambles, with boxes piled on boxes, and all piled high in front of open shelving which is also full. In addition—as if that weren't bad enough—everything is all mixed up. I'm sure that you are familiar with these types of restaurants. They're the ones that order a case of #10 sliced pickles because they can't find the bottles they were sure they had. The suppliers love these people, since it is no work at all to sell to them. They just fill out the order blank, while they try to work from memory or witchcraft. This may be profitable for the salesman, but it is obviously very unprofitable for the restaurateur.

You must know the storage capacity of your restaurant. And, if possible, you should place your food and supply orders with such frequency as not to overload the facilities. Next, you should categorize all items and devise a system, so that each item has a specific place for storage. If you develop and maintain such a system, you will be able to make spot checks and take regular inventories with ease—lessening any danger of over or under buying. When you can't closely monitor your inventory (and I mean monitor "with your eyeballs"), then you risk waste by overuse and/or pilferage. And there is plenty of pilferage in restaurants! Set up your storerooms and walk-in refrigerators and freezers so that everything has its place—and then make sure that your staff keeps them that way.

How To Prepare An Inventory Record System

You can easily set up a storeroom by first preparing an inventory record that categorizes the various items to be stored. Within each category, items should be alphabetized. The order of items in storage must be in the same order as found in the record. For example:

Inventory Record

Amount	Unit	Item	Price	Total
		Canned Fruit		
3	#10	Apples, Pie	$4.15	$12.45
4	#10	Peaches	3.25	13.00
4	#10	Pears	2.85	11.40
		Tomato Products		
7	#10	Catsup	4.10	28.70
12	Btl.	Catsup	.56	6.72
6	Btl.	Chili Sauce	.54	3.24
6	#10	Tomatoes, Whole	3.00	18.00
14	#5	Tomato Juice	1.14	15.96

If canned fruit was the first item in the book, it would be found on the first shelf in the storeroom, with Tomato Products being the next item. It doesn't matter whether you arrange the storeroom to fit the inventory record or vice versa. It will depend on how much and what kind of storage space you have.

In addition to the dry storage, you should utilize the same system in your refrigerators and freezers. When you set up a system like this, you have actually established a file for merchandise, which will also be of great benefit to you when preparing to place new orders.

HOW PROPER HANDLING OF FOOD SAVES MONEY

You must make sure that your staff is thoroughly trained in the handling of food and supply items. Fresh fruits and vegetables must be handled with care in order to avoid damage. In addition, they must be examined on receipt, in order to determine if they are the same fresh and wholesome products you ordered. Meat purchases must be weighed and closely examined.

Every restaurant has a certain amount of pre-preparation of foods that is necessary before actual start of production. However, the strongly established trend toward "cook ready" foods has eliminated much of that work. But cleaning and cutting of fruits and vegetables, trimming meats, etc. still must be done. In doing this, people sometimes get careless, and in the process "trim" a sizeable amount of foodstuffs that could be used and *sold*. For instance, tomatoes can be cored and sliced which allows for the entire tomato to be utilized. While this may seem trivial, it is just one area where proper training will serve not only in the preservation of tomatoes, but will carry over into the proper handling of other items as well.

How Special Equipment Can Help You

You should carefully analyze your food handling and preparation techniques, to make certain that waste is eliminated wherever and whenever possible. If special equipment helps, and if it will increase your profits and preserve your quality standards, then use it!

There are many companies that make a variety of kitchen aids. One such company is Le-Jo Enterprises, Inc., Two Lee Boulevard, Malvern, Pennsylvania 19355. It makes a very simple and inexpensive item called a Tomato Shark, and it looks like this:

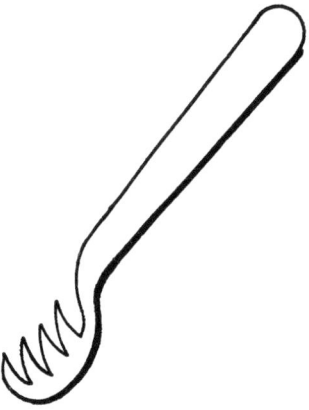

This utensil will core tomatoes, loosen grapefruit segments, remove potato eyes, remove apple and pear seeds, form melon balls, score cucumber rinds and stem strawberries.

In addition, Le-Jo makes other time-saving devices that help to eliminate waste. For example, its tomato slicer produces perfectly sliced products, with no discarded portions.

Again, these are only a few of the items that will help your staff better prepare your food. These—and others—are always worth considering, not only for their time- and money-saving advantages, but also because they can help to make food more attractive and appetizing.

KEEPING IN LINE WITH SANITATION REQUIREMENTS

All cities have a public health department that is organized for the purpose of safeguarding the health and welfare of their residents. Those bodies, in conjunction with the various state and national organizations devoted to maintaining high standards for food handling, have developed the guidelines to be used in public restaurants. There are many publications available that will furnish the information you need to maintain your restaurant operations at an acceptable level. These publications can be obtained by contacting your local Food Service Sanitation Department, or through the offices of your local or state restaurant association. There is no shortage of information available, and the material you get will form the foundation for much of your employee training programs.

While you must of course adhere to the city health codes—there is also the matter of your own sense of loyalty and responsibility to your restaurant customers. Remember, your customers place their trust in the hands of you and your employees every time they come to your restaurant. Therefore, it is your responsibility to take every precaution necessary to protect the food and drink served.

How Improper Storage Results In Loss Of Profits

In addition to the losses that you can suffer through improper, pre-preparation of foodstuffs—mentioned earlier in this chapter—is the loss that can be incurred with bad storage technique. For example, refrigerators that are improperly regulated as to temperature will cause:

- spoilage that necessitates *discarding* food instead of using and *selling* it.

- loss of poundage in meats due to shrinkage. That kind of loss translates into money that comes straight out of your pocket.

When dry storage rooms are improperly planned and maintained, it means:

- broken containers resulting in spilled contents that become unusable.

- items actually "lost" in the storeroom, resulting in the need to spend your hard-earned dollars for items that you can't find due strictly to carelessness.

If your restaurant has too much space dedicated to storage, you may want to consider using some of it for additional sales activity, if possible. If, on the other hand, you have insufficient space, the first thing you should do is to examine carefully your purchasing and delivery techniques to be sure that you are not over-buying. In addition, be certain that racks, pallets, etc. are properly sized and used. And make sure that refrigerators are equipped right for storage. If you have a walk-in type, make sure that you are efficiently using it. For example, the coolest parts of the interior should be used to store those items that need the coldest holding temperatures.

While it is not possible to address completely the matter of proper food handling and sanitation in this Guide, suffice it to say that all sorts of help are available to you in the form of books, pamphlets, films, slides, lectures, etc.—and you should take full advantage of them.

The following is a partial listing of agencies that can provide further information:

- Educational Materials Center
  National Restaurant Association
  311 First St., N.W.
  Washington, D.C. 20001

- The NRA publishes a catalog of Books, Bulletins, and Pamphlets of interest to the Hospitality Industry that covers many different subjects.

- Texas Restaurant Association
  Box 1429
  Austin, Texas 78767

- City of Houston Health Department
  Houston, Texas 77001

  (This department has a Food Service Manager's Certification Program. The manual used and given to each person following completion of the course would be a useful addition to your restaurant library.)

- The National Sanitation Foundation
  Ann Arbor, Michigan, 48105

- College of Hotel and Restaurant Management
  Michigan State University
  East Lansing, Michigan, 48824

- Cornell University
  School of Hotel Administration
  Ithaca, New York, 14853

How To Make Sure That You Receive What You Ordered

There are lots of "eagle eyed" people around who are constantly looking for a way to pick up a fast buck. Therefore, you must keep a very sharp watch on your business—including the people who work for you, delivery people, repair or maintenance persons, customers, and security persons.

The best way to do this is to check your incoming merchandise carefully. For instance, it would be a very simple matter for someone to take out a few pounds of meat from any one delivery. And if you don't weigh in your merchandise, you will never notice the difference. But you will notice the difference in your food cost if these kinds of people get into your pocket often enough.

Several years ago, I worked for a restaurant company that took extra pains to check incoming goods. And the purveyors they dealt with knew how closely they checked their deliveries. Even so, the restaurant caught the following neat little tricks:

- Bags of potatoes clearly labeled #1 Idaho Bakers that turned out to be California potatoes.

- Fresh parsely that was rebundled into smaller than standard size.

- "Sealed" cases from which a few bottles or cans had been taken.

There are lots of ways that dishonest people can find to pilfer your goods. "Short weighting" deliveries is one of the easiest.

INVENTORY CONTROL METHODS THAT WORK

There are two basic inventory control methods with variations that you can effectively use. Many restaurants never take an inventory during the course of a fiscal year, estimating their inventory at year end. Such a practice can be very costly. No matter how big or small your business is, you must have a system for controlling your inventory.

The Perpetual Inventory System

Very simply, this particular system requires that "pars" or inventory levels be established for all stock or standard items on hand. Each item has an individual record, often referred to as a bin card. These cards are updated constantly from purchase records to reflect current cost. As units are used, a running record is maintained of units left in inventory—as well as the cost of items transferred to production. Each item also has a reorder point or a level of units on hand, at which time a purchase is made in order to bring the total units back up to par. Theoretically, with this system, inventory is being taken constantly as items are moved into production and eventually sold.

The Physical Inventory System

This system is simply a matter of maintaining an inventory record of all items on hand. It should be broken down into units that are actually transferred to production. For instance: if #10 cans of tomatoes are transferred as individual units into production, then the inventory of that item should be by the can rather than by the case.

At the end of each predetermined period, you take a physical inventory by counting *all* items on hand. The items are then priced as purchased, extended, and a total cost of inventory determined. This inventory record is generally kept in a book or on separate sheets of paper. It includes spaces for item name, price, amount on hand, and totals.

The basic difference between the two systems is in the actual counting. With the perpetual system, counting of items on hand is constantly going on, whereas with the physical system, all counting takes place at one time and only at the end of a fiscal period. That period might be weekly, monthly or annually as decided by the owners.

It is very difficult for a small business to use a perpetual inventory system because of all the necessary paperwork involved. Even though such a system can be computerized, there will still be a considerable amount of paper to handle—and the cost may be too high for other than the very high-volume places to handle.

Selecting A System That's Right For You

If you don't already have a good system, you will profit greatly by installing one now! In my opinion, there is only one good way to control the costs in a restaurant, and that is by having a weekly cost control system that includes a physical inventory and an operating statement. The key lies in the system itself and how well it works for you.

Since food can easily spoil when improperly handled, and because food and liquor can "walk away" if you turn your back, you must keep track of both at all times. Remember that *watching* and *counting* are the keys to any system's success. As mentioned earlier, when you don't know how much inventory you have on hand, you are apt to either underbuy or overbuy. If you underbuy, you will have "run outs" and lose sales. If you overbuy, the following might develop:

- Spoilage can occur because your sales were insufficient to use up the perishables in time.

- Pilferage can occur because you have more on hand than you need. And if you didn't know what was there to start with, you won't know if anything is missing.

- It costs money to carry excessive inventory. And if you do, you are either borrowing working capital at high interest rates, or losing interest by not investing the money that is tied up in excess stock.

So if you want to have a profitable restaurant, *watch your inventory!*

How Best To Calculate Your Inventory Turnover

Restaurant inventories, because they consist in large part of perishable items, must be "turned" (used) often. You should strive to turn your inventory about once a week, or four times a month. Doing so will insure your diners fresh, wholesome food.

You can measure your own effectiveness by calculating your inventory turnover ratio on a regular basis. This ratio is calculated by dividing the Cost of Goods sold by the Average Inventory Cost.

> **Example:**
>
> ABC Restaurant takes inventory and prepares a statement each month.
>
> Average Monthly Inventory - $ 4,000
>
> Yearly Cost of Sales - $180,000
>
> $180,000 \div $4,000 = 45$ turns/year
>
> 45 turns $\div 12$ months $= 3.75$ turns/month

Your inventory must be taken at the close of each fiscal period whether weekly, monthly or yearly. Inventories cannot be taken prior to the designated date, nor can they be postponed and taken at a later time. Doing so will distort the figures and make statistical comparisons with past periods erroneous and, in some cases, totally useless.

Case History: The Importance Of Keeping Tabs On Inventory

Charlie Shortor had a nice little family restaurant that he was able to handle pretty much by himself. Over the years, the restaurant prospered. Then the kids went off to college and Charlie decided that he should invest in a great big restaurant and make lots and lots of money. Well, Charlie found a place that he could purchase, and he took the plunge.

There were many good features about the new restaurant. Most of all, Charlie liked the fact that the storeroom, back bar and all refrigerators were equipped with locks.

Charlie's restaurant was very busy and sales were strong. But what was puzzling was why the food and beverage costs were high—so high that Charlie was not making any profit. He kept everything locked up, but still items were missing from inventory. Evidently there were pilferers in his organization. Charlie didn't know how all of this could be happening.

One day, while Charlie was hard at work trying to figure this out, he heard the porter with that often-heard restaurant cry, "Hey, who's got the keys?" Right then Charlie realized that, although he had locked up all his merchandise, he had not locked up all the keys.

Moral of this story: "You can't be too careful in this restaurant business" *or* "It's the little things that will do you in." More specifically, keep the keys in your pocket; and know who has them when you are not there.

How To Control Storage Areas

It is sometimes difficult to forecast restaurant sales on a day-to-day basis. But if you estimate your sales with your production supervisor, you will be able to relate those sales to the raw product needs of the restaurant. Once that is done, you can proceed with an actual issue of products to cover the day's production.

This method will never be one hundred percent accurate, but the more you use it, the closer you will come. The result will be the prevention of people running in and out of storerooms and refrigerators all day long. Such a practice will help you control your inventory, and will also aid productivity by making the jobs of food preparation and service as easy and convenient as possible.

Access to storage areas should be limited to authorized persons only. One reason for this is obvious—to control pilferage in your restaurant, as in the example above. Another reason is the need to maintain order so that inventories can be categorized and merchandise stored by category in a prescribed manner.

Allowing free access to storage areas means that you will have no control over your storage plan, and it will be ineffective. Remember, people tend to throw items around carelessly, open cases unnecessarily, and generally cause disruption especially when they are in a hurry. This is particularly true in the restaurant business. So guard your storage areas carefully!

* * * * *

On the following pages are checklists for purchasing, receiving, storage and issuing, to help you rate your restaurant.

CHECKLIST FOR PURCHASING

Who does the purchasing?

Are purchase orders used?

Are budgets for purchasing of food and supplies developed from operating history and forecasts of future business? Or, are orders placed by habit or "the guess we need some more" technique?

Are purchase specifications in written form?

Do specifications provide enough information for evaluation of merchandise received?

Are bid sheets used, and are all purchases made on a competitive basis?

Are some items purchased in advance for future needs? What items?

Are these future needs carefully forecasted?

Is there sufficient and safe storage for future use inventory?

Has the cost of money to carry the extra inventory been carefully considered?

How often are the following categories of foodstuff purchased?

> Meat
> Groceries
> Produce
> Baked items
> Dairy

Are they bought often enough? Too often?

Do you qualify for trade discounts? If so, do you take all of them?

Do you make petty cash purchases? How often? What is the average dollar amount of a petty cash purchase?

Who checks invoices for payment? Does anyone?

Who writes the checks or disburses the cash? Are they double checked against vendor invoices and statements?

Are any comparisons of prices paid made with other restaurants?

Is the quality of merchandise closely monitored, to insure that "merchandise received" is the same as "merchandise bought"?

CHECKLIST FOR RECEIVING

Who receives food and supplies?

Is it always the same person?

Where is merchandise received?

Can you depend on the person receiving the merchandise? Will that person check the merchandise carefully? Will that person make sure that you get your money's worth?

Do you have a scale at your receiving point? Is it used for weighing in merchandise? Or, do you have empty boxes, unusable equipment, etc., stored on top of it?

Is your scale adequate for your business?

How often is it checked for accuracy?

Are "merchandise quality guides" available to the receiving person?

When weighing merchandise—

    Are wrappers removed?
    Do you buy ice at the price of red snapper or shrimp?

How are foods judged as substandard rejected?

How are the invoices handled?

Are invoices verified by signature?

If you are on a cash basis, do you pay in cash or by check at the time of receiving?

If by cash, do you have a "tight" system that will prevent fraud and/or theft?

CHECKLIST FOR STORAGE

Are foods *properly* and *promptly* stored after delivery?

How are meats handled? Are they stored in the best possible manner so as to prevent spoilage and/or shrinkage?

Are your walk-in refrigerators equipped with wooden platforms to keep food items off damp or wet floors?

Are fruits and vegetables in shallow trays to retard spoilage from pressure and/or lack of air circulation?

Do you have sufficient refrigerator and storeroom space for the volume of business you do?

Are those fruits and vegetables that are stored at room temperature properly handled?

What is the temperature in

		*Should Be**
Your produce room	_____	36° - 40°F
Your refrigerator	_____	30° - 35°F
Your freezer	_____	0 -(-10°)F
Your storeroom	_____	50° - 70°F

Are they too hot? Too cold?

Do you have adequate locks on your refrigerators and storerooms? Do you use them?

Who controls the keys to those locks?

Do your employees bring packages or carry above-average size handbags, etc., into the restaurant? Why?

What procedure do you use for checking packages, handbags, etc. of employees going off duty? Or do you bother to check at all?

Are vendor drivers carefully watched and checked to prevent pilferage?

---

*M.C. Warfel and Frank H. Waskey, *The Professional Food Buyer* (Berkeley, California: McCutchan Pub. Corp.)

CHECKLIST FOR ISSUING

Do you have a procedure for issuing, or are refrigerators and store-rooms open to everyone?

Is any food given or sold to employees for removal from premises? How do you control this procedure?

How often do you examine your inventory?

How often do you count and price your inventory?

Are food items that are transferred to the cocktail lounge properly charged and credited?

Are beverages such as wine, liquor, and beer that are transferred from bar to kitchen properly accounted for?

What is your inventory turnover ratio? Does it make you happy?

How To Get More And Better Work From Your Employees

Table of Contents

How To Get More And Better Work From Your Employees

While many firms in the food service industry have become large enough so they can afford a specialist to handle personnel matters, there are many others that cannot. If you are financially able to carry such a person, hiring one will save you many hours of detail work. Either way, this chapter will brief you on some steps you must take for the effective management of your employees.

In the restaurant business, high employee turnover seems to be a continual problem, with someone always leaving and needing to be replaced. This usually has little to do with how well you manage your restaurant—but it's a serious problem, all the same. Let's consider these—

FIVE REASONS FOR HIGH STAFF TURNOVER

1. Most restaurants hire some part-time people in an effort to control labor costs. For the majority of these people the job is temporary, and they will move on to something else.

2. Some restaurant employees look unfavorably at their jobs, even though those same jobs are performed with dignity by thousands of people.

3. Working in a busy restaurant can be rough and tough. Only the hardy survive.

4. Since restaurants are busiest when the rest of the world is at leisure (holidays, nights, weekends), many people who want those times for themselves don't stay on for long.

5. Generally speaking, many restaurants pay smaller salaries than certain other kinds of businesses. In many restaurants prices must be held at the lowest levels possible, in order to protect sales and insure customer acceptance. Although some restaurants are able to maintain high prices due to their position with the status-seeking portion of the public, *all are not*. But that does not mean that restaurant employees don't make a good living. On the contrary, many are highly remunerated—through either salary or gratuities.

There are, of course, many other reasons for employee turnover and some certainly relate to poor management practices, such as failure to train new employees. Therefore, it is in your best interest to develop and maintain a formal personnel policy.

The Key Steps To Hiring Employees That Are Right For The Job

The important things you need to know in hiring the right people are:

- whether you even need to fill the position
- what the job is all about
- what kind of person is best suited for the job

Once you've answered these, there are many ways to find good employees. Here are six recruiting sources:

- Having one's own employees recruit from among their friends and relatives.

- Advertising for help in various local and regional periodicals. Even though there may be many organizations advertising in the same paper, your particular restaurant may have special appeal for some one individual.

- Through the placement services of local high schools and colleges.

- From the local Labor Department placement service.

- Other restaurants or food service establishments, such as school or college food service and industrial plant cafeterias.

- Through your own friends, acquaintances, and activities such as church and other community functions.

How To Develop A Better Application Form

Before considering your interviewing technique, you will need an application form, since you must maintain records in your business. Having such an application form, in itself, will tell you much about a particular person, such as:

- Can the applicant read and write? English?

- Can the person follow simple written instructions?

You'll get the answers to these merely by having someone use the form.

There are probably more kinds of employment application forms than there are pages in this Guide, but they all have certain parts in common—previous experience, education and so on.

CAUTION. There are some questions that you cannot ask an applicant. So before designing your form, you should consult with your local Labor Department office for guidelines.

The length and complexity of the job you are attempting to fill will dictate the kind of application form you will need. There is, however, the following standard information on all of them:

—Applicant's name and address.

—Social Security number.

—Telephone number where person can be reached.

—Previous work record, rate of pay and name of supervisor.

—What form of transportation does the applicant rely on? Have own auto? Take bus? Walk?

You must take care in the construction of your application blank, in order to avoid trouble through violation of Equal Employment Opportunity Regulations. It is wise to counsel with knowledgeable persons regarding the law and what you can or cannot do. The following are some of the topics which you should not discuss:*

√Race

√Religion

---

*The list is only partial. You should do your own investigating as to the rights under law of employers and employees.

✓National origin

✓Sex

✓Age

✓Marital status

Actually, applicants will usually volunteer most, if not all, of the information you need without any prompting on your part.

HOW BEST TO INTERVIEW PROSPECTIVE EMPLOYEES

Interviewing is a skill that comes from educating oneself in accepted technique, and then from actually doing it over a period of time.

> *Key Point*: Your profits will be directly related to how good a job you can do in the selection and retention of employees. It is almost certain that substandard, non-caring employees will soon drive you out of business— and just as certain that good, caring employees will help you prosper in business.

When interviewing candidates, keep in mind that the applicant has a need. Maybe it's a need for a change in employment, or maybe the person is unemployed and the need is basic. Your job during the interview process then is to explore these needs. And this can be done through skillful questioning.

How To Ask Result-Getting Questions

It is wise to avoid those questions that invite an abrupt "Yes" or "No" answer. It's better to use open-ended or suggestive questions that elicit conversation from the applicant.

Examples:

Bad: Did your boss at the ABC Restaurant treat you well?

Better: Who was your supervisor at the ABC Restaurant? How would you describe this person?

Bad: Did you graduate from high school?

Better: Can you tell me something about your education? How do you think it might help you in the restaurant business?

Bad: Do you like this kind of work?

Better: What prompted you to enter the restaurant field? Do you find the work pleasant?

Bad: Do you enjoy serving food to diners?

Better: What do you most like about serving diners? Most dislike?

Bad: Do you like night work?

Better: What are your feelings about working nights?

If you study these questions, you will note that the objective is to give the applicant every opportunity to talk. When you encourage the applicant to do the talking, you will be able to listen and form your opinion of the interviewee. When an interviewer remains silent at times, the applicant often will become impatient and talkative. As a result, many of the answers the interviewer is looking for will evolve in the conversation without further questions.

How To Put An Applicant At Ease

If there is sincerity and truth in the interview process, then each person will put his best foot forward and attempt to reach the objective at hand.

The first step is for you to put the applicant at ease. Therefore, you should:

- Provide as much privacy as possible.

- Have your telephone calls held.

- Instruct others that you are not to be disturbed unless there is an emergency.

If your restaurant doesn't have a private office where interviewing can take place, you can take the following steps to facilitate the interview process:

1. If you have a private dining area, it can be used for this purpose during off hours. However, avoid using a busy area, such as when your staff is trying to set up for a function —even though there are no customers in the house.

2. Select a table in a remote section of the dining room or lounge. Be sure, however, that there is sufficient light for reading and for observing the candidate.

Privacy is very important during the interview. You both want to be able to talk freely with no fear of being overheard. The more private you can make the interview, the more apt you are to elicit meaningful conversation. By doing this, you establish a businesslike environment and convey to the applicant that he or she is important, and that the interview will be conducted properly.

A proper interview is done after each party has completed the homework and has a knowledge of the other. Unfortunately, there are many situations when people are badly needed and little or no investigation takes place before the interview. It is in this kind of situation that "practice makes perfect." If you have "honed" your interviewing technique and if your application form is properly constructed, you will be able to move quickly into the process of evaluation.

How To "Size Up" An Applicant

When first sizing up a prospective employee for any position, "the eyes have it." Since sanitation is so very important in a restaurant, try to see the prospect in that light. Check the following:

1. Is the person neatly dressed? Remember that it is not necessary to have expensive clothes in order to be neat and clean.

2. How about grooming? Is hair combed? Neat? Clean? How about hands and face? If the applicant is sloppy and uncaring during the interview, he or she will probably carry the same habits on to the job.

Probably the greatest fault in all of us is our desire to be heard. It is a fact that, for the most part, people do not listen well. It is very important for the interviewer to listen carefully to what the prospect has to say, in order to make the right hiring decision.

A good interviewer is one who has the skill to encourage the applicant to talk, and who also has the patience and intelligence to *watch* and *listen*.

Some points to watch out for are:

1. Does the person seem overly nervous? Are the eyes steady? Check the position of hands and feet?

2. Does the applicant appear to be indolent? Sleepy?

3. Does the applicant appear healthy? How about complexion? Posture?

If you practice, you will become very adept at spotting these signs of potential trouble. The end result will be a high quality employee that is interested in making a profit for your business.

HOW TO DEVELOP A SUCCESSFUL TRAINING PROGRAM

Once you have developed all the techniques necessary to finding good employees, you will want to take steps to insure that they stay with you for as long as possible.

One sure way to keep employees on the job is through the development and consistent use of training programs. It is very important for people to feel confident of their own ability to do a job well. I have heard more than one operator play down training because "they just get trained and someone else hires them away." This, of course, may happen. But a positive way to view such a situation is that, if your employees are so good and in demand, then you will surely have a thriving business—because of the great service they are giving your customers.

Another reason, which is equally unfounded, that managers use for not having training programs is: employees "turn over so fast" there is no time to train them. Well, that kind of thinking is dangerous, because owners do not realize that turnover is often the result of no training and little or no orientation on the job.

Employees like to be welcomed and smoothly integrated into the work group. Their skill on the job has much to do with how they are accepted by their peers. If they carry their weight, there is a good chance they will win acceptance of the group. Therefore having contented, skillful employees who are able to work together will mean additional profits to you. And training programs, even if modest in design, will help bring this attitude into your restaurant.

You can develop your own training programs that fit your own particular needs. Consider, however, that since time is at a premium in most restaurants, the short, ongoing training sessions will probably be the most effective.

Model Training Session For Waiters And Waitresses (15 minutes)

How to load and carry a tray: Select one person as the "doer." Select one person as the "learner." By working with the "learner," have the "doer" demonstrate how the tray can be loaded for balance.

Demonstrate how the tray is lifted and how the hands, arms and legs all play an important role. Then have the "learner" go through the exercise. Stress to the group how the job is easier and safer if done properly.

Training will best be accomplished by those persons who understand and practice the principles of teaching. These principles are time honored and practiced by all good instructors. Below are two guides for instructing trainees from two separate source books that were copyrighted some 33 years apart. You will quickly note the similarity of technique, and you will be a successful instructor if you will adopt and practice either one.

The following has been excerpted from: "A Guide to the Selection and Training of Food Service Employees" prepared by a Committee of the Food Administration Section of the American Dietetic Association. Copyright 1947.

HOW TO INSTRUCT

Here is what you should do every time you instruct an employee or correct his work:

Step 1: PREPARE the worker to receive the instruction.

    A. Put him at ease. Remember, he can't think straight if you make him embarrassed, ill at ease, or frightened.

    B. Find out what he already knows about this job. Don't tell him things he already knows. Start in where his knowledge ends.

    C. Gain his interest. Relate the job or operation to the work of the whole unit, so he knows his work is important.

    D. Put him in the right position. Don't have him see the job backwards, or from any other angle than that from which he will work.

Step 2. PRESENT the operation.

    A. Tell him, show him, illustrate for him, ask him questions.

    B. Give only a few instructions at one time. Understanding is gained more quickly if ideas are presented gradually.

    C. Make the "key points" clear. These will make or break the operation, or possibly mean the success or failure of the employee.

      D. Be patient, and proceed *slowly*. Work for accuracy at first, speed later.

      E. Repeat the job and the explanation if necessary.

Step 3. TRY OUT performance.

      A. Have the worker do the job under observation.

      B. Then have him do it again, but have him EXPLAIN to YOU what he is doing and why. All of us find it easy to observe motions and not really understand what we are doing. YOU want him to UNDERSTAND.

      C. Have him explain the key points.

      D. Correct errors, but don't correct the employee in such a way he believes he is slow to learn.

      E. Continue doing this until YOU know the WORKER knows.

Step 4. FOLLOW-UP

      A. Put the worker on his own. He has to "get the feel" of the job by doing it by himself.

      B. Tell him to whom to go if help is needed. Make this definite—yourself or someone *you* designate. The wrong person might give poor advice.

      C. Check his work frequently, perhaps every few minutes at the start, and then every few hours or days. Be on the lookout for any incorrect or unnecessary moves. Be careful about your taking over the job too soon, or too often. Don't take it over *at all* if you can point out the help he needs.

      D. Get him to look for key points as he progresses.

      E. Taper off this extra coaching until he is able to work under normal supervision.

* * * * *

You will be surprised and gratified at the greatly improved results which can come from the use of such a simple plan. Use it when implementing a new operation, checking an employee's work, or changing a work procedure.

Application of this outline does not end with instruction in specific skills. This technique, which presents the basic principles of teaching, can be used in planning any course of employee training.

Also, sanitation and cooking methods can be taught more effectively if you follow the suggestions made in this procedure.

The following has been exerpted from Lester R. Bittel, *What Every Supervisor Should Know*, Fourth edition, p. 265. Copyright © 1980 by McGraw Hill Book Company. Reprinted by permission of McGraw Hill Book Company.

How Do You Get Down To The Real Business Of Training Employees To Do A Job The Way You Want Them To?

Training can be either the simplest—or the most difficult—job in the world. If you can grasp just four fundamentals, you can be a superior trainer. If you don't buy this approach, you'll spend the rest of your life complaining that employees are stupid, willful, or not like workers used to be in the good old days.

The foundation of systematic, structured job training has four cornerstones:

Step 1.   *Get the workers ready to learn.* People who want to learn are the easiest to teach. So let trainees know why their job is important, why it must be done right. Find out something about the employees as individuals. Not only does this make them have more confidence in you, but it reveals to you how much they know already about the job, the amount and quality of their experience, and what their attitude toward learning is. This familiarization period helps the trainees to get the feel of the job you want them to do.

Step 2.   *Demonstrate how the job should be done.* Don't just tell the trainees how to go about it or say, "Watch how I do it." Do both—tell *and* show them the correct procedure. Do this a little at a time, step-by-step. There's no point in going on to something new until the trainee has grasped the preceding step.

Step 3.   *Try the workers out by letting them do the job.* Let the employees try the job—under your guidance. Stay with the trainees now, to encourage them when they are doing right and to correct them when wrong. The mistakes they make while you're watching are invaluable, since they show you where they have not learned.

Step 4.   *Put the trainees on their own gradually.* Persons doing a new job have to fly alone sooner or later. So after they have shown you that they can do the work reasonably well while you're standing by, turn them loose for a while. Don't abandon them completely, though. Make a point of checking on their progress and workmanship regularly. Perhaps three or four times the first day they are on their own, then once or twice a day for a week or two. But never think they are completely trained. There's always something the employee can learn to do, or learn to do better.

* * * * *

The following are some short instructional sessions that can be scheduled with service people:

- Setting up a table

- Stocking a service stand

- Clearing between courses

- Proper service of food

- Preparing the guest check

- Presenting the guest check

- Serving of all beverages

For the bus people:

- How to clear the table

- Pre-sorting china, glass and flatware

- Setting up a table

- Serving water, rolls, butter, etc.

- Delivering soiled dishes and flatware to the dishwashing station

- How to fold a napkin

For the pre-preparation and salad people:

- How to core a tomato before slicing

- How to core a head of lettuce the right way, instead of cutting off and discarding usable leaves.

- How to store produce properly

We can all think of hundreds of small, seemingly insignificant tasks that are performed daily in all restaurants. If you select from these tasks, you can develop a fine ongoing program that will produce the following very worthwhile results:

1. Your people will feel more important and closer to the business.

2. You will promote teamwork.

3. You will be constantly working toward increased sales and lower costs, thereby putting more money in your pocket!

One last word on training, keep the sessions short so that people don't lose interest. And be sure you pay your people for the time spent in these sessions. In addition, there are many fine programs that can be obtained that utilize film and recorded dialogue. However, these take somewhat longer to use, and that may present a problem. If so, try short 10 to 15 minute sessions. Then, if you have enough time, use both kinds. Whichever you choose, I guarantee that you will be absolutely amazed at the results.

If you are in need of additional ideas and/or prepared and ready-to-use programs, you can contact your local restaurant association office for information on programs available through the Educational Office of the National Restaurant Association. If you are not a member, you may want to consider joining since the organization is most supportive of its membership.

How To Measure Employee Performance

In order to insure that your employees receive the raises and promotions that they deserve, you should institute and maintain an EMPLOYEE APPRAISAL PROGRAM. Properly organized and done in a consistent manner, this is not at all burdensome. The following steps will help you to organize and handle this very important function:

1. Set up a file with a separate folder for each employee. You will use this file to maintain all personnel records.

2. In the file, you should have an appraisal form with spaces for the following information:

   —Employee's name

   —Date of appraisal

   —Notes you have kept regarding the person's performance on the job, and notes to be taken as you talk to the employee. You will also want the notes from any previous sessions with that employee.

   —Space for signatures that signify your acceptance, and the employee's, of the contents of the session.

Although some evaluation forms have room for other data, the foregoing will suffice for most of the appraisals you will need to conduct.

When And How To Do The Appraisal

You will need a calendar or tickler file to alert you when an appraisal is due. The length of time on the job or time between appraisals is of course your decision. Generally speaking, though, the first appraisal or review should be after the first three to six months of employment, and yearly thereafter.

Of paramount importance is the need to be consistent. If you establish an Employee Appraisal Program, make sure you follow through and do it on a regular basis.

The following are some suggestions that will help to make your program successful:

1. When giving an appraisal, make sure you do it in a place where you will have privacy. Make the employee feel at ease. Hold your telephone calls, and do not allow interruptions. In other words, make the employee "king" for the hour.

2. Be prepared for the session. Be sure to give ample notice to the employee, so that he or she can also be prepared.

3. Be fair and forthright, and make every attempt to encourage a give-and-take conversation.

To sum up, when giving an appraisal, be consistent, be on time, listen and evaluate. Remember too that appraisal time is a time to discuss the employee's performance. It is also a time for you to listen. By listening carefully, you may find out some very worthwhile information about your business. More importantly, the appraisal may help to turn a marginal employee into a good one, or cause a good employee to change his mind about looking for a different job. Either way, you win!

What About Salary And Wage Reviews?

There is some difference of opinion about whether salary or wage reviews should be given at the time of appraisal. My preference is to schedule the appraisal review separate from any discussion about wages or salary. Remember, a performance appraisal is carried out for the purpose of discussing how well the employee has performed his duties during the stipulated period. Therefore, if you include a salary and/or wage review during the same interview period, you will likely find that the employee has little or no interest in discussing the job. And since money is so important to everyone, the employee will likely be preoccupied with whether or not there is a raise in the offing, and how much it will be.

Another difficulty that can be encountered during simultaneous reviews is the perception of the employee as to whether or not the salary review fits the appraisal. If the performance has been good, you will want to say so. Even if you offer a raise that is proper in your mind, it may be perceived as too low and inadequate by the employee. *Result*: a disgruntled and unhappy employee who may no longer perform to the same high standard.

Similarly, when you are appraising an employee whose performance has not been up to standard, your goal is to try and make him or her understand why you have such an opinion. Further, you should be attempting to "turn" this person around so that a marginal employee can become a good one. Therefore, if you couple such an appraisal with the statement that no increase in salary is warranted, the entire session is almost sure to become totally negative. In the process, you will probably lose an employee who might have been good if properly handled.

In most restaurants, everyone seems to know exactly how much money everyone else makes. For this reason, you *must* have a wage and salary policy that sets the rate and range for all jobs in the restaurant. When you do this, you introduce and maintain consistency. You also eliminate all the speculation and suspicions that people have regarding how much money each one makes.

How To Communicate Effectively With Employees

Communication can be defined as our most constant activity, but the one to which we contribute the least thought. Our communications skills have much to do with whether or not we succeed or fail.

When considering how best to communicate with employees, one must focus on the status levels of the participants and the goals and desires of each. For example:

- The goal of the owner or manager is to develop and maintain a successful business, thereby earning more money to enjoy whatever he values in life.

- The goal of the employee is to perform in a manner acceptable to the management, so as to advance his or her position and/or earnings in order to enjoy whatever that person values in life.

How to reach those goals is a problem that you are constantly facing as a restaurant owner or manager. If you are to succeed, you must develop and maintain a high degree of skill in communications.

The ability to communicate effectively with employees has a lot to do with your "track record" as a good manager. If you are consistent in the way you deal with your people, they will know what to expect from you. As a result, they will develop security and confidence, and will perform better on the job.

It is not enough to speak of consistency of management by itself. Rather, one must add some other ingredients that go with good management. We have many words in our English language that go well with consistency:

—Firm, yet always fair

—Honest

—Forthright

—Friendly

—Courteous

—Generous

—Truthful

—Thoughtful

You can take any one, or all of them, to use with consistency—and you will go a long way toward communicating effectively with your employees.

Remember, all of your actions communicate something to others. For example:

- If you walk around with a scowl or a long face, someone will "see" unhappiness and feel apprehensive.

- If you are impolite or discourteous with a person, he or she may take it personally and feel insecure and unwanted.

- If you are dishonest with your employees, they will develop the attitude that they must also be dishonest to protect themselves.

- If you are not forthright or "up front" with your people, you will probably encourage them to treat you—and each other—the same way.

Key Ingredients For Better Communication

Schedule and conduct regular meetings with employees. In this way, your people will get the message that you want to communicate with them, and are concerned about their well-being, as well as your own. Set up regular times for the meetings and establish in advance the length of the sessions. Be sure to start and end on time.

Next, prepare an agenda and set down the rules for the sessions. For example, your meetings might follow this sort of format:

—Each Monday at 2:30 P.M., schedule a meeting with all kitchen personnel

—Length of meeting is 30 minutes

—Ten minutes for review of previous week's business

—Ten minutes for any revisions to menu, etc., for current week

—Ten minutes for open discussion; each person limited to a total of three minutes.

If items of business arise that require additional time, schedule a separate session with only the person or persons concerned. Don't forget to stick to *your* rules. Don't let any one person, including yourself, dominate the sessions. And be sure that you use the old ears. Listening to "them that does" can really pay off!

A bulletin board is another good way to communicate special messages, and will help to keep your employees better informed. For example, congratulating people on birthdays and special anniversary dates, or announcements of local social and sports events. Be sure, however, to place only current and/or meaningful notices on it. In addition, separate the official governmental or civic portion of the board from your own day-to-day operational postings. It is important to make sure that the bulletin board is worth the effort to read.

BETTER EMPLOYER/EMPLOYEE RELATIONS

Often managers fail to recognize the very important part that employees play in the success of a restaurant, and fail to communicate because they are either too busy or feel too important. This is one of the biggest mistakes a manager can make.

Fostering good employer/employee relationships is an ongoing management responsibility that holds true regardless of individual organizational structure. It doesn't matter if you own or manage a large or small restaurant, independent or chain operations, fast food or dinner house business—the relationship between boss and worker is still the same. This relationship also holds true in those organizations that are unionized. The contract does not supplant the need for management to relate on good terms with the workers.

What To Do If Your Restaurant Is Unionized

Although much has been written about unions and management/union relationships, the material deals mostly with pre-organization matters. To my knowledge, there is a scarcity of information relating to acutal management of the unionized organization.

The major point to remember as far as unionization is concerned is that if it happens to your business, it will bring about a change in your style of management. Once a restaurant has been organized, the management and employees must begin to live with the contract negotiated between management and the union. When the contract is signed by both parties, it becomes a legal document, and management and employees become bound to abide by the terms.

When this happens, problems may develop because either side— management or employee—does not understand the terms or implications of the agreement. And these problems can result in misunderstandings and the filing of grievances that may require time and effort to settle. Too many grievances, although settled, tend to build adversarial relationships between management and employees to the detriment of the business.

If your business is organized, study the contract carefully. Have an attorney or labor relations expert explain any parts that you do not completely understand. Remember that the union has the mechanisms and talent available for administration of its contracts. You must do likewise.

Of major importance if you're unionized is a separate file for each employee in your restaurant. The file should contain the following documents:

—Application Form

—Health Card Record

—Appraisal Form

—Wage History

—Record of any and all meetings between you and the employee. (Contracts usually specify how meetings are to be conducted, and whether or not steward or committee person attendance is required. This sort of meeting normally refers to the handling of disciplinary measures.)

—Attendance Records

—Record all actions taken that have an effect on the employee's job, wages, hours of work, etc.

The foregoing is a general list of items that are necessary for the administration of many contracts. Your own particular situation may be different and may require a different type of record keeping. The main point is that you must be as adept at contract administration as are the union representatives who service your employees. Otherwise, you may find yourself in costly and time-consuming grievance sessions, rather than spending it on better ways to run your restaurant.

HOW WELL-GROOMED AND SMARTLY ATTIRED PEOPLE CAN INCREASE SALES

If you want your restaurant to be a winner, you will have to make it look like one. Theme and concept seem to have become the number-one concern of investors, as each tries to outdo the other in pizzazz and glamor. At the same time, the simple basics of good grooming and smart attire for employees often get completely overlooked.

I recently revisited The Savoy Grill, a fine old restaurant in Kansas City. One of the first things I noticed was the appearance of its very efficient service staff. The Dining Room Manager wore a dark suit, white shirt and black tie. The waiters were in black slacks, white shirts, black ties, white jackets and black shoes. The bus help were in black slacks, white high-neck jackets and black shoes. I could not help but notice that the personal grooming of the employees complemented the sharpness of the uniforms. The jackets were clean, shoes shined, trousers creased, and everyone's hair was neatly trimmed. You may think that I was there "before the action started." Not at all; it was well into the dinner hour and the restaurant was full.

When I visit a restaurant such as this one, I immediately feel like the management really does care about its customers. It tells me that the kitchen is clean and that I am in good hands. Evidently, it gives other people the same feeling, since the restaurant has been there for many years.

How To Select Uniforms That Will Complement Your Restaurant

Before making your uniform selection, there are certain factors that you should consider. For one thing, you must be sure that the colors harmonize with the decor of your restaurant. Also they must be colors that enhance and complement the food and service you offer. Aside from black and white uniforms, there are many color combinations that are very attractive.

A good way to select uniform colors is to seek the advice of people who are expert in that business. Certain colors tend to excite people and are attention getters, i.e., red and yellow, while others can be a turnoff, such as gray. Some colors are cool and relaxing, others are gay and cheerful, while others are somber and noncommittal. The uniforms in your restaurant can be a focal point and a very important sales tool for you.

After you have settled on color, you must give some thought to style, kind of material, initial cost and maintenance. Consider the following when selecting uniforms:

1. Do the colors coordinate with your restaurant's decor? Be sure they "liven up" the food and service.

2. Will the style be complementary to all of the shapes and sizes of your employees? Arrange to see the uniforms modeled by a few people of different size and build.

3. Should you buy or rent your uniforms?

4. Is the replacement cost in line?

5. Can the uniforms be laundered? Are they colorfast? Or do they require dry cleaning?

6. Who will maintain the uniforms? Employees or the house?

7. Will you also specify accessories? What color and style of shoes will be worn?

8. Can you obtain samples?

9. Are aprons to be part of the uniform?

10. Will the uniforms readily show spots and stains? Can they be "spotted" for small stains, or must the entire garment be cleaned?

Key Point: The "best" uniforms will look like the "worst" if they are not properly worn and maintained. So make sure your employees adhere to your expectations.

How To Help Keep Your Employees Looking Sharp

Some people dress sharp and take care of their overall appearance, while others could not care less. This certainly includes your employees. Therefore, furnishing uniforms will not insure that your employees are sharp and well groomed. If you want to have a good-looking staff, you'll have to work to get it—and work even harder to keep it. Here are some suggestions:

• Use some of your training time for modeling and demonstration.

• Do not use the best-looking employee as a model, but have an average, ordinary-looking employee model for the group.

• Check that everything is just right. Accessories, shoes, hair, uniform condition, tailoring, jewelry, hose, etc., should all be correct and in keeping with your own particular dress code.

• Talk to the group while the uniform is being modeled. Run your own little fashion show, and sell the idea that careful dress "says" care and efficiency. Sell the group on the fact that neat dress and good grooming will earn more tips.

In addition, you can provide these aids for helping employees to look sharp and stay that way:

• Accidents will happen. Try to have clean aprons and some spare uniforms around, if needed.

• Some restaurants provide full-length mirrors with tips about grooming to the side. Employees should be encouraged to check their appearance periodically.

• You can obtain pictures that demonstrate proper attire. These can be posted where they will be noticed.

• You can use the old technique of an inspection before each shift. This is a very good practice if it is done in a professional and consistent manner. If you do this, make certain that each employee knows that he or she must be acceptable in appearance, or he or she will not work. This may seem a bit severe, but in the long run it will pay in dividends to you.

"Training For Profit" Programs

All of this business of grooming and manners can be very nicely incorporated in your "training for profit" programs. As stated previously, you should concentrate on short, meaningful subjects as topics for your sessions. You can handle the sessions yourself or call on various employees to participate. In addition, there are other business people who will probably be more than willing to give a talk on the subject. Here are a few ideas you might want to try.

—Ask a local hair stylist to give a short demonstration on haircare.

—There may be a shoe supplier who will demonstrate the proper methods of cleaning and caring for shoes for long and comfortable wear.

—The uniform people will very likely have someone who will demonstrate proper maintenance techniques.

—You may find a department store that is willing to furnish a cosmetician for a short demonstration on skin care and tips on applying makeup.

These are just a few suggestions. Undoubtedly, you'll come up with more. All of these "little" things will help to make your employees feel wanted and secure in their job—and you know what that means for you!

DEVELOPING A PERSONNEL POLICY MANUAL

Restaurant owners and managers are more the "action types" who enjoy the activity of a busy operation. It is difficult for these kinds of people to take the time to sit down and compose something like a policy manual. Consequently, lots of them turn out to be "hip shooters" who neglect to establish a written policy. This practice can only lead to inconsistent management and result in people getting wrong answers. If you run your business like this, you risk having disgruntled employees and a high employee turnover rate. Better to plan carefully—and write it down.

Although the development of a personnel policy manual requires time to gather and compile the content, it will pay off big. You will need written guidelines that include the following:

—rules to be followed by employees

—what actions can result from breaking these rules

—a complete breakdown of fringe benefits that are offered

—government laws and regulations that must be adhered to

—guidelines for recruiting, interviewing and hiring of employees

—payroll procedures to be followed

—job specifications and descriptions, and the approved pay scale for the business

As stated, it is important for you to have made firm decisions on all these matters, and to have them in some kind of written form. Also, the form you elect to use must be such as to allow for changes, since very little or none of this type of material is cast in stone.

There are consultants who can do this work for you if you are unable or unwilling to do it yourself. As you shop around for this service, you will probably find a range of fees charged. Keep in mind, though, that you get what you pay for—no more or no less.

A Sample Personnel Policy Manual

I have developed the following outline that you can use as a table of contents for your personnel policy manual. Each topic includes a short narrative relating to the subject, and some tips on gathering information and developing policy.

PERSONNEL POLICY MANUAL

"YOUR RESTAURANT"

Part	*Subject*
I	*Recruiting, Interviewing, Selecting and Hiring Employees* (This topic was covered earlier in this chapter.)
II	*Orientation and Training of Workers* (Also discussed earlier.)
III	*Job Specifications and Descriptions* In this section, you will *specify* each different job in the restaurant, and the skills and requirements that are needed. Further, you will *describe* the duties, functions and responsibilities that are part of each job. Here are a couple of examples to guide you. They are by no means complete, but should aid you in developing your own.

Job Specification	— Waiter/Waitress
Age Requirements	— Minimum 21 years
Education	— At least 10 years formal education completed
Experience	— Not necessary, but 1 to 2 years preferred
Skills Required	— Must have basic knowledge of food, and service of same
	— Must have some knowledge of wines and alcoholic beverages
	— Must possess basic arithmetic, reading and writing skills
	— Should be well groomed, friendly and have a degree of self-confidence
	— Must have ability to work well with other people
Job Description	— Waiter/Waitress
Reports to	— Hostess or manager (if no hostess is on duty)
Supervisory Tasks	— None
Major Function	— Sets up and assists in clearing tables. Performs side work as directed. Serves food and beverages to diners in a manner acceptable to management. Follows methods and procedures as established.
Responsibilities	— Reports to work on time in a clean and proper uniform. Is alert, organized and ready to provide cheerful and efficient service.

— Reviews and becomes familiar with the menu

— Assists in seating guests when needed

— Assists bus persons in clearing and setting tables as needed

— Takes orders from guests and provides service in a friendly and acceptable manner

— Prepares, presents and processes guest checks

IV   *Wage and Hour Policies and Benefits*

This is a very important section that should contain information regarding federal and state labor laws that regulate your business. One such law is the Fair Labor Standards Act which establishes a minimum wage rate for most businesses in the U.S. There are various other state laws that regulate overtime work and payment for same. In addition are the provisions relating to allowable credit for tips against minimum wage. You will also want to include policy information regarding uniforms and student employee wage rates, if allowed.

Of particular interest to the restaurant are the IRS provisions relating to tip reporting. The law is specific in how this matter is to be handled, as well as the responsibilities of both employer and employees.

Other items you will want to detail in your manual:

- Any allowance for uniform maintenance

- Employee meal allowance

- Policy regarding minimum employee age

- How to use your own particular time record

- Pay periods and pay days

- How work schedule is prepared, and who is responsible for the preparation

- Your policies regarding sick leave, vacation and holidays

- Life and health insurance

- Computation of bonus and profit sharing plans, if any

- Company policy on other items such as rest periods and parking privileges

Developing A Fringe Benefit Package

You must first determine how much money you can put aside to fund such a package. This can be decided after you figure your annual operating costs. Certain items such as overtime and/or premium pay may be fixed by law, or decided by various government agencies. But you can control the hours worked before the "OT" or premium pay is due.

Life And Health Insurance

These two items constitute a very worthy portion of any benefit package. How much you can offer will depend again on your financial situation. There are many insurance companies eager for your business, and they all have an ample supply of agents to serve you. Some points that you should consider before agreeing to institute an insurance program for your employees are:

1. Insurance is generally thought of as a very important item by people seeking employment. Your recruiting efforts will be enhanced if you are able to offer something, no matter how comprehensive the program.

2. Insurance programs are expensive. No matter how desirable, they are not recommended for businesses that can't afford to pay the premiums. You should of course investigate thoroughly before you make any announcements to your staff. Once you commit yourself to a Life and/or Health Insurance program, you will have to see it through.

3. Decisions will have to be made as to the amount of coverage per employee. You will also have to decide if the house pays all premiums, or if the employee should be required to pay for all or a portion of the coverage.

Vacation Policy

Most businesses offer some sort of paid vacation to their employees—and most, if not all employees, will expect it. A typical policy is one week after the first full year of employment, and two weeks following the second year and thereafter. There are variations of these basic plans, including a two-week closing of the restaurant at which time all qualified employees receive vacation pay.

Bonus Or Profit Sharing Plans

Today, we are hearing more and more about stock ownership plans for employees. Most of these plans are found in large companies, and have come about during recessionary times when the subject companies were faced with financial failure. In some of these companies, the best employees may really not be employees at all. They are actually minority stockholders in the business. This sort of arrangement is good theory as it relates to employee participation in the business. However, it may not be so good if the employees do not see any financial return on their ownership.

As a general rule, the plans related to bonus or profit sharing in our industry are for the benefit of management personnel. There are different forms of these plans, but they all relate to sales and/or profits. For example:

* Certain plans pay a bonus based only on sales increases over a base amount. These are rare.

* Other plans pay on sales, but only if costs and expenses are kept under base amounts.

* Still other plans pay a percentage of net profit from operations before occupancy costs and taxes.

If you feel that a bonus or profit sharing plan is important to your business, you can construct one similar to any of these. When doing so, you should seek the advice of your accountant or an outside consultant for assistance. Any plan such as this must be equitable to all parties, or it can cause more harm than good. No manager will be enticed toward outstanding performance by financial goals that are unreachable. None of these plans should be instituted and ignored by the owners. There should be constant communication during the accounting period as to the present state of the plan and how the bonus can be maximized.

V   *House Rules and Regulations*

This section will reflect not only your own philosophy of business, but also will stipulate the rules that must be followed to conform with those agencies that safeguard the public welfare. Every restaurant is somewhat regulated by certain city codes regarding sanitation, fire prevention and the overall safety of guests and employees. In addition, there are laws protecting minority groups from discriminatory job practices.

New laws and regulations are being enacted all the time, and we must keep alert for changes. Some restaurants will come under the provisions of the Occupational Safety and Health Act. There is legislation for prevention of sexual harassment on the job. All of the regulatory agencies that deal with these items have some form of enforcement machinery at their disposal. It is important that you contact your local restaurant association for information related to these items.

You will also want to include your own rules relating to conduct on the job. All prohibitions should be spelled out to prevent misunderstandings. Here are a few subjects for you to cover:

- Specify which persons are allowed access to the storage areas, i.e., food, liquor and supplies. If you establish and stick to a policy, you will be sure to control pilferage better.

- Decide and stipulate whether or not employees are allowed to frequent the dining room or bar when off duty. A *not allowed* policy may help you control costs by preventing complimentary food and drink practices.

- Determine whether employees are allowed to eat at other than scheduled times and in predetermined places. Establishing and enforcing a firm policy in this matter will prevent constant snacking and will also save you money.

- Set up a policy relating to drinking alcoholic beverages on the job.

- Cheating on the time record. There should be a policy relating to employees handling their own time records that outlines the need for accuracy of time for starting and ending work periods.

There are lots of other rules that you may want to cover. The main point is you will run a better restaurant if you state the rules for *all to know*. Your policies should also clearly state what action will be taken when rules are broken. Last, but certainly not least, you must mean what you say and always act fairly, firmly and consistently with everyone concerned.

There are sure to be other items that you will want to include in your manual. So be sure you make provision for change without having to redo major portions of the document. A loose-leaf notebook is probably the best form to use. If you are unsure as to how to construct a policy manual or if you don't have the time, you can, as mentioned, contract for the task. Some consulting firms such as mine, Gordon Associates, Inc., offer this as a part of their overall service functions.

How To Get Service Help To Do Such A Great Job That Repeat Business Is Guaranteed

Table of Contents

6

How To Get Service Help To Do Such A Great Job That Repeat Business Is Guaranteed

You can make a lot of money in this business if you keep the notion of "repeat business" firmly in mind. It is essential that your customers not only return to your restaurant for more of your fine food and service, but that they also send their friends and neighbors too! When customers are treated to good food, served in a smooth and friendly manner, they are most apt to return.

HOW TO MAKE YOUR PLATES MORE ATTRACTIVE

It is said that people "eat with their eyes." There is no question that the appearance of food has much to do with how it tastes. And the technique that is used to make food more attractive to the eye is garnishing.

Garnish is a term in cookery that is often misused. Garnish is from the French word, garniture, and in classical cookery means "to complete the dish as prepared." Properly used, it sets the mode and tells the diner what to expect. An example of this usage would be Veal Marsala, which would indicate that the entree was sauteed and finished with Marsala wine. In this case, the garnish is the sauce which is made with Marsala wine.

Other examples would be Forrestiere, Newburg, a l'Orange, etc.

In addition, the term may describe the accompaniment, as in Veal Cutlets Provencale. Without going into detail, this description says the item, if properly prepared and served, will consist of sauteed veal cutlets garnished with a sauce containing Madeira wine, tomatoes and onions.

The common usage of the word "garnish" is quite different. To many people it means adding an item to a plate mainly for the purpose of providing color. We see examples of this in nearly all sorts of restaurants. They include sliced tomatoes, lemon wedges and the most used (or overused) item, parsley.

When garnishing in this manner, you must make sure that the garnishes used are edible. Also, you should pay close attention to how the garnish will hold up in service. For example, not all garnishes will hold shape, color or texture when subjected to heat, and therefore should not be used on heated plates. Similarly, it is very often improper to garnish a plate and then let it stand under a heat lamp. As a rule, the garnish should be added just prior to service, which means that the kitchen must be properly organized and supervised. The color of the garnish is also very important in that it should enhance the plate and complement the appearance of the entree.

Selecting Garnishes That Will Complement Your Dishes

Since garnishes will be an important part of your plates, you must take a part in the selection of them. At those times when people are tired or busy, most anything may show up as a garnish—whether it fits the plate or not. And you don't want that to happen to you. Therefore, you should outline what garnish/garnishes you want with each dish.

The following are some garnishes that will complement your menu offerings:

Rainbow Trout	Lemon Wedge/Green Onions
Red Snapper	Lemon Slice/Sprig of Dill Weed
Ocean Trout	Pat of Dill Butter
Sauteed Filet of Sole	Capers

(Most fish and shellfish items are enhanced with lemon. It can be served as a half or in wedges. Parsley is also widely used, and its green color is a nice contrast to most seafood dishes.)

Leg of Lamb	Most often served with mint jelly and a sauce made from the drippings.

Various Steaks	Pat of garlic butter Mushroom caps
Pork Chops	Spiced whole apple or apple rings Applesauce
Bratwurst	Sweet and sour red cabbage

(Fruit in season can provide a very nice touch to the finishing of a plate. These go especially well with cold or hot sandwich items, along with your own favorite pickles.)

Cold Sandwiches

Ham and Swiss Corned Beef Pastrami Roast Beef Chicken Salad	Interchange depending on availability and cost—cantaloupe, honeydew or watermelon, blueberries, sliced apple.

Hot Sandwiches

Hamburgers Cheeseburgers Grilled Ham & Cheese Grilled Cheese	Use canned peach or pear slices or halves, cottage cheese, raw finger vegetables such as carrot or celery sticks, and french fried zucchini.

We can all think of a particular meal in a restaurant that stands out above most others. One of my all-time favorites was simple yet outstanding in color, presentation and overall enjoyment.

To my surprise, a Peanut Butter and Strawberry Jam sandwich was offered on the luncheon menu at this very pleasant restaurant. In fact, I was so surprised that I was compelled to order one. The sandwich as served was excellent. It consisted of bread rounds, one with peanut butter and thinly sliced banana, and the other slice covered with strawberry jam. It was beautifully served with a garnish of assorted fresh fruit in a cast iron ham and egg skillet. This particular item had everything—shape, color, texture, temperature and contrast—all of the important factors in the presentation of food. Last, but certainly not least, it also tasted very good and I had the satisfaction of feeling that I had received good value for the money spent.

Of course, garnishes will not overcome any deficiencies you might have with menu balance. You must be sure that each item on the plate, as well as those served on the side, are complementary to each other. Therefore, carefully study the appearance of each of your menu items and its appeal to the diner. Try for pleasing patterns in the shape and color of food served. And pay attention to visual values. In other words, every plate should be a "palette."

HOW TO ORGANIZE AN EFFICIENT SERVICE STAFF

The supervision of service starts in the kitchen. One of the most important jobs in a restaurant is the *expediter*. A brief description of an expediter's job would be liaison between preparation and service staffs.

An expediter is stationed in the kitchen and works in the prime areas to be supervised—the pickup stations for hot and cold foods. Part of this person's job is to insure that foods are dispatched as quickly after preparation as is possible. In other words, the expediter sees that diners receive their hot food, hot and cold food, cold. Also, this person supervises the appearance of the finished plates for compliance with menu and garnish requirements. In addition, the expediter "keeps the peace" in the kitchen, and makes sure the two departments—service and preparation—function in a smooth and efficient manner.

If you don't have an expediter, or don't have someone who could function in that capacity, consider getting one. The whole secret to profits lies in your ability to turn your seats as often as possible. An expediter will help accomplish this, by keeping your customers happily returning to your restaurant.

How To Get Acceptable Employee Productivity

There is probably no such thing as a restaurant that has a complete staff of highly motivated and efficient people. Every restaurant seems to have some service stations where everything runs smoothly, and others that don't. Our business is described as a "people-intensive business," and therein lies the problem. Some of us are very good at our job, and some of us are not.

As outlined earlier in this Guide, "turning seats" is the secret to profits in the restaurant business. A full restaurant with every seat taken is experiencing one turn. If a restaurant has 100 seats and serves 150 persons on a given night, we would say it had 1.5 turns. There are exceptions to this, such as those houses that serve a slow-paced gourmet menu with prices sufficiently structured. In these, one or two seatings for a given mealtime is sufficient to insure proper sales and profits.

You can only produce satisfactory seat turnover with acceptable employee productivity. Therefore, it makes sense that you should provide as much supervision as possible—and it must be where it counts the most, in the kitchen. If the kitchen is not running smoothly, then neither will anything else.

Supervising the flow of orders in and out of the kitchen insures that service persons and cooks work in unison with a first-in, first-out system. Such a system tends to force slower servers to pick up their orders on time. The total effect will be faster and smoother flow of service to the dining room, the turnover rate will increase, and all diners will receive the same smooth, efficient service.

SUREFIRE TECHNIQUES THAT TURN SERVERS INTO SELLERS

Servers must be sufficiently knowledgeable about the menu items to be able to guide diners intelligently toward selections. Therefore, they must know about ingredients, as well as preparation and service times. Furthermore, servers should be sales oriented. That is, they should approach the guest with a desire to sell; although a high-powered sales pitch should never be used. If done properly, everyone will benefit—the diner will probably try something new, the server will receive a larger tip, and the house will increase its sales.

The Approach

At all times, a server should approach a customer with a pleasant smile and a friendly greeting. Good morning or good evening is always appropriate, but the server should not stop there. The following greetings will help make the diners feel welcome:

- Good morning. May I start your day with a cup of hot, fresh coffee?

- Good evening. We are pleased to have you as our guest tonight.

- Hello, I am (Mary, George), and I am here to help you enjoy your dinner with us tonight.

Suggestive Selling

Suggestion is probably the most important selling technique a server can learn how to use. When dining out, people are often preoccupied with business or personal matters, or are absorbed in conversations with companions. They may not want to take time to study the menu. Therefore, it makes sense for your servers to make suggestions, particularly if you offer daily specials. Here's how to do it:

When suggesting items for sale, it is wise to offer alternatives. This sort of selling makes a refusal more difficult. For example,

"May I serve you a Manhattan or Martini?" is better than "Would you care for a cocktail?" The first question tends to elicit a choice, whereas the second calls for a "yes" or "no" answer.

Offering a special that is properly described by the waiter will sometimes help a diner to decide. For example:

> "Good evening. Tonight our chef has prepared roast Leg of Lamb as a special item. He has seasoned it with care. (You might want to mention the seasonings.) It is served with new potatoes and a choice of salad or the vegetable of the day. The special price this evening is $10.95."

You can also use suggestions when selling desserts:

> "Have you tried our pecan pie? No, then you have missed a taste treat. Would you like to try a piece with ice cream, or do you prefer it plain?"

The Pre-Meal Briefing

A pre-meal briefing for your service staff should be done daily—even though your menu may not have undergone a recent change. During it, you can place emphasis on the items that you especially want to sell, including the specials of the day. The briefing should take the role of a sales meeting, providing information and answering any questions your service staff may have. It should also provide the impetus to "pump up" your servers, so that they go out and sell with zest.

The Tasting Session

A good technique for increasing sales is the use of a tasting session prior to the meal period. It is unfortunate, but true, that management and service staff in many restaurants never taste the food before serving it. In restaurants that carry a large staff, you may want to limit the taste session to only management and supervisory personnel. In smaller restaurants, however, the sessions should include the servers. In any event, such a program will insure that the proper persons are acquainted with the products for sale. If the servers are not actually tasting the food, then they should at least be briefed by someone who has.

If you have a large restaurant and it is not feasible for the entire service staff to participate in a regular tasting session, you might try another plan. Select a person from the service staff as a participant in the regular daily taste session. Each day a different server would be selected, so that you would rotate the process throughout the entire group. That person could then conduct the menu briefing session under the supervision of management. Reinforcement in terms of sales technique, etc. could be furnished by management. Such a program would effectively bring the entire group into the management process, and should aid greatly in the development of esprit de corps and pleasant working conditions—all of which will translate into dollars for you.

The Bonus Plan

Since most of us want to make all the money we can, it follows that cash incentives are probably the best way to encourage employees to build sales. One such way is to pay a percentage of individual total sales during a given period as a bonus. This could serve two purposes: 1. it would reward the high achievers, and 2. it helps you to spotlight those servers who don't push for sales. However, this system will not work unless all servers have equal opportunity in terms of desirability of assigned stations and fair placement of diners in the rooms. An alternative way to develop a bonus plan would be to select certain items, such as appetizers or desserts, and establish a bonus based on numbers sold over a given time period. There are certainly other ways you can devise to develop good sales habits, but the ones outlined above have worked extremely well.

In addition, it is your responsibility to provide training for your employees, as covered in Chapter 5. There are slide presentations available from some of your suppliers and also from the trade associations, such as the state and national restaurant associations. Role playing is another effective technique you can use in which some of your staff pretends to be customers while others serve them, and the balance observes. During these sessions you can be suggesting and coaching in the proper service techniques that will build and sustain sales.

In addition, there are booklets available for outside reading. You also can post on the bulletin board tips on effective selling, service, etc.

HOW TO MARKET YOUR WINE FOR BIGGER PROFITS

The successful selling of wine is a speciality that can only be attained through the proper training of your service staff. If your restaurant does not have a wine steward, and most restaurants do not, then you must be certain that your servers are fully informed about the wines you have for sale. In other words, they should be able to suggest a particular wine for a specific meal or occasion. This doesn't mean that the servers must become connoisseurs, but it does mean that they must have a general knowledge of what they are trying to sell.

You can include information on wine sales in your training programs. In order to encourage the selling effort, you can even offer a bonus to each server based on his or her own individual wine sales. In addition, remind everyone that every bottle or glass of wine sold means a higher check and, most likely, a larger tip.

How To Prepare A Wine List

You, as owner or manager, must furnish strong support for your service staff, if they are to be able to reach the full sales potential for you. This means developing a total sales support program. This program begins with the development of a wine list that fits the overall economic pattern of your business. For example, if you attract customers who traditionally spend in a moderate range (e.g., strong family trade including children), you will probably want to structure your wine list so as to merchandise the low- to medium-priced offerings. Conversely, if your menu, decor, etc. is pointed to the "carriage" trade, your wine list will reflect this by listing the more expensive labels.

Proper preparation of a wine list will require that you start with some basic research on wines. There are several books available on the subject. *Grossman's Guide to Wine, Spirits and Beer* by Sherman and Sporer, Inc., and *The Management of Service for the Restaurant Manager* by Raymond J. Goodman, Jr., William C. Brown Company, are two good sources of technical information. A trip to your local bookstore will undoubtedly turn up many more. Reading some of this material will help you greatly in establishing your wine sales program.

Another excellent source for information on wines and how to market them, including the preparation of a wine list, is your local wine distributor. Usually, he will be eager to help you, and is well qualified to do so.

The wine list on the following page is from the Bayou House in Dickinson, Texas, and it illustrates a selection from low- to high-priced wines. In this restaurant, the higher priced wines sell at a much slower pace than the medium- or low-priced offerings. The biggest seller is the house wine which is sold by the glass or carafe.

THE BAYOU HOUSE RESTAURANT

Wine List

California...

WHITES

Chardonnay - Parducci	17.50
Chenin Blanc - Mirassou	14.50
Chablis - Concannon	10.50

REDS

Cabernet Sauvignon - Parducci	17.50
Zinfandel - Ridge	21.00

French...

WHITE BURGUNDIES

Puligny Montrachet - Mommessin	42.00
Pouilly Fuisse - Antonin Rodet	25.00
Chardonnay - Macon Les Charmes	21.00

RED BURGUNDIES

Chateauneuf du Pape - De Fins Roches	23.00
Beaujolais - Sarrau	14.00

BORDEAUX

Chateau Lafite Rothchild, 1971	180.00
Chateau Margaux, 1978	140.00
Pauillac - Haute Batailley	48.00
Margaux - Domaine de Fontarney	28.00
St. Julien - Beychevelle Gloria	34.50
St. Emillion - Chateau Lescours	23.00

ROSE'

Rose' de Anjou - Chateau de Tigne	11.00

German...

Auslese (ask your waiter for Vintner) - priced accordingly	
Bernkastler Kurfursley Kabinett	14.00
Wehlener Sonnenuhr Spatlese	19.50
Piesporter Michelsberg Spatlese	17.00
Piesporter Goldtropfchen QBA	12.50

CHAMPAGNES

California...

Mirassou Brut - when available	27.00
Chateau de Fleur	13.00

Gathering The Necessary Information

Once you have acquired the necessary background knowledge, you should then begin to research the local market to determine:

1. What the big sellers are in similar restaurants to yours.

2. What wines are available on a consistent basis that "fit" your menu and your clientele.

3. What kind of prices you can realistically expect to sustain in your restaurant.

You will find some of the answers to the above by visiting other restaurants similar to your own. As you make the rounds, you will want to study other wine lists and visit casually with service personnel and management. These trips will be most rewarding in that you will be able to gather considerable information on how to sell—and how not to sell—wine.

Here are a few items to consider when visiting other restaurants:

- Does the server present a wine list, or is the list a part of the table setting?

- Does the restaurant and its service personnel actually try to sell, or is wine something that happens to be available if you ask for it?

- What wines appear to be big sellers? Bottles? Decanters? Red? White?

- Was a specific suggestion made as to label or type of wine?

- Are you able to estimate or ascertain a particular price range or level?

Making Your Wine Selection

Obtaining answers to the questions given above will be of great benefit to you when you begin the next phase of the program—selecting the wine. At that time, you will want to talk with reputable dealers regarding availability, prices, method of payment and any requirements as to quantities to be purchased. Most dealers will be happy to assist you in the preparation of your wine list. You must be certain, however, that you have adequate storage and/or display area to handle the volume that will be required to support your list. Often dealers can help you with merchandising the wines by furnishing table tents and menu clip-ons. Further, most good distributors have sales literature, slide presentations and film clips that can be utilized in your training programs.

Of major importance is, of course, your selection of the wines and the price you want to sell them for. You must be particularly careful not to price yourself out of the market. While liquors generally yield gross profit margins of 70 to 75 percent, wines will generally run from 60 to 70 percent. (For a wine-pricing formula refer back to Chapter 2.)

In pricing a carafe or decanter, you must first measure how many of *your* glasses are contained in each one. Once you determine that, you can then apply the formula to yield your own desired gross profit margin per glass. Remember, if you price too high, you will not be fair to your customers, and your servers—regardless of their skill—will not be able to sell. Today, the general public is much more aware and sophisticated with respect to wine consumption, and will respond more favorably to the restaurateur who keeps this firmly in mind.

The decision whether to sell by the bottle, decanter, and/or glass may be determined by your customers' preferences. These preferences may be influenced by the general sales trend in your particular area. Your ability to alter these preferences can be accomplished through proper sales and merchandising techniques.

Your wine inventory should be large enough to satisfy the widest range of taste and price preference possible. It should therefore include an array of red, white and rosé wines. In all probability, you will want to offer both imported and domestic wines, as well as house wine to be sold by either the glass or decanter. If your list is extensive and backed up by a good cellar, you might consider numbering the selections on the wine list. Storing the wines in a number sequence will then aid greatly in locating difficult-to-read labels, thereby facilitating and speeding service.

WHY GOOD SERVICE DOESN'T STOP WHEN THE MEAL DOES

After the meal, one type of surprise that diners don't want is to find out that only certain kinds of credit cards, or no credit cards or personal checks, are accepted for payment. So make sure that your guests know your payment policy in advance.

There are millions of people who buy solely on credit or personal check, and many of them carry little or no cash. For these people, credit card/check usage is a habit, and they don't even consider that a busy restaurant might not honor them. If you surprise them after the fact, you may never see them again. But, if you state your policy clearly—either with signs, a highly visible menu notation, in your advertising, or with table tents—you will probably win a new friend and long-time customer. You might also consider telling your customers about your policy when they call for table reservations. Remember, it is very hard to repossess a consumed meal.

How Best To Present The Check

There are various ways of presenting the check to the guest. You may prefer to have the server give the guest the check. If so, then the check should be presented on a tip tray. Presentation should only be made after the server has ascertained—by offering additional service (e.g., an after-dinner drink, more coffee, etc.)—that the diner has completed the meal.

It is important to have the check clearly written for easy readability. This can be done by hand or by a pre-check machine or cash register. Further, keep the check simple. Some restaurants present two separate checks, and the final result only confuses the guest.

Following presentation, the server should complete the transaction as smoothly as possible. The process should not be hurried, but at the same time the guest should not be made to wait an unnecessary amount of time. Some restaurants do very well as far as serving the food and beverage, but break down completely after the meal, by either not presenting the check shortly after the meal, or by taking an interminable amount of time to return with the change or charge ticket. When this happens, all the goodwill created during the meal is lost—and the diner remembers only the poor service after the meal.

If you prefer that guests pay a cashier direct, then you should take steps to inform them as to the procedure. Such steps could include a notice on the guest check and also a verbal reminder by the server, e.g. "You may pay the cashier when ready" or "When you are ready, I will take the check to the cashier for you."

Some restaurants add a percentage (usually 15%) of the raw sale price before tax as a service charge. This is certainly an acceptable practice that insures tips for your servers. Once again, clear communication with the diners as to your policy is very important. If you have such a policy and also honor credit cards, be sure that the entire transaction is entered on the charge ticket with tax and gratuity clearly indicated.

Regardless of the cash control method used, bright smiles and pleasant thank-you's by the servers will please your guests and bring bigger and better tips for them, and higher profits for you!

Hidden Gold In Your Cocktail Lounge

Table of Contents

Hidden Gold In Your Cocktail Lounge

The next best thing to a gold mine or a producing oil well may be a busy, well-managed cocktail lounge. Today, busy lounges deliver a gross profit margin on sales ranging from 70% to 80%. That means that a lounge selling $500,000 in beverages annually can produce a gross profit of $350,000 to $400,000. In addition, this figure is highlighted by the low supporting expenses needed for the operation. Labor and operating costs will of course vary with labor rates and other expense items such as entertainment. But if you run your lounge properly, it should return 50% or more on the bottom line. Those dollars will in turn aid in offsetting the higher costs of your restaurant operation.

THE IMPORTANCE OF INTERNAL CONTROL

Internal control throughout your restaurant operation is a management function that must be performed by you. This goes double for the bar, since the drainage expense there can have a disastrous effect on the profit line. Although the profit margin on alcoholic beverages is great, so too are the cracks through which those profits can slip. Here are some of the loopholes through which those profits can disappear.

- drinks dispensed free to employees, including management personnel

- "complimentary" drinks given to "good" customers in the interest of sales promotion, but done mostly for the devious purpose of increasing tip revenue for lounge personnel

703

- failure to record sales—pocketing cash

- bar personnel actually selling their *own* merchandise on the house bar

- collusion between bar and table service personnel to accomplish any of the foregoing

- over-pouring of liquor for "stiff" drinks—again, in the interest of increasing tips

- over-pouring of liquor that results in waste and spillage

- failure to empty liquor bottles completely before discarding

Remember, every drop of alcoholic beverage, every slice of fruit, every drop of soft beverage, each and every container of beer and wine represents a unit of cost. Each unit lost—no matter how you lose it—will reflect as lost revenue and profit to you.

How To Set Up A Cost Control System

Cost control starts with the price range of the beverages that you are going to offer. The hard liquors—whiskey, gin, rum, etc.— come in many shapes and sizes, and in a wide range of prices. What you buy will depend on the quality you are able to sell in your own particular location.

Generally speaking, hard beverages are classified by operators as "bar" or "well" liquor and "call" brands. The bar or well liquors are used when a patron orders a drink without requesting a particular brand. Call brands refer to just that. They are kept on inventory for the patron who specifies the brand of liquor when ordering his drink. The bar or well brands used by most operators are usually lower-cost brands that are judged to be acceptable by the house. This does not mean that only cheap liquor is sold as bar or well stock, but it usually means that it is less expensive than a majority of the call stocks. Wine sold as "house" wine by the glass or carafe is usually a less expensive brand than those sold in a bottle.

Here are a couple of comparisons from the Houston, Texas area between high- and low-priced brands of liquor. They readily demonstrate the difference in gross profit per drink for the house.

CALL BRANDS - SCOTCH WHISKEY

Brand	Cost/Btl*	#1¼ oz. Drinks	Price	Gross Profit
Chivas-Regal	18.80	26	3.00	$59.20 - 76.0%
J & B	12.85	26	3.00	65.15 - 84.0%

BAR BRAND - SCOTCH WHISKEY

Crawfords	7.01	26	2.50	$57.99 - 89.0%

CALL BRAND - BOURBON

Wild Turkey	12.84	26	3.00	$65.16 - 84.0%

BAR BRAND - BOURBON

Evan Williams	4.79	26	2.50	$60.21 - 93.0%

As you can see, the call brands that sell for $.50 per drink more than the bar brands, actually deliver a lower margin of gross profit per bottle.

If you used the following call brands as bar whiskies, the margin would be even less:

Brand	Cost	Yield	Sell Price	Gross Profit
J & B	12.85/btl.	26 dr.	2.50	$52.15 - 80.0%
Wild Turkey	12.84/btl.	26	2.50	52.16 - 80.0%

How To Avoid Overbuying

Once you have made your decision as to quality and price range, your next move is to research the market for the brands of beverage that will fit into your overall sales philosophy. This will mean checking out prices and probably doing some sampling. You will also want to investigate other bars catering to your type of customers. Such trips will provide the information relative to brands that will sell or not sell.

After going through this exercise, you will be able to order intelligently and will be much less apt to buy brands that don't move. There are many bars that have gotten stuck with inventory items they can't even give away. This is usually a result of not knowing what to buy, over-reacting to a sales pitch, or letting some unqualified person do the buying for you.

A common mistake made by operators is overbuying different brands in stock, as well as stocking too high an inventory. This can be controlled by carefully forecasting sales, as outlined in Chapter 4. To sum up: Don't overbuy! There are an untold number of different brands of each beverage category, and it is impossible to stock them all. Without a doubt, you will have isolated requests for a certain kind of beverage, but unless there is a strong identifiable demand, you will probably be wise not to carry it.

Remember, excess inventory requires cash outlays that may be better used in other ways. (In your own pocket for one!) You will no doubt hear about promotions that will earn you big bucks. Maybe some of them will, but be sure you study each individual case thoroughly as it relates to your own clientele and to your own sales capability.

Check Your Order Carefully

Be very sure that what you buy is what you get! Before signing for or paying for merchandise, check it thoroughly. Because beverages are generally purchased in case lots, the chances of losing individual containers through breakage or pilferage are high. The following case study shows how this can happen.

> An acquaintance of mine was at one time responsible for the convenience store operations in a large midwestern city. In several locations, he was experiencing a high loss of soft drinks. He was unable to stem the losses. So the company decided to assign a trouble-shooter, who quickly identified the problem.
>
> It seemed as though certain drivers were delivering full cases of beverage which they unloaded and stacked in the storerooms. At the same time, they would remove the empty cases. However, the stacks of empties they removed had also contained full cases. In addition, the stacks of full cases being stored contained empty cases that had just been removed.
>
> *Result*: The company not only was being shorted of merchandise, but was also being double-charged for the deposit fee on the full and empty bottles.

KEY WAYS TO KEEP TRACK OF YOUR INVENTORY

The next step is the control of your inventory after you receive it. This is best accomplished by storing it under lock and key, and providing very limited access to persons other than trusted management personnel. Your storeroom should be spacious enough to accommodate your stock, and the goods should be stored in a manner that facilitates quick and easy physical inventory. If you have a storeroom that is too "small," take a long hard look at your purchasing procedure and sales records along with vendor delivery schedules, to see if you really need as much inventory as you are actually carrying.

I am often called in by businesses having cost problems. In almost every case, I find problems with either overbuying or with little or no inventory control—and often it is a combination of both. You cannot remain competitive in this business while absorbing losses of this kind! Restaurants losing money through pilferage must raise their prices to cover their losses—and that practice soon results in lost sales.

There are two basic bar control methods used throughout the industry: the physical inventory and an operating statement. While somewhat different, they are similar in one respect.

The Physical Inventory

Any system of internal control requires a periodic physical inventory of goods on hand, and this "counting" of the stock must be done on a consistent basis. The inventory must coincide with the closing of the fiscal period for control, and if accuracy is to be maintained, it cannot be postponed or rescheduled for any reason.

If, for example, you opt for a monthly operating period and decide to close your operating books after the close of business on the last day of a calendar month, you must take a physical inventory before opening for business on the first day of the following month. It doesn't matter whether the first of the month falls on Sunday (the day you're closed, and when the fish are biting), inventory must be taken before you open for business on Monday.

Consistency is the key to good record keeping. It is the ingredient that provides valid comparisons of operating results from one period to another. In addition, it provides records that coincide exactly with your budgets. Probably the most basic reason of all for taking a physical inventory is to verify that you *have* on hand what you are *supposed* to have. In this case, the "eyes" have it! The most sophisticated control system in the world will not *verify* the physical presence of items on hand.

The Operating Statement

Probably the simplest control system is the preparation of an operating statement that includes a verification of goods on hand by physical inventory. This system requires that purchases be recorded during a fiscal period. The value of the purchases is added to the value of a beginning inventory (the ending inventory from the previous period). Finally, the value of the ending inventory for the current period is subtracted from that total, to arrive at the dollar cost of goods sold. Control is exercised by dividing the cost by the net sales (after taxes, etc.), to arrive at a ratio of cost to sales. This ratio is then compared to the previous period ratio and also to the budget.

This system is considered the simplest, since it does not require daily record keeping in the form of issues from storeroom to bar. It is probably the best system for a low-volume operation, since it reduces the amount of paperwork necessary for the maintenance of other systems. The problems with it are:

1. There is no way to discover cost distortion, either up or down, until the operating period is closed.

2. The owner/manager must be ever vigilant during operating hours. This means watching the bar closely at all times for such loopholes as were mentioned earlier in this chapter.

Establishing A Par Stock

Another method of control is one in which a par stock is established for the bar. This means that all brands of alcoholic beverage available for sale are kept at a predetermined level. These levels are known as pars, and each brand has a par. If you have a storeroom from which you issue to one or more bars via a written requisition, you would establish a par for each brand on each bar.

In addition, to insure that you keep your inventory at the lowest possible level, you would establish a set of pars for your storeroom. This means that there would be a reorder point at which time you would buy more of a brand trying not to exceed par. What happens here is that you establish a minimum and a maximum amount for each brand of beverage to be on hand. When a particular brand reaches a minimum amount (reorder point), you buy more—trying not to exceed the maximum (par) amount. This system has definite advantages, as follows:

- It controls inventory both in the storeroom and on the bar by avoiding overages and/or shortages.

- It keeps management well informed as to the popular and unpopular sale brands.

- If invoices are tabulated for cost each day, it provides a daily cost of sales figures that is a good indication of how current costs are running.

The one disadvantage this system may have is the amount of paperwork that is involved. Each brand of liquor must have an individual record of receipts and issues, and these records (bin cards) must be kept up to date in a consistent manner. If you have people to handle chores such as these, then you should by all means install such a system. If, however, you have a small restaurant and have to tend to most of the administrative details yourself, then it may be difficult to take on a system such as this. If it is not maintained consistently and accurately, it is worthless.

Automatic Beverage Metering Systems

Automatic beverage metering systems utilize a storage for open bottles that are each locked in place. Each bottle has a draw-off valve that can be preset to deliver the desired quantity per drink. It eliminates the free-pour system on most brands, and insures accuracy as to quantity per drink sold. The system also uses a metering device that counts the number of drinks dispensed from each bottle. These systems are widely used in hotels and large high-volume restaurants.

ESTABLISHING THE RIGHT PRICES

Beverage prices are arrived at in the same manner as are prices for cooked foods. Full containers such as beer present no problem other than marking up in price in order to return the desired gross profit per unit. However, opened containers, i.e., bottled goods sold by the drink or in combination as mixed drinks, present a more complex problem for control.

Before you can price beverage by the drink, you must first decide on the yield or how many drinks you want to get from a bottle. This, of course, will vary with the size of the drink served and also with the size of the bottle. Until recently, liquor was sold in bottles containing 4/5 of a quart, 1 quart and 1/2 gallon. Since the inception of metric usage in the U.S., that has all changed. We now find liquor being sold in bottles as follows:

1.75 Liter	=	59.2 fluid oz.
1 L	=	33.8 fl. oz.
750 Ml.	=	25.4 fl. oz.
500 Ml.	=	16.9 fl. oz.
200 Ml.	=	6.8 fl. oz.

Equipment such as jiggers and drink glasses will also soon be available in metric sizes. This means that there will be a lot of equipment that was purchased prior to conversion on hand—and no one wants to discard what can still be used. The following gives examples using both ounce and metric measures.

Easy Ways To Use The Metric System

It is almost an impossibility to realize a 100% yield from a bottle of liquor that is sold by the drink. Because of this fact, an allowance to account for spillage, waste, etc., is established as a deduction from the total amount available for sale. As an example in which we use milliliters converted to ounces, let's assume that we are using the 750 ml. bottle which contains 25.4 fluid ounces. If we allow 1.4 ounces per bottle for waste, we will have a net saleable bottle containing 24 ounces (for purpose of analysis). If we pour a 1½-ounce drink, we should then realize a sale of 16 drinks from the bottle:

$$750 \text{ ml.} \qquad\qquad = 25.4 \text{ oz.}$$
$$25.4 \text{ oz.} - 1.4 \text{ oz.} \quad = 24 \text{ oz.}$$
$$24 \text{ oz.} \div 1.5 \text{ oz.} \quad = 16 \text{ drinks at } 1\tfrac{1}{2} \text{ oz. each}$$

Using the same loss ratio per bottle, but analyzing by milliliters, will produce the following:

$$1.4 \text{ oz. (waste)} \div 25.4 \text{ oz.} = 5.5\% \text{ loss}$$
$$750 \text{ ml.} \times 5.5\% \qquad\qquad = 41.25 \text{ ml. waste per}$$
$$\qquad\qquad\qquad\qquad\qquad\qquad 750 \text{ ml. bottle}$$
$$750 \text{ ml.} - 41.25 \text{ ml.} \qquad = 708.75 \text{ net saleable quantity}$$

$$(1 \text{ oz.} = 29.5730 \text{ ml.})$$
$$29.5730 \text{ ml.} \times 1.5 = 44.595 \text{ ml. per each } 1\tfrac{1}{2} \text{ oz. drink}$$

$$708.75 \text{ net} \div 44.595 \text{ ml/drink} = 15.89 \text{ per bottle}$$

(The above analysis has been simplified for illustrative purposes only. Actually 1.4 oz. waste per bottle is too high. Waste shouldn't be more than one-half of that amount.) If you are using the 1-liter bottles on your bar, you can analyze in the same manner as the foregoing, except that you must decide how much waste and/or spillage you are willing to allow.

How To Arrive At A Selling Price

In order to arrive at a selling price, you must first decide on what gross margin on sales you want to realize. Once decided, the rest is relatively simple. For example:

$$1 - 750 \text{ ml. bottle of Scotch}$$
$$\text{Cost} - \$10.00$$
$$\$10.00 \div 16 \text{ net drinks/bottle} = \$0.625/\text{drink}$$

Let's suppose you need to realize 75% gross profit from each drink as a highball or straight up. (For this example we will ignore the cost of mixers and deal with that later.) You would use the following formula for this calculation:

$$\text{Cost} \div (100\% - \text{Gross Profit}) = \text{Selling Price}$$
$$\$.63 \div (100\% - 75\%) = \$2.52 \text{ Selling Price}$$

The foregoing represents what you must do to arrive at unit selling prices that will yield the profits you want. As for beer and wine, you follow the same procedure:

1. Determine the quantity to be sold, i.e., a full bottle or a glass holding a certain number of ounces or milliliters.

2. Determine the cost of each saleable unit.

3. Calculate the selling price with the aforementioned formula.

There are many different types of hand-held calculators on the market that will save you a great deal of time in figuring costs, in addition to preventing errors. When making calculations like these, it is always good to prove the answers in order to prevent errors in final pricing.

It is also possible to arrive at reciprocals to apply on certain kinds of liquor in order to cost out mixed drinks. These calculations are more complex and, in my opinion, are too time consuming for the average restaurateur—unless he or she has a controller on the payroll. Don't forget the importance of monitoring the cost of mixers, fruit and other supplies in dollars of cost and ratio to total beverage sales. Such diligence will yield additional profits for you.

SETTING UP HOUSE RULES FOR EMPLOYEES AND PATRONS

There are certain "house rules" for employees and patrons that should be instituted and adhered to.

Guidelines For Employees

1. It should be strictly forbidden for employees and/or supervisory personnel to consume any alcoholic beverage during their working hours, or after closing. Serve coffee or soft drinks only.

2. Employees should be discouraged from frequenting the restaurant while off duty. This will help to avoid disruptions, such as socializing, in the other employees' workday.

Protecting Your Patrons

The house must be considerate and protective of *all* of its patrons. Your customers will expect a reasonable amount of peace and privacy, and there are certain things you can do to insure this.

One of the things you will have to consider is the fact that some people don't like a noisy restaurant, while others can't abide a quiet place. Some people can be loud and boisterous in a nonoffending way. They are often entertaining to others around them, and usually do not present a problem for you. However, this is not true of everyone. Sometimes this boisterousness is not entertaining to others. Such a situation arises when a guest decides to "table hop" around the room. Another potential problem can develop with people who are loud, and especially if they are using off-color or foul language.

These kinds of situations can only be handled by a firm and consistently enforced house policy against such behavior. You must move quickly and diplomatically to "nip these problems in the bud." Be sure to smoothly, yet firmly, let the people involved know that they are most welcome in your place, but that they must also be considerate of other guests. If situations become very bad and you must threaten to force them to leave the premises, *don't back off.* Only threaten action when you are fully prepared to carry that action all the way.

Then there are the smokers and non-smokers. Usually, the non-smokers are very vocal about their objections to smoke. And there is the further complication of the cigar and pipe smokers against whom the anti-smokers are particularly hostile. In an effort to satisfy both groups, many restaurants have divided their public rooms into smoking and non-smoking areas.

In addition, when you sell liquor you always run the risk of someone becoming intoxicated in your establishment. This situation is something that all good restaurateurs seek to avoid at all times for the following reasons:

1. Intoxicated persons are difficult to handle and are often offensive to other customers.

2. Drunk driving has become a great concern in many communities. Of course, none of us want to contribute to that problem. We must also consider the surge of DWI legislation, much of which seems to be pointed at the lounge and restaurant owners. Good business sense plus the protective feeling we have for our customers tells us that letting pa-

trons become intoxicated is "bad business." And that holds true, whether they are driving or afoot.

You must always be on the alert—watching out for those persons who seem to be spending a long period of time drinking and not eating. In addition, you should take special care in training your employees (bartenders, servers of both food and drinks) to be watchful and to alert management when a person seems to be drinking too heavily. Signs to watch out for are an unsteady walk, slurred speech, loose tongue and/or an unsteady head.

Even if you and your people watch carefully, you will probably still encounter the occasion when a guest has "had too much." Here are some tips on how to handle that situation:

- Most intoxicated persons will not be belligerent unless someone—a bartender, waiter, manager—makes them that way. Usually you can reason with them if they sense that you are "really on their side," and only want to help them enjoy their stay in your place.

- If the guest has not eaten, try to get him or her to do so. Try to seat the person in an area that is as remote from others as possible. In the process, don't try walking him or her through the entire restaurant.

- Don't assume, because the person has eaten and/or consumed some coffee, that he is sober. Actually, this person may now be nothing more than a "fully satiated drunk."

- Don't force intoxicated persons to leave your premises without being in the care of others who are sober. This may mean calling a taxi or even the police. Regardless of what action you must take, it is in the best interest of your guest, and he or she will certainly appreciate it. (If not, you really don't need that sort of guest in the future anyway.)

There are times when people who are not considered to be heavy drinkers become intoxicated. This can happen when people are under stress, overtired, ill or whatever. Holding out a helping hand to these folks will secure their friendship for you forever.

Your biggest problem requires experience and good judgment to assess a state of intoxication in a person. It also requires tact and diplomacy to refuse to sell, especially when dealing with good and "steady" customers. In any event, when you are in the business of selling alcoholic beverage, you should always maintain high ethical standards, along with a sense of responsibility for the health and welfare of your patrons.

CONTROLLING CASH AND CHARGE SALES

Whether or not your restaurant has a liquor business, it is vulnerable to drainage expense through waste, neglect and pilferage. Gaining and retaining the profits to which you are entitled requires diligent management by you. Up to now, we have discussed control of bar cost and the importance of purchasing and receiving. Of equal importance is the control of cash and charge sales dollars.

Direct Sales At The Bar

Most well-operated bars use modern well-designed cash registers on which sales checks can be documented. The style or brand of register you use is of course a matter of individual preference. (Chapter 2 includes a discussion of cash control systems that are available at this time.) However, you must always remember that the system selected, no matter how sophisticated, will not supplant the need for diligence and consistent management on your part.

All sales should be recorded on a bar check, and the recording should be done at the time of sale. Each patron or party seated at the bar should have a check on which the price of each drink or round of drinks purchased has been entered. It is not a good practice to serve several customers and then go back and ring up the different sales at one time. Bar employees will sometimes argue that ringing up each sale takes too much time. However, this method will help to prevent lost profits through uncollected sales.

A policy of recording at the time of sale will greatly aid observation and inspection of your business. Some businesses use spotter service companies to identify wasteful or dishonest employees. These people frequent a subject lounge as patrons for the purpose of observing employees at work. Reports are filed following the visits, with any discrepancies so noted.

How To Handle Complimentary Drinks

As previously stated, you should prohibit the giving of complimentary drinks by anyone other than management. It is probable that you will want to "buy" for certain patrons at certain times. When such occasions arise, be very sure that a check is properly filled out and recorded. Adjustment to your Promotion Expense Account can be made later by your bookkeeper. This is important because:

- It establishes your internal control by strictly accounting for every unit of cost in your inventory.

- It tells your employees that you are in fact controlling your inventory, and any shortages will be quickly noted and appropriately dealt with.

Controlling Table Service

Once the merchandise (liquor) leaves the relative confines of the bar proper, the need for extensions of control becomes necessary. Again, it becomes absolutely necessary to have all sales recorded when picked up from the bar. This recording of sales can take place either at the bar or at a checker/cashier station, remote from the bar. In any event, no matter which system you elect to use for recording, that recording must take place before any drinks are served anywhere.

Generally speaking, liquor will be served at tables both in the cocktail lounge and in the dining room. This kind of sales activity presents some unique problems for the restaurant. When only drinks are purchased, tabulation and collection of guest checks are simplified because there is only one point of sale, namely the bar.

When food and liquor are combined for a total sale, the merchandise has originated from two separate points of sale. That means that the items must be combined into one total for collection. Some houses present two separate checks to the guest, one for food and one for liquor, but this is confusing for the patron and can even be a source of irritation.

A further complication to all of this arises when a guest begins with a drink in the bar, and then moves into the dining room without paying for drinks consumed in the bar. Some restaurants require that drinks consumed in the bar be paid for before moving into the dining room. Such a system will work, but it is sometimes annoying to the guests. Your guests will be happier if you allow bar checks to follow them into the dining room.

Each restaurant will need specific solutions to these problems because of the various interior layouts, equipment being used or contemplated, and the methods used for control of food checks. If you have problems such as these, they can best be addressed by conferring with an outside consultant or a representative of the company that furnished your cash control system.

A very simple, yet effective control of sales at tables in the cocktail lounge is to have the serving persons pay for the drinks in cash when they are picked up at the bar. This puts the responsibility for collection on the server. A problem could arise when payment is by a credit instrument; however, that can be solved by refunding in cash for each of the checks.

INVENTORY CONTROL

The frequency of inventory should be identical to that for food. You probably can't afford to go any longer than one week between inventory and preparation of operating statements. If "leaks" in your system continue to eat into profits for longer than that, a great amount of money will be lost in the process. Some places can afford the type of system that renders full accounting on a daily basis; however, if you are not able to do that, you must personally look at your inventory, since no automatic or electronic system will tell you when an item has been physically removed. Further, records can be "doctored" and mistakes will always be made. No system has yet supplanted the need for lock and key and periodic physical counts.

Most of the big hotels and restaurants make an effort to identify their own bottles as they leave storage. Such a system aids in the inspection of bar merchandise and helps to prevent employees selling stock they have brought from outside. Such a practice is not uncommon in this business and can be very costly to the house.

How To Take Bar Inventory

Bar inventory is best taken by estimating or measuring the fractional parts of opened bottles along with full bottles. Full bottles present no problem and are merely carried at their cost price. Opened bottles may be inventoried in any fractional amount you desire; however, most businesses do their accounting in one-eighth parts. For example, we can use the same bottle of scotch that originally cost $10.00. It has now been opened and all but 4/8ths or one-half is gone. In order to arrive at our cost for inventory purposes, we merely multiply the total cost by 4/8, and we have the fractional cost of the bottle:

$10 × 4/8 = $5—cost for inventory purposes

The retail value of the opened bottle is now reduced by one-half or 8 drinks which have been sold:

16 drinks (original amount) × 4/8 × 2.52 (retail price per drink) = $20.16 retail value—remainder of bottle

The financial importance of inventory control is monumental. If you lose a bottle of liquor, you not only lose the cost, but you also lose the profit from the sale that will never happen. If you have "drainage" expense on your bar, that loss will drop right to the bottom line. As an example, if you have costs that are 3 percent too high, your profit is also 3 percent less than it should be. A dollar expression of the example could go like this:

	Budget	Actual
Sales	$90,000	$100,000
Cost of Goods Sold	22,500	28,000
Gross Profit	$67,500	$ 72,000

In the above example, Cost of Goods Sold was budgeted at 25% of sales. Actual cost came in at 28%, or 3% over budget. Further analysis shows that while gross profit is over budget, it is actually short by $3,000, and a profit of $72,000 should really have been $75,000.

8

Internal Control: How To Keep Track Of All Your Money

Table of Contents

8 Internal Control: How To Keep Track of All Your Money

Do you want to make $25,000 more in profit? In an operation with sales of slightly over $800,000 per year, that would mean an increase of about 3.1%. And you can do this without increasing your sales by even one penny!

The Importance Of Keeping Good Records

You must keep appropriate and timely operating statements, whether you prepare them yourself or have someone else prepare them. Most businesses, however, employ bookkeepers or bookkeeping firms for ongoing services. In addition, certified accounting firms are utilized for tax work. To get the most from these services, the records prepared must meet certain conditions:

- Operating statements must be prepared and given to you as quickly as possible following the close of the financial period. For example, if your restaurant operates on a monthly period, you should receive those statements during the week following the close of the month. If you don't, you could be looking at statements showing costs that may have been incurred 7 or 8 weeks earlier.

- Your financial statements should be put on a special type of chart of accounts widely used by restaurants. You can procure such a chart from the National Restaurant Association, 311 First Street N.W., Washington D.C. 20001. It is in book form, entitled, *Uniform System of Accounts for Restaurants,* Copyright © 1983. (A sample chart is reprinted by permission of the National Restaurant Association at the end of this chapter.)

There are three main reasons why you must have a tight control over incoming dollars from sales:

1. It will insure that *you* receive all the money spent by the customers in your restaurant.

2. It will allow you to *meet* your financial obligations.

3. It will *provide* you with the sales and income statistics that are needed for your operating statements, as well as the basis on which to forecast future income levels.

What Daily Sales Records Can Do For You

A Daily Sales Record is the document on which you record all of your income each day. If you use a cash register, it should provide you with all the information needed for the report. The daily sales report should tell you things such as:

- The total volume of business for the day, as well as a breakdown of cash and charge sales.

- Information about the day, i.e., the weather and any special events including holidays.

- What items or categories of items were actually sold. This sort of information is easy to obtain with the kind of cash register systems that are on the market today.

- The volume of sales per individual waiter or waitress, and whether or not all guest checks are accounted for.

- How many diners were served. What the average sale per guest was.

- The amount of your bank deposit for the day, and net amounts after taxes.

- The opening and closing cash register readings, and a cash over or short report.

There may be other kinds of information you may wish to include; but recording the foregoing items will surely help to put additional profits in your pocket.

Figure 8-1 is an example of a daily sales report that will help

DAILY SALES REPORT

Date _____

Day of Wk. _____
Weather _____
Spec Events _____

Meal & Reg. No.	Register Reading	Register Reading Diff.	Cash	Over (Short)	Charge	Sales Tax	Tips	Net Sales
E								
B								
E								
B								
E								
B								
E								
B								

Day Totals

Comments: _____

Bank Deposit _____

$ _____

Statistics

Check Numbers Issued — _____ thru _____
Check Numbers Returned — _____ thru _____
Check Numbers Missing — _____
Action Taken _____

Waiter/Waitress Individual Sales

	Luncheon	Dinner
#1	_____	_____
2	_____	_____
3	_____	_____
4	_____	_____
5	_____	_____

Number of Diners Served

Meal	No./Diners	Sales	Sales/Diner
_____	_____	_____	_____
_____	_____	_____	_____

Figure 8-1

you to manage your restaurant properly. It is particularly handy in that it consolidates all the information on one sheet of paper. In addition, you might find that having this form printed on an 8½ x 11 or legal size envelope would comprise a good filing device. The outside of the envelope would be used for recording, with all supporting documents such as cash register tapes, charge sale invoices, etc., contained within.

How To Turn Your Daily Sales Record Into Profits

Here's what you can do in order to make your daily sales record into a profit source:

- Compare your cash sales to your charge sales. You must determine if your net sales (after credit account charges) are sufficient to meet your needs, or if adjustments to prices are necessary.

- Make certain adjustments for seasons, holidays, etc. These are generally necessary when forecasting sales for the future.

- Analyze your sales against your menu, and continually adjust in order to eliminate poor sellers and unnecessary low profit items.

- Monitor your salespeople to see how each of them is doing. In that way, you can help the poor performers to improve.

- Watch the average sale per guest in order to rate your menu as to efficiency of sales mix. Also, the average sale statistics tell you how well your sales force, in total, is actually doing. Whenever there is movement either up or down in this statistic, it should be compared with the individual sales figures per server. If, for example, the general trend overall is down, it may be the fault of less spending by all diners, or a failure to sell or provide good service by one or more of your staff. If the condition is less spending by everyone, it is time to examine your operation in depth. Here are some questions to ask yourself:

  —Should my menu be overhauled with an eye toward better merchandising?

  —Should I add or delete certain items?

  —Do the specials have a desired good effect? Or are they encouraging less spending with no increase in traffic?

  —Am I providing the training that is needed to encourage employees to adopt and use good sales techniques? Are my training sessions consistent?

—Has the "shine" gone from the decor? Do the guests now find my place uninteresting?

—Has the quality of my food and/or service begun to slip? If so, is it the fault of all menu items or just certain ones, such as appetizers or desserts?

- Keep accurate and consistent records so that the information that is transmitted for statement purposes is clear and easy to get. This will save you a lot of time.

HOW TO DEVELOP AN OPERATING BUDGET

Management, as noted earlier, consists of four key functions: planning, organizing, directing and controlling. A budget has both a *planning* and a *control* function, and is essential for the profitable operation of your business.

The first step necessary in the development of a budget is the determination of a plan that incorporates the goals that you want to achieve during the upcoming fiscal period. For example, the following might be the way the ABC Restaurant would approach its planning for the new year.

In view of the fact that all forecasts indicate a short supply of beef next year, we can assume that prices for beef items will escalate. It is our intention to attempt to offset this increase in the following manner. While we know that we must continue to serve beef due to customer demand, we will make every attempt to offset the higher cost by selling more pork, poultry and fish items. We plan to accomplish this task in the following way:

- By featuring lunch specials consisting of non-beef items.

- When we reprint our menu, we will highlight non-beef items and play down the beef.

- We will place a strong emphasis on the sale of non-beef items during our regular waiter/waitress training programs during the year.

- We will aggressively seek out and buy beef products from those sources that furnish the best price, while satisfying our requirements for quality and service.

Once a plan such as this has been established, you are ready to begin forecasting your sales and expenses. Of course, there could be much more involved than the foregoing example, such as changes in operating hours, search for new markets, upgrading of personnel, and upgrading of salary structure, and so on. The important point to remember is that goal setting is the first and most vital step in the planning process for a viable budget.

Of equal importance are the matters of internal control and preparation of accounting statements, analyses and projection of future trends. These procedures and documents constitute the fiscal record of the past which is necessary to the forecast of the future.

Once all of these factors are in place, the actual construction of a budget can be started.

Forecasting Sales And Other Revenue

Most forecasters take sales history and add a percentage factor to account for growth, expansion and inflation (if necessary). Few businesses, if any, stand still or regress and still remain in business for long. Taking a sales history is relatively simple to accomplish once the percentage factor has been determined. It involves "looking down the road" and deciding how the business will be affected by any and all of the factors you have taken into account.

The following reminder checklist will help you to identify these factors—events and demographic developments—that may have some impact on your business:

- Population changes by total city or area of the city, either up or down.

- Planned changes to your area that would have an effect on traffic patterns that in turn could affect your sales, e.g., street repairs, sewer repairs.

- New industry or activity coming into your area, e.g., new plant or office building.

- Changes in laws or ordinances that might mean cause for certain adjustments to operating policies and/or procedures, e.g., legal age for alcohol consumption.

- Ethnic or economic changes in your immediate market area that could cause sales fluctuations, e.g., aging neighborhood with an increase in senior citizens.

- Expected shortage of certain commodities that are big sellers for you, e.g., Texas ban on commercial fishing for Redfish.

- Major conventions, meetings or shows that could bring business, e.g., site of the Republican or Democratic National Convention.

Many of these developments will be reported in your local newspaper. Therefore it is important that you read it every day. Other places where information can be gathered is from your local, state and national restaurant association, city planning and traffic departments, state highway department, Chamber of Commerce and from trade publications. You probably will be able to think of many other happenings that could affect your sales—and the more you can identify the better. As for the mechanics of the forecast, it's quite easy and you can become very good at it with study and practice.

An Action Example Of How To Forecast Sales

Suppose there is a new factory coming into your area with a work force of 2,500 persons. A little checking should disclose how many people will go out for lunch or dinner. You can probably attract a good many of these.

You can translate these figures into economic data by estimating how many of these folks you are apt to attract to your restaurant. You then multiply this amount by your check average and the number of days a week that the factory is open. This computation will yield a dollar figure that can be used in your forecast of income.

There are many sources which forecast inflation figures, and that figure (in percentage) should also be included in the total sales picture.

Here's how one such forecast might look:

Last Year

Food Sales	$800,000
Beverage Sales	250,000
Total Sales	$1,050,000

New business coming into area:

Food	$100,000
Beverage	25,000

Inflation @ 8% —
1,050,000 x .08 =   84,000

Total estimated increase $ 209,000

Next year forecasted sales $1,259,000

<u>Breakdown</u>

Food Sales	75%	$944,250
Beverage Sales	25%	314,750

(The luncheon and dinner percentage breakdown would come from your own past years' sales records.)

Forecasting Costs And Expenses

The same basic rules apply to the forecasting of cost and expense items as for sales forecasting. You must search out and identify those areas where change may occur, and adjust your forecast accordingly. For instance, in the example of the impending high beef prices, mentioned earlier, you would want to adjust your food cost to show the increased cost of beef in the next year. The forecasting of cost and expense can be made a lot easier by the way you and your accountant keep records of *actual* cost and expense of operations.

Earlier in this chapter, you learned about the importance of good record keeping and about the Chart of Accounts published by the National Restaurant Association. It is at this time that such records take on added importance. Compared to many other types of businesses, the restaurant business is a comparatively low-volume operation that is made up of thousands of small details. Consequently, the record keeping must be such that it keeps track of all of these small details, and of the thousands of nickels and dimes that go through the registers.

A Model Statement Of Costs

All restaurant accounting systems should break down the various income, cost and expense categories so that control is facilitated. Such a breakdown might be similar to the following sample statement:

REVENUE	$	%
Food Sales	_____	_____
Beverage Sales	_____	_____
Other Income	_____	_____
Total Revenue	_____	_____

COST OF GOODS SOLD	$	%
Food Cost:		
Meat	——	——
Seafood	——	——
Dairy	——	——
Produce	——	——
Groceries	——	——
Bakery	——	——
Total Food Cost	——	——
Beverage Cost	——	——
TOTAL COST OF GOODS SOLD	——	——
Controllable Expense:		
Payroll	——	——
Taxes & Fringe Benefits	——	——
Employee Meals	——	——
Direct Operating Expense	——	——
Advertising & Promotion	——	——
Utilities	——	——
Administrative & General	——	——
Repairs & Maintenance	——	——
Rent	——	——
Profit Before Depreciation and Interest	——	——
Depreciation	——	——
Interest	——	——
Profit (Loss) before Income Tax	——	——
Net Profit	——	——

The foregoing is a standard type of statement that furnishes the information necessary for good, tight internal control, as well as the facts needed for accurate forecasting. None of these categories will appear automatically. Rather they come about by instituting the proper classification and handling of all documents including sales reports, inventory records, invoice files and records, and payroll registers.

Important: Now that smaller style computers have come down in cost, it is more likely that they will find their way into our business on a much larger scale. Therefore, it would be beneficial to enroll in a computer course in your local adult education program, so that you can employ them in an intelligent and cost-effective manner. There is no doubt that if used properly, computers will reduce your workload and enhance internal control procedures. It is important, though, that you understand how data is gathered and fed into the machine, as well as what the final reports really mean.

How To Budget Food Costs

When your records show a breakdown of cost by category, i.e., Meat, Seafood, Groceries, etc., you can structure your budget in the same manner. Here is how to do it:

Your Operating Statements

Last Year

Food Sales	$800,000	
Food Cost	280,000	35%

Breakdown of Cost by $ and % of Sales

Meat	$ 78,400	9.9
Seafood	78,400	9.9
Dairy	36,400	4.6
Produce	28,000	3.5
Groceries	42,000	5.4
Bakery	5,600	0.7
Beverage	11,200	1.4
TOTAL	$280,000	35.0%

The above breakdown will come from the statements that are being prepared at the end of each operating period. The process of budgeting now becomes one of applying these percentages to next year's forecast of food sales.

Food Sales (Forecast)	$944,250	
Food Cost	330,490	35.0%
Meat	93,480	9.9
Seafood	93,480	9.9
Eggs & Cheese	45,320	4.6
Produce	33,050	3.5
Groceries	50,990	5.4
Bakery	6,610	.7
Beverage	13,220	1.4

The above would represent the food cost portion of the budget for the new year. In order to arrive at other expense amounts, the same type of calculations would be used. For instance, if Direct Expense were 10% last year, then you would forecast 10% of $944,250, or $94,425, in Direct Expense for next year. This budget assumes no increase or decrease in any individual category. If that were the case, then the particular category or categories would be adjusted accordingly. For example, if beef cost were forecast to be higher, you would have two options:

1. Raise prices to deliver the same percentage cost.

2. Adjust budgeted cost category for meat upward which, in turn, would raise food cost and lower net profit.

How Budgeting Gives You The Opportunity To Evaluate Your Past Performance

Budgeting gives you the opportunity to study your past performance carefully. During this process, you should examine every item on your statement to see where improvements can be made. Once done, you then construct your budget by building in sensible and realistic goals that will keep your restaurant moving forward. Here are some examples this process would reveal, and the solutions for them:

- An examination of sales—along with an assessment of your in-house training—discloses some slippage in wine sales, as well as several cancelled training sessions.

  Remedy: Conduct consistent training with an emphasis on wine. Make a practical forecast for wine sales in the new year.

- Investigation of rising utility costs discloses that a further steep increase will occur in the new year.

  Remedy: Have a comprehensive energy audit performed, and incorporate those recommendations for improvements that are possible for you to make. Even though you may have forecast a higher utility cost in the new year, make it a realistic one that requires everyone paying attention to cost.

- Examination of supply cost reveals a high cost for paper products.

  Remedy: Examine storage and handling procedures and implement improvements. Forecast a lower percentage cost in the new year—and keep to it.

ANALYZING SALES AND COSTS

Your operating statements should reflect sales and costs for the current period, as well as the previous period. These figures will tell you whether your business is improving or falling behind. Operating statements should also reveal the performance of the business as compared to the goals you have set in your budget. These comparisons may not appear on any one statement, but they all are important to you. Several statements, then, may be necessary.

How To Use Statistical Tables To Compare Your Operating Results

There are several sources for operating statistics that relate to the restaurant industry. Some of these cover operating results in a particular city or state, while others relate to the United States as a whole. Most of the magazines and trade papers will print some form of operating results that will be helpful to your own restaurant.

Two examples of statistical sources are as follows:

> Texas Restaurant Association (See Figure 8-2)
> P.O. Box 1429
> Austin, Texas 78767
> (Quarterly Publication)
> Title: *Texas Foodservice Trends*

> National Restaurant Association
> 311 First Street N.W.
> Washington, DC 20001
> (Annual Publication in cooperation with
> Laventhal and Horwath)
> Title: *Restaurant Industry Operations
> Report* (year of study)

Using these statistics to compare with your own operating re- sults can bring big dollar rewards to you. What you must recognize when dealing with them is that they are usually a compilation of historical data that may be one or more years old. The important point to note is the *trend* of business and how it affects you at any particular time period.

The following statement illustrates how this is done. The statis- tics used here are related to the Texas Restaurant Industry and are from *Texas Foodservice Trends* as shown:

ABC RESTAURANT
Profit & Loss Statement

Sales	1982	%	1983	%	Variance
Food	$500,000	76.9	550,000	81.5	+ 50,000
Beverage	150,000	23.1	125,000	18.5	– 25,000
Total Sales	$650,000	100.0	$675,000	100.0	+ 25,000

An examination of the foregoing ABC Statement discloses an increase of $50,000, or 10%, in food sales from the year 1982 to 1983. In addition, it shows a decrease of $25,000 in Beverage Sales. These two figures result in an increase of Total Sales in a net amount of $25,000, or 3.9%.

1983 TEXAS EATING AND DRINKING PLACES SALES ANALYSIS

PAGE 1

METRO AREA/ County	TOTAL UNITS 4TH QTR 1983	PERCENT CHANGE '82-'83	TOTAL UNITS 4TH QTR 1982	YEAR TO DATE GROSS SALES[1] 1983	PERCENT CHANGE '82-'83	YEAR TO DATE GROSS SALES[1] 1982	GROSS MIXED[2] BEVERAGE SALES 1983	SHARE OF EATING AND DRINKING SALES	AVERAGE SALES PER OUTLET YTD 1983	TOTAL[4] POP. (000)	CDI	UDI	PEOPLE PER OUTLET	AMOUNT SPENT PER PERSON YTD	PERCENT OF[3] FOOD BUDGET SPENT EATING OUT IN 1983
ABILENE/ (+)Taylor	269	3.86%	259	71,150,669	5.3%	67,600,169	11,584,060	16.28%	264,501	115.9	113	88	431	614	37.07%
AMARILLO/	546	4.20%	524	123,044,673	8.7%	113,199,746	22,385,979	18.19%	225,357	184.5	122	112	338	667	42.53%
(+)Potter	429	4.38%	411	100,536,036	5.1%	95,700,906	19,812,710	19.71%	234,350	102.0	181	160	238	986	45.16%
(+)Randall	117	3.54%	113	22,508,637	28.6%	17,498,840	2,573,268	11.43%	192,382	82.5	50	54	705	273	33.74%
AUSTIN/	1,860	5.50%	1,763	469,727,823	18.1%	397,667,129	88,110,123	18.76%	252,542	588.9	146	120	317	798	44.08%
(+)Hays	139	6.92%	130	31,265,469	16.2%	26,905,664	5,103,309	16.32%	224,931	44.2	130	119	318	707	49.47%
(++)Travis	1,465	4.64%	1,400	409,573,092	17.6%	348,249,035	82,198,840	20.07%	279,572	454.5	165	122	310	901	44.96%
(+)Williamson	256	9.87%	233	28,889,262	28.3%	22,512,430	807,975	2.80%	112,849	90.2	59	108	352	320	31.62%
BEAUMONT-PORT ARTHUR	1,026	-2.29%	1,050	190,395,360	9.7%	173,575,662	26,087,997	13.70%	185,571	388.4	90	100	379	490	33.00%
(-)Hardin	90	-2.17%	92	10,501,580	18.5%	8,864,898	128,507	1.22%	116,684	44.6	43	77	496	235	21.03%
ORANGE (+)Jefferson	770	-2.16%	787	147,446,109	7.7%	136,895,131	23,278,298	15.79%	191,488	255.5	106	114	332	577	36.76%
(+)Orange	166	-2.92%	171	32,447,671	16.7%	27,815,633	2,681,192	8.26%	195,468	88.3	67	71	532	367	25.78%
BRAZORIA/ (+)Brazoria	479	4.36%	459	68,232,104	10.3%	61,871,681	6,163,493	9.03%	142,447	190.9	66	95	399	357	26.61%
BROWNS-HAR/(+*)Cameron	732	2.09%	717	89,577,157	-2.0%	91,410,516	16,497,724	18.42%	122,373	232.0	71	120	317	386	34.75%
BRYAN-C STA/(+)Brazos	309	11.15%	278	69,202,344	6.9%	64,795,415	10,556,765	15.25%	223,956	104.8	121	112	339	660	38.60%
CORPUS CHRISTI/	977	-1.91%	996	186,870,938	4.6%	178,583,027	35,046,072	18.75%	191,270	340.0	101	109	348	550	35.44%
(+)Nueces	846	-0.94%	854	171,825,477	4.6%	164,280,272	33,749,453	19.64%	203,103	278.2	113	116	329	618	38.42%
(+)San Patricio	131	-7.75%	142	15,045,461	5.2%	14,302,755	1,296,619	8.62%	114,851	61.8	45	81	472	243	18.78%
DALLAS/	4,546	5.18%	4,322	1,377,146,388	9.8%	1,254,400,084	305,585,886	22.19%	302,936	2,090.8	121	83	460	659	40.77%
(-)Collin	260	9.24%	238	70,166,397	27.0%	55,262,118	7,900,256	11.26%	269,871	171.9	75	57	661	408	31.89%
(+)Dallas	3,732	4.83%	3,560	1,183,049,184	8.4%	1,091,095,493	286,641,742	24.23%	317,001	1,629.3	133	87	437	726	42.80%
(+)Denton	317	8.19%	293	79,851,259	15.8%	68,933,707	7,173,234	8.98%	251,897	166.1	88	72	524	481	34.28%
(-)Ellis	112	1.82%	110	19,701,813	20.1%	16,404,008	1,405,210	7.13%	175,909	64.4	56	66	575	306	25.03%
(-)Kaufman	91	5.81%	86	12,212,513	8.1%	11,298,198	1,331,617	10.90%	134,203	41.9	54	82	460	291	21.30%
(1)Rockwall	34	-2.86%	35	12,165,222	6.7%	11,406,560	1,133,827	9.32%	357,801	17.2	130	75	506	707	49.14%
EL PASO/ (++)El Paso	1,091	-0.91%	1,101	244,608,437	26.7%	193,067,993	41,889,755	17.13%	224,206	520.3	86	80	477	470	42.74%
FORT WORTH-ARLINGTON/	2,455	0.86%	2,434	703,147,207	12.8%	623,352,048	121,652,878	17.30%	286,414	1,039.4	124	90	424	676	41.75%
(1)Johnson	132	7.32%	123	23,686,556	20.7%	19,624,424	997,963	4.21%	179,444	75.8	57	66	574	312	24.35%
(1)Parker	75	5.63%	71	14,005,970	12.2%	12,479,110	423,825	3.03%	186,746	48.9	53	58	652	286	23.09%
(+)Tarrant	2,248	0.36%	2,240	665,454,681	12.6%	591,248,514	120,231,091	18.07%	296,021	915.1	133	93	407	727	43.60%
GALVESTON/(+)Galveston	695	-0.29%	697	120,810,323	10.3%	109,497,502	20,129,963	16.66%	173,828	205.4	108	129	295	588	34.63%
HOUSTON/	8,071	0.96%	7,994	1,954,583,844	4.4%	1,871,997,964	450,425,394	23.04%	242,174	3,028.0	118	101	375	646	39.12%
(**)Fort Bend	328	4.79%	313	39,074,991	14.9%	33,998,588	4,602,317	11.78%	119,131	159.8	45	78	487	245	26.68%
(+)Harris	7,182	0.91%	7,117	1,839,237,199	4.3%	1,763,374,993	435,409,572	23.67%	256,000	2,635.2	128	104	367	698	40.54%
(-)Liberty	177	2.91%	172	18,103,381	2.9%	17,599,429	702,247	3.88%	102,279	52.5	63	128	297	345	21.39%
(+)Montgomery	316	-2.17%	323	51,332,469	1.0%	50,839,196	9,478,919	18.47%	162,445	158.8	59	76	503	323	26.03%
(+)Waller	68	-1.45%	69	6,835,804	10.5%	6,185,758	232,340	3.40%	100,527	21.7	58	119	313	315	21.66%

(+)COUNTY TOTALLY WET FOR DISTILLED SPIRITS.   (+*)SALE OF MIXED BEVERAGES LEGAL IN ALL OR PART OF COUNTY.
(-)DISTILLED SPIRITS LEGAL IN PART OF COUNTY.   (1)COUNTY WHOLLY DRY.

[1] YEAR TO DATE GROSS SALES - includes all sales at eating and drinking places.
[2] MIXED BEVERAGE SALES - includes all mixed beverage sales at units with mixed beverage permits.
[3] PERCENT OF FOOD BUDGET SPENT EATING OUT - figures are estimated using non-taxable food store sales. Gasoline sales at convenience stores are included in the figures, and account for some level of error.
[4] POPULATION - Population figures as of 12/31/82; figures estimated by Sales And Marketing Management Magazine.

Figure 8-2

1983 TEXAS EATING AND DRINKING PLACES SALES ANALYSIS   PAGE 2

METRO AREA/ County	TOTAL UNITS 4TH QTR 1983	PERCENT CHANGE '82-'83	TOTAL UNITS 4TH QTR 1982	YEAR TO DATE GROSS SALES[1] 1983	PERCENT CHANGE '82-'83	YEAR TO DATE GROSS SALES[1] 1982	GROSS MIXED[2] BEVERAGE SALES 1983	SHARE OF EATING AND DRINKING SALES	AVERAGE SALES PER OUTLET YTD 1983	TOTAL[4] POP. (000)	CDI	UDI	PEOPLE PER OUTLET	AMOUNT SPENT PER PERSON YTD	PERCENT OF[3] FOOD BUDGET SPENT EATING OUT IN 1983
KILLEEN-TEMPLE/	505	9.31%	462	89,613,668	16.1%	77,195,673	12,133,732	13.54%	177,453	233.0	71	82	461	385	35.84%
(+)Bell	451	9.73%	411	80,889,857	16.3%	69,578,138	11,189,908	13.83%	179,357	169.9	87	101	377	476	38.38%
(1)Coryell	54	5.88%	51	8,723,811	14.5%	7,617,535	943,824	10.82%	161,552	63.1	25	33	1,169	138	22.19%
LAREDO/ (++)Webb	278	0.72%	276	37,841,101	-16.8%	45,505,036	4,508,302	11.91%	136,119	109.0	64	97	392	347	32.86%
LONGVIEW/ (-)Gregg	386	-1.53%	392	73,170,034	2.4%	71,480,948	9,290,831	12.70%	189,560	108.4	124	135	281	675	32.52%
LUBBOCK/ (+)Lubbock	488	1.46%	481	146,085,484	15.1%	126,899,373	25,638,470	17.55%	299,356	222.2	121	83	455	657	39.83%
MCALLEN/ (++)Hidalgo	755	3.28%	731	105,344,536	-0.3%	105,626,339	11,635,659	11.05%	139,529	319.3	61	90	423	330	29.77%
MIDLAND/ (+)Midland	273	10.53%	247	65,048,787	9.4%	59,469,736	14,634,406	22.50%	238,274	90.6	132	114	332	718	43.93%
ODESSA/ (+)Ector	389	1.57%	383	73,675,853	-10.0%	81,895,317	14,699,552	19.95%	189,398	125.7	108	118	323	586	37.63%
SAN ANGELO/ (-)T.Green	274	9.16%	251	52,215,909	5.8%	49,375,959	7,746,795	14.84%	190,569	90.4	106	115	330	578	37.76%
SAN ANTONIO/	3,420	5.49%	3,242	662,382,478	11.8%	592,341,263	109,074,837	16.47%	193,679	1,130.1	108	115	330	586	42.10%
(++)Bexar	3,096	5.99%	2,921	621,163,587	11.8%	555,567,529	105,119,948	16.92%	200,634	1,039.5	110	113	335	598	42.51%
(++)Comal	161	-0.62%	162	20,787,608	10.5%	18,807,477	2,315,666	11.14%	129,116	40.6	94	151	252	512	34.69%
(+)Guadalupe	163	2.52%	159	20,431,283	13.7%	17,966,257	1,639,223	8.02%	125,345	51.0	74	121	313	401	39.28%
SHERM-DENI/ (-)Grayson	202	2.54%	197	38,440,712	10.8%	34,702,654	5,227,947	13.60%	190,301	92.5	76	83	458	416	30.31%
TEXARKANA/ (1)Bowie	148	10.45%	134	39,619,349	8.2%	36,600,419	1,800,757	4.55%	267,698	77.6	94	72	524	511	31.09%
TYLER/ (1)Smith	289	5.86%	273	73,208,477	13.3%	64,625,544	9,474,756	12.94%	253,317	139.3	96	79	482	526	29.77%
VICTORIA/ (+)Victoria	251	2.45%	245	40,864,631	-3.5%	42,342,647	6,082,168	14.88%	162,807	74.7	100	128	298	547	31.55%
WACO/ (+)McLennan	555	4.72%	530	100,425,266	14.0%	88,081,759	10,489,571	10.45%	180,946	178.9	103	118	322	561	35.41%
WICHITA/ (-)Wichita	337	-3.44%	349	68,758,625	4.1%	66,055,159	8,619,686	12.54%	204,032	122.6	103	104	364	561	38.81%
TOTAL SMSA AREAS	31,606	2.66%	30,787	7,335,192,177	8.8%	6,743,216,762	1,407,173,556	19.18%	232,082	12,144.0	111	99	384	604	39.05%
NON SMSA AREAS	8,666	0.03%	8,663	997,709,162	5.8%	943,409,624	86,748,909	8.69%	115,129	3,153.2	58	104	364	316	25.29%
STATE TOTAL	40,272	2.08%	39,450	8,332,901,339	8.4%	7,686,626,386	1,493,922,465	17.93%	206,916	15,297.2	100	100	380	545	36.67%

[1] YEAR TO DATE GROSS SALES - includes all sales at eating and drinking places.
[2] MIXED BEVERAGE SALES - includes all mixed beverage sales at units with mixed beverage permits.
[3] PERCENT OF FOOD BUDGET SPENT EATING OUT - figures are estimated using non-taxable food store sales. Gasoline sales at convenience stores are included in the figures, and account for some level of error.
[4] POPULATION - Population figures as of 12/31/82; figures estimated by Sales and Marketing Management Magazine.

THE QUARTERLY EATING AND DRINKING SALES ANALYSIS REPORT IS COMPILED BY THE TEXAS RESTAURANT ASSOCIATION.

CONTACT KENT HUGHES, P.O. BOX 1429 AUSTIN, TX 78767 (512) 444-6543. REPORT AVAILABLE THROUGH SUBSCRIPTION.

Reprinted by permission of the Texas Restaurant Association.

Figure 8-2 (Cont'd)

If we next look at the statistics in *Texas Foodservice Trends*, as shown in Figure 8-2, we can see that Total Gross Sales for all reporting Texas restaurants showed an increase of 8.4% from 1982 to 1983. Carrying this further, let's suppose your restaurant is in Waco, Texas. That city showed an increase in Gross Sales of 14% in 1983 over 1982. What this tells you is that your sales increase of 3.9% is 4.5% less than the statewide average, and a whopping 10.1% less than the average restaurant in your city.

Looking at the entry for Total Units in the Analysis, we see that the number of places reporting went from 530 in 1982 to 555 in 1983. If the population also had a significant increase in the same year, it could account for the increase in total sales in the city. However, if the population did not increase, then it could mean that more people were eating out in 1983 than in 1982, or it could signal higher sales brought on by inflation and price increases. (1983 population figures were not available when this TRA report was released.) Whatever the cause, the statistics do tell you that your sales are not increasing in ratio to other restaurants in either Waco or across Texas. The next step is to find out why.

What To Do When You Are Falling Behind The Overall Trend

Going back to your Daily Sales Record will help you to find the answers. You may detect a slippage in dinner sales that can be traced to a new restaurant in the vicinity during the past year. The thing to do now is to find out why you have lost business to this competitor. Once you determine that, you can then take the necessary steps to become more competitive, and to narrow or eliminate the gap in sales. Again, the emphasis is on *trend*. Just because the Sales at ABC Restaurant increased does not mean that it is a healthy business. The fact that sales of ABC are falling behind the overall trend as experienced by the industry usually means that changes have taken place that are having a negative effect on your business.

What sort of changes could be occurring? If you will read the cover page of *TRA Foodservice Trends* (see Figure 8-3) you will note that many alterations in eating and drinking habits are taking place as follows:

"Italian foods are a favorite of Americans."
Is yours an Italian Restaurant? If so, does it offer the pasta dishes that seem to be most popular? Is the new restaurant that is in direct competition with you an Italian restaurant? If not, does it offer popular pasta dishes anyway? Could you?

TRENDS AND STATISTICS
June 11, 1984   *Research & Information*

Gallup Organization Analyzes Pasta Popularity
According to a recent study, Americans prefer Italian foods over all other
ethnic foods. Seafood pasta was the most popular dish, followed by Pasta
Primavera (a pasta tossed with a garden vegetables and topped with cream and
mild cheese). More women than men will order the Pasta Primavera when eating
out, and the Seafood Pasta is most popular among working adults age 18-34.

Light Beer Consumption Up and Still Growing
        Per capita consumption of light beer is expected to increase by 50
percent by 1990, and presently accounts for 20 percent of market sales.
        Alcohol producers are even looking at dealcoholized beer and wines. The
process involves removing alcohol from regular beer and wine by vacuum distil-
lation, resulting in a product that has .5 percent alcohol or less per serving. The non alcoholic beer has about 55 to 65 calories per serving, while
the wine has between 30 to 36 calories per serving.
                              Restaurants & Institutions, 6/6/84
AND...
The Miller Brewing Company claims that beer accounts for over 25 percent of
all foodservice sales. Per capita consumption of beer is projected to reach
27.6 gallons by 1986, outranking milk (17.5), coffee (16.7), and wine (4.3).
                              Restaurant Hospitality 4/84

Fast Food Moving Fast
1983 national Eating and Drinking place sales increased 10.5 percent to over
$115.7 billion, which compares favorably to the increase of 6.5 percent in
1982, and the 9 percent increase in '80 and '81. Fast food accounted for 35.8
percent of those gross sales, an increase of 15 percent in market sales.
                              Restaurant Hospitality, 5/84, p. 30

Breakfast Business Moves Upward
        Sales in the category are out pacing industry growth, according to a
recent CREST Family Report. Breakfast now accounts for 8.5 percent of all
restaurant traffic, jumping 15 percent in the past year.
        More 35-49 year olds tend to eat breakfast out than other age groups, and
seems to indicate that breakfast attracts the working market. The study also
found that senior citizens are not likely to skip breakfast -- a good market
for focusing breakfast efforts.
        Family restaurants capture about half of the breakfast traffic. Fast food
controls about 30 percent, and coffee shops maintain 16 percent.
        WHY IS BREAKFAST BOOMING? Opportunity for restaurateurs to expand
service, minimal costs--bottom line profits; consumers are more conscious of
their health and diets--start the day right with breakfast, morning business
meetings and functions, and working women are "bringing home the bacon rather
than frying it."
                              CREST Household & Family Report - NRA News, 5/84

Texas Restaurant Association, P.O. Box 1429, Austin, Texas 78767

Figure 8-3

Food & Beverage Receipts Up in Hotels

Texas Hotels reported an increase of 28 percent to $11.88 for average receipts per cover through March of 1984 over the same period during 1983. Motor Hotel sales were up slightly to $6.39 per cover during the same period.

Laventhol & Horwath, "Lodging Industry," 3/84

Who's Paying for Business Men & Womens Lunches?

A Gallup survey found that fewer than one in 10 respondents had eaten a meal out in the previous week that was paid for by their companies. More men (10 percent) than women (3 percent) reported having eaten a meal out that their employer paid for.

Gallup Monthly Monitor of Eating Out, 4/84

Singles Bring Returns

Incidence of eating out is reported to be highest among unmarried adults under 50 years of age. While this group accounts for only 25 percent of the adult population, they represent 32 percent of all restaurant customers.

Gallup Monthly Report on Eating Out 4/84, p. 4

Irradiation of Food Looks Promising

The process involves exposing foods to radioactive isotopes which kill harmful bacteria without significantly altering the taste, appearance, odor or texture of the food itself. This allows perishables to be stored for extended periods without refrigeration.

The FDA claims that the process is safer than chemical pesticides, and stresses that the process causes no detectable radioactivity, even with methods that detect radioactivity of substances that appear naturally in food.

The process would increase the quantity of food available worldwide by 25 to 30 percent. The government has spent $80 million on researching the process since 1953, and seems eager to have the FDA's proposal approved.

Restaurants & Institutions, 6/6/84

Gallup Organization Reports on Salad Bars in Restaurants

30 percent of all restaurants now offer salad bars. The salad bars tend to be more popular in small cities and the average price is $2.99.

This report is part of **Texas Food Service Trends**, a quarterly report compiled by the Texas Restaurant Association. Contact the Research & Information Department, P.O. Box 1429, Austin, TX 78767, or call (512) 444-6543.

Figure 8-3 (Cont'd)

Beverages: Many restaurant operators do not like to sell beer, and some only sell one or two brands. If the ABC is such a restaurant, then the following should be noted:

> "According to the Miller Brewing Co., beer accounts for 25% of all food service sales, outranking milk, coffee and wine individually. And, according to *Restaurants and Institutions*, light beer is expected to account for 70% of the beer market by 1990."

Note also the trend toward Fast Food with that sector accounting for 35.8% of the Gross Food Sales Total of 115.7 billion. Does your restaurant offer the speed of service demanded by *your* clientele? Does your luncheon menu offer items that can be packaged easily and attractively for take-out service? Do you offer any take-out service at all? Could you? Do you offer breakfast in your restaurant? If not, should you do so? If you do, are you doing a good job of marketing the product?

Statistics tell a most interesting story if you will just take time to study and relate them to your own business.

Next, we can turn to an analysis of the Cost of Sales.

	1982		1983		Var.
Food Cost	$200,000	40.0	$205,000	37.0	+5,000
Beverage Cost	34,500	23.0	31,250	25.0	-3,250
Total Cost of Sales	$234,500	36.0	$236,250	35.0	+1,750

In our example, we can see that food cost increased by $5,000, however, it actually dropped as a percentage of sales from 40% in 1982 to 37% in 1983. Such a drop usually means an increase in efficiency of purchasing, increased retail prices with steady or decreasing wholesale prices, or better management of the business. On the other hand, since sales are not keeping pace with the industry, it could mean an "excessive pinching of pennies" that have actually caused a loss of new and/or old business.

Beverage cost shows as a percentage increase in cost, even though total dollar cost actually decreased. Even though sales dropped from 1982 to 1983, the ratio of cost to sales should remain constant unless there has been a drastic change in sales mix (ratio of variable priced items sold to one another), or a loss of dollars or product through waste or pilferage.

How To Manage Sales And Costs With Good Budgets

If the ABC Restaurant has constructed a budget that is meaningful and practical in 1983 for 1984, you can next analyze actual results versus budget. Your budget represents your goal or target and is a necessary ingredient for any business. It should set the goals to be met for sales, cost and expense that are necessary to pay for the fixed cost and debt of the business. (Minimum payroll, utilities necessary to "open the door" each day, rent or mortgage, depreciation, and interest.) In addition, since you want to make a profit, that amount must also be recognized in your budget.

ABC RESTAURANT
Profit & Loss Statement
(1984)

	Actual		Year-to-Date Budget		Variance
	$		$		$
SALES					
Food	600,000	80.7	575,000	79.3	+25,000
Beverage	144,000	19.3	150,000	20.7	– 6,000
Total Sales	744,000	100.0	725,000	100.0	+19,000
COST OF SALES					
Food	192,000	32.0	184,000	32.0	+8,000
Beverage	30,240	21.0	36,000	24.0	–5,760
Total Cost of Sales	222,240	30.0	220.000	30.0	+2,240
EXPENSES					
Payroll	200,880	27.0	188,500	26.0	+12,380
Taxes & Fringes	37,498	5.0	35,525	4.9	+ 1,973
Utilities	14,880	2.0	15,225	2.1	– 345
Advertising	18,600	2.5	14,500	2.0	+ 4,100
Direct Op'n. Ex	71,424	9.6	72,500	10.0	– 1,076
Total Expenses	343,282	46.0	326,250	45.0	+17,032

You should budget for each item in your operating statement. This would include each of the sales, cost and expense categories. Studying the foregoing shows a rather healthy experience in sales which are increasing over budget, as well as cost of sales which are either right on target or better.

The same, however, is not true in the Expense category. Payroll has increased in both dollars and percentage. This is also true for Taxes and Fringes and for Advertising Expense. Such a condition would call for an analysis of labor like the one in Figure 8-4, as well as a hard look at your advertising program. The same sort of analysis should always be made for every item on the Profit and Loss

LABOR ANALYSIS CHART

Page # ___ of ___

DATE ___

Name	Job Title	Day Off	Rate of Pay	AM 6	7	8	9	10	11	12	PM 1	2	3	4	5	6	7	8	9
	Cook				The Prep				The Prep Preparation									
	Cook					The Prep Prep.				The Prep Preparation								
	Cook Helper								Clean									
	Cook Helper					The Prep				Office Preparation								
	Salad Prep																	
	Salad Prep								The Prep Preparation									
	Pot Washer								Wash Pots Clean Store Room									
	Etc.																	

Monday Thru Thursday

Luncheon Service   11:30 AM - 2:30 PM

Dinner Service   6 PM - 11 PM

Re-Cap. Rate No. Total

Enter No. of Persons
per each Rate and Total.
Total of All Persons
and Rates = Total Payroll.

Total Payroll $ ___

Figure 8-4

Statement on both a monthly and year-to-date basis. Consistent bookkeeping and analyses of this kind will certainly bring maximum dollar profits to you.

ANALYZING LABOR COSTS

Since restaurant conditions are subject to constant changes, you as owner or manager should always be aware of all the costs required to produce the quality of food, beverage and service needed to sustain your business.

Among the cost items you'll need to keep track of are the introduction of convenience foods and labor-saving devices. If such implementations take place, and menus and/or service are not extended to capture additional sales, then there may be decreasing profit margins. Frequently, labor-saving improvements are "absorbed" into the system resulting in higher food cost (convenience item) or added capitalization (new equipment) without any increase in revenue.

How To Do A Labor Analysis

There are different ways to do a labor analysis. In general, a detailed study of movements, i.e., hand, feet, etc., against a stop watch is unnecessary. Instead, an analysis of the total staff work routines in one-half or full hour increments over the workday is done. There are many possible variations of charts on which you may plot duties and shifts. One such chart is included here for illustrative purposes (see Figure 8-4). Regardless of the form used, in order to be useful, the chart must include the following:

—Title of jobs to be analyzed. Names of persons on the work force should not be substituted for job titles. Such a practice only leads to bias which, in turn, invalidates the analysis. A good analysis should include only those jobs necessary to run the restaurant efficiently and economically. Once this is accomplished, then the names of those best qualified are slotted into the schedule.

—Hours of work and task assignments.

—Hours of operation for the restaurant. These may vary from day to day. For example, Friday and Saturday may be longer operating days than the other days of the week.

Developing Work Schedules From The Labor Analysis

Employee work schedules should be developed from your labor analysis. It is easy to schedule additional time, if needed. The sample labor analysis chart can be used with an actual or projected operation to:

1. Estimate labor requirements when a restaurant is in the planning stage.

2. Analyze labor usage in an existing restaurant operation.

The technique required for preparing such an analysis is simple. It consists of charting the work hours from the beginning to the end of each shift for each person. If certain days of the work week differ from others, two separate charts may be needed.

For example, you may need a chart for Monday through Thursday, and separate ones for Friday and the weekend. Furthermore, instead of using arrows to schedule the various tasks, as shown in Figure 8-4, you can color code the chart. To do this, you would use different colors to indicate the blocks of time for pre-preparation, dining room setup, preparation, meal serving and cleanup.

Important: Make sure that you stick to the schedule you draw up. If a job can be accomplished in seven hours, schedule it to be completed in that length of time. Remember, each one of those extra hours costs you in lost profits.

For example, if your restaurant "loses" only eight hours a week at $4.50 per hour, and you have a 17% tax and fringe benefit cost, your yearly loss for 52 weeks is more than $2,190. Put another way, if you had paid attention to your labor cost, you could have realized an additional $2,190 in pre-tax profit!

APPENDIX

SAMPLE CHART OF ACCOUNTS
BASED ON
UNIFORM SYSTEM OF ACCOUNTS FOR
RESTAURANTS

The chart of accounts is a numbering system for the income and expense classifications conforming to the *Uniform System of Accounts for Restaurants*. The codes used here are not the only method for classifying the accounts; however, this is an acceptable standard grouping used by many restaurants.

The illustrated code-numbering system is designed to be flexible and to be added to or reduced to fit the requirements of the individual restaurant owner. Modern restaurant accounting methods dictate that some type of account code-numbering system be used.

CHART OF ACCOUNTS

Account Number	Account Name

ASSETS (1000)

1100	Cash
1110	Change funds
1120	Cash on deposit
1200	Accounts receivable
1210	Customers
1220	Credit card accounts
1230	Other
1240	Employees' loans and advances
1250	Provision for doubtful accounts
1300	Inventories
1310	Food
1320	Beverages
1330	Supplies
1340	Other
1400	Prepaid expenses
1410	Insurance
1420	Deposits
1430	Taxes
1440	Licenses
1500	Fixed assets
1510	Land
1520	Building
1530	Accumulated depreciation
1540	Leasehold improvements
1550	Amortization of improvements
1560	Furniture, fixtures and equipment
1570	Accumulated depreciation
1580	Automobiles
1590	Accumulated depreciation
1595	Operating equipment
1600	Deferred charges
1610	Marketing program prepaid
1620	Pre-Opening Expenses

LIABILITIES (2000)

2100	Payables
2110	Notes payable
2120	Accounts payable
2200	Taxes withheld and accrued

CHART OF ACCOUNTS

Account Number	Account Name
2210	Income Tax
2220	FICA
2230	Federal unemployment tax
2240	State unemployment tax
2250	Sales tax
2260	Employer's share of payroll taxes
2270	Provision for income taxes
2300	Accrued expenses
2310	Rent
2320	Payroll
2330	Interest
2340	Water
2350	Gas
2360	Electricity
2370	Personal property taxes
2380	Other
2400	Long-term debt

SHAREHOLDERS' EQUITY (3000)

Account Number	Account Name
3100	Common stock
3200	Capital in excess of par
3300	Retained earnings

REVENUE (4000)

Account Number	Account Name
4100	Food
4200	Beverages

COST OF SALES (5000)

Account Number	Account Name
5100	Cost of sales - food
5200	Cost of sales - beverages

OTHER INCOME (6000)

Account Number	Account Name
6100	Cover charges and minimums
6200	Commissions
6210	Gift shop operation - net
6220	Telephone and coin box commissions
6230	Concessions
6300	Salvage and waste sales
6400	Cash discounts
6900	Miscellaneous

CHART OF ACCOUNTS

Account Number	Account Name

CONTROLLABLE EXPENSES (7000)

7100	Salaries and wages
7105	Service
7110	Preparation
7115	Sanitation
7120	Beverages
7125	Administrative
7130	Purchasing and storing
7135	Other
7200	Employee benefits
7205	FICA
7210	Federal unemployment tax
7215	State unemployment tax
7220	Workmen's compensation
7225	Group insurance
7230	State health insurance tax
7235	Welfare plan payments
7240	Pension plan payments
7245	Accident and health insurance premiums
7250	Hospitalization, Blue Cross, Blue Shield
7255	Employee meals
7260	Employee instruction and education expenses
7265	Employee Christmas and other parties
7270	Employee sports activities
7275	Medical expenses
7280	Credit Union
7285	Awards and prizes
7290	Transportation and housing
7400	Direct operating expenses
7402	Uniforms
7404	Laundry and dry cleaning
7406	Linen rental
7408	Linen
7410	China and glassware
7412	Silverware
7414	Kitchen utensils
7416	Kitchen fuel
7418	Cleaning supplies
7420	Paper supplies
7422	Guest supplies
7424	Bar supplies
7426	Menus and wine lists
7428	Contract cleaning
7430	Exterminating
7432	Flowers and decorations
7434	Auto and truck expense

CHART OF ACCOUNTS

Account Number	Account Name
7436	Parking lot expenses
7438	Licenses and permits
7440	Banquet expenses
7498	Other operating expenses
7500	Music and entertainment
7505	Orchestras and musicians
7510	Professional entertainers
7520	Mechanical music
7525	Contracted wire services
7530	Piano rental and tuning
7535	Films, records, tapes and sheet music
7540	Programs
7550	Royalties to ASCAP, BMI and SESAC
7555	Booking agents fees
7560	Meals served to musicians
7600	Marketing
7601	Selling and promotion
7602	Sales representative service
7603	Travel expense on solicitation
7604	Direct mail
7605	Telephone and telegraph used for advertising and promotion
7606	Entertainment cost in promotion of business (including gratis meals to customers)
7607	Postage
7610	Advertising
7611	Newspaper
7612	Magazines and trade journals
7613	Circulars, brochures, postal cards and other mailing pieces
7614	Outdoor signs
7615	Radio and television
7616	Programs, directories and guides
7617	Preparation of copy, photographs, etc.
7620	Public relations and publicity
7621	Civic and community projects
7622	Donations
7623	Souvenirs, favors, treasure chest items
7630	Fees and commissions
7631	Advertising or promotional agency fees
7632	Franchise fees
7640	Research

CHART OF ACCOUNTS

Account Number	Account Name
7641	Travel in connection with research
7642	Outside research agency
7643	Product testing
7700	Utilities
7705	Electric current
7710	Electric bulbs
7715	Water
7720	Removal of waste
7725	Fuel
7730	Engineer's Supplies
7795	Ice
7800	Administrative and general expenses
7805	Office stationery, printing and supplies
7810	Data processing costs
7815	Postage
7820	Telegrams and telephone
7823	Management fees
7825	Dues and subscriptions
7828	Executive office expense
7830	Traveling expenses
7835	Insurance—general
7840	Commissions on credit card charges
7845	Provision for doubtful accounts
7850	Cash over or (short)
7855	Professional fees
7858	Directors or Trustees Fees
7860	Protective and bank pick-up services
7865	Bank charges
7870	Miscellaneous
7900	Repairs and maintenance
7902	Furniture and fixtures
7904	Kitchen equipment
7906	Office equipment
7908	Refrigeration
7910	Air conditioning
7912	Plumbing and heating
7914	Electrical and mechanical
7916	Floors and carpets
7918	Buildings
7920	Parking lot
7922	Gardening and grounds maintenance
7924	Building alterations
7928	Painting, plastering and decorating
7990	Maintenance contracts—elevators
7992	Maintenance contracts—signs

CHART OF ACCOUNTS

Account Number	Account Name
7994	Maintenance contracts—office machinery
7996	Autos and trucks
7998	Other equipment and supplies

RENT AND OTHER OCCUPATION COSTS, INTEREST & DEPRECIATION (8000)

8100	Rent & other occupation costs, Interest and depreciation
8105	Rent—minimum or fixed
8110	Percentage rent
8115	Ground rental
8120	Equipment rental
8125	Real estate taxes
8130	Personal property taxes
8135	Other municipal taxes
8140	Franchise tax
8145	Capital stock tax
8150	Partnership or corporation license fees
8160	Insurance on building and contents
8200	Interest
8205	Notes payable
8210	Long term debt
8215	Other
8300	Depreciation
8305	Buildings
8310	Amortization of leasehold
8315	Amortization of leasehold improvements
8320	Furniture, fixtures and equipment
9000	Income Taxes
9010	Federal
9020	State

9

How To Increase Your Profits By Staying On Top Of Changes In The Marketplace

Table of Contents

9

How To Increase Your Profits By Staying On Top Of Changes In The Marketplace

Staying abreast of the constant changes that can affect the restaurant business is one of the most important things you, as owner or manager, can do. One very good way to stay alert to impending change in the community that could influence your profits is to spend the maximum time possible in your restaurant's dining room talking with your guests. Your customers can represent an excellent source of information about a great many different subjects, including the local happenings.

How To Turn Negative Changes Into Positive Ones

Changes in the community can affect your business by causing changes in your market that can be either beneficial or disruptive. Often changes that look disruptive can have a positive effect if you are alert and imaginative enough to turn negative situations into positive ones.

For example, suppose you hear from a steady customer that a new building will be going up near your restaurant, and that your driveway is going to be partially blocked for some time because of the need to extend or modify utility lines. This may at first appear to be disastrous for you. However, after checking to see if this information is factual, here is what you can do to turn this into a benefit and come out a winner:

You find additional parking space within easy walking distance of your restaurant for which you are able to negotiate a short-term lease. You then utilize table tents, signs and your regular method of advertising to inform your customers of the temporary inconvenience to them. At the same time, you emphasize that the food and service will still be the same fine quality they have enjoyed in the past.

Next, realizing that you might still lose some regular business because of this inconvenience, you take your miniature sample menus and personally visit other businesses, institutions, etc., within walking distance, inviting folks to try your restaurant. In order to help this program along, you hand out some coupons that offer discounts on your daily specials.

Results:

- You have shown your regular customers that you care enough to alleviate the inconveniences.

- You have opened new markets and secured some new customers.

  In other words, you have turned a negative into a positive!

Changes in the marketplace that could hurt your business can also have a disastrous effect on your employees. For example, service people may lose tips and want to seek other employment. Or, production people may have to face the possibility of layoffs due to poor sales. In both cases, you may suffer the loss of good employees who will have to be replaced later.

Employees are often a good source of grapevine information. Therefore, by keeping open the lines of communication, they may alert you to troublesome events. In addition, ongoing communication may help to forestall future employee dissatisfaction.

WHERE TO FIND OUT ABOUT CHANGES

There are many different sources from which information is available about events that could affect your business. The most common, as well as obtainable are, of course, television, radio and your daily newspaper. By watching the news or listening to at least one newscast each day on the radio, you will keep informed of national and state news, as well as certain important community items. In addition, your local newspaper should be read daily since it is full of tidbits about what is going on around town.

When you read the paper, you should pay particular attention to the following:

1. *The Business Section*—for events related to companies and institutions in your town; for news about companies moving in and out of the area; for personnel and executive changes within various organizations; for real estate development.

   When you hear of new companies coming into the area, you may want to establish contact by presenting sample menus, welcome letters, etc. Personnel or executive changes may call for your contacting secretaries to suggest your restaurant for congratulatory parties or get-togethers. Also such items as birthdays, christenings and wedding announcements would invite some action on your part.

2. *City/County Government Section*—for happenings at city council meetings; planning related to street, sewer, etc., construction; any contemplated changes in tax laws or rates of assessments.

   You should be aware of what is happening in city government in order to be forewarned of events that could either help or hurt you.

3. *Sports Page*—for what's happening on the local sports scene.

   Watching the local sports scene could offer opportunities for award banquets, luncheons, etc. If you are able to pick up only 10 banquets in one year for 50 persons at $18.00 per person, you will bring in a nice extra $9,000. Not only that, you will probably make a minimum of $3,150 in operating profits from just those few parties.

Trade Periodicals: Another Excellent Source Of Information

Trade periodicals are publications that relate to a specific industry. In addition to these are business periodicals, which report on business conditions and happenings to industries and governments. Both of these are informative. But of special interest to you are those periodicals that report on the food service industry.

The following is a partial listing of some of the various restaurant publications, and what they cover:

- **Restaurant Association Publications**
  For example, the Texas Restaurant Association publishes a

monthly magazine entitled *Texas Food and Service*. It contains articles written by many different people in the industry, covering all facets of restaurant operations. Included in it are such items as menu construction, marketing and sales, employee training, labor relations and the latest information on present and proposed legislation that will affect the restaurant industry. Each state has an association, and each tries to keep its membership informed as best it can.

- **Nation's Restaurant News**
  Published by Lebhar-Friedman Inc., 425 Park Avenue, New York, New York 10022. This paper is published biweekly, every other Monday. It contains over 150 pages, and covers current events in the restaurant industry throughout the country. In it, you will find articles dealing with current and proposed laws; what is happening with various companies as well as independent restaurants; sales and earnings statistics; editorial comments about the industry; and reports on past, current and future meetings, conventions and events.

- **Restaurant Hospitality**
  Published monthly at 1111 Chester Avenue, Cleveland, Ohio 44114. In it, you'll find articles about different restaurant operations around the country. Usually it has at least one story related to restaurant design. Each month there are comments from various writers covering a wide expanse of topics.

- **Restaurants and Institutions**
  A Cahners publication, 1350 E. Touhy Avenue, Des Plaines, Illinois 60018. This magazine is published twice a month. It contains statistics of interest to the industry, including current restaurant industry sales and forecasts for the future. Products—both new and established—are reported, and there are the usual stories about specific companies. Included are menus and recipes from restaurants, as well as a classified section containing information on personnel recruiting, real estate and franchise opportunities.

- **Food Service Equipment Specialist**
  Published monthly by Cahners Publishing Company, Five South Wabash Avenue, Chicago, Illinois 60603. This publication is a sourcebook for virtually every type of equipment used in a food service operation of any kind. If you are looking for a certain product or products, try this magazine. It also carries a listing of industry manufacturers and associations.

- **Restaurant Design**
  Published quarterly by Restaurant Business, Inc., 633 Third

Avenue, New York, New York 10017. This magazine is all about restaurant interior design and facility planning. It has feature articles on specific installations, and includes pictures and diagrams. If you are going to build a new facility or remodel an existing one, you may get some very valuable ideas from this periodical.

- **Food Service Marketing**
  Published monthly by EIP Inc., 2132 Fordem Avenue, Madison, Wisconsin 53704. It includes statistics on dining out in various market segments of the industry. This magazine offers information on marketing techniques through merchandising of menu and interior design. You will also find results of research into pricing of products, energy, standardization of menu items, and more. There are also articles by contributing editors on a variety of subjects ranging from personnel problems to facilities planning.

- **Restaurant Business**
  Published monthly (except semi-monthly in March, May and September) by Restaurant Business Magazine, 633 Third Avenue, New York, New York 10017. Includes many different articles about various market segments and companies in the industry. Also has a good coverage of statistical data related to the economics of our business.

The following is a listing of some of the general business periodicals:

- **The Wall Street Journal**
  Published Monday through Friday. This is a regional paper that you can probably find on your favorite newsstand. The paper covers all aspects of current happenings throughout the country. For the most part, it is dedicated to business news, but it often carries articles on subjects of general interest.

- **State Business Publications**
  In Texas, we have a magazine entitled *Texas Business* published monthly by Commerce Publishing Corporation, 5757 Alpha Road, Suite 400, Dallas, Texas 75240. This magazine specializes in the reporting of business news around the state. In addition, it reports on economic statistics and news on legislation having an effect on business in the state. There are probably journals such as this in your state, and any good newsstand or bookstore usually carries them.

- **The Kiplinger Washington Letter**
  Published weekly at 1729 H Street, N.W., Washington, D.C. 20006. This publication consists of a capsulized version of

current happenings in Washington and on the national scene. It is short, easy to read, and quite informative.

You should decide how much time you can give to this particular activity, and then select those publications that you personally enjoy and that will fit into your busy schedule. Obviously you can't read everything that is written on the subject, but you should certainly try your best to read some.

An Example Of How You Can "Lose Your Shirt" By Not Keeping Informed

While there are always exceptions to any rule, a good and accessible location is of prime importance to the success of a restaurant. Of course, the surrounding traffic situation is one of the factors to be considered (Chapter 10 discusses site selection in detail), as is the residential and commercial development in the surrounding neighborhood. However, no matter how judicious you are in your original choice, unfortunately nothing stays unchanged.

Let's take a look at the disastrous results that can happen when the changes come unexpectedly.

> Herman's restaurant is located on the east side of E Street in a nice, relatively stable town of 100,000 population. E Street is a moderately busy street running north and south between the suburbs on the south side, and the downtown area to the north.
>
> Herman's restaurant does an excellent breakfast business that begins at about 6:30 a.m. and lasts until 9:00. In fact, Herman is so busy cooking that he doesn't hear about the new 35-story office building that will be constructed just up the street from the restaurant. And by the time he gets the news, plans have been finalized and the city is getting ready to close down the east side of E Street in order to widen the street and install new sewer and water lines. This means that northbound traffic will be routed one block to the east, and E Street will become one way for southbound traffic during the construction period.
>
> Herman obviously has a big problem. Now he will really have to scramble to protect his business. And before he gets reorganized, he will probably have lost many of his steady customers because of the inconvenience.

Earlier in this chapter, you saw how just such a situation as this could be handled. The key, of course, is to stay alert and become aware of the impending change long before it happens. If you are that kind of alert manager, you will be able to make plans that may get you through such a crisis, even though you suffer some loss of business.

Keeping Track Of Events That Affect Supply And Demand

The last several years have seen the restaurant industry move toward specialization in menu offerings. One is hard pressed to find a dinner or family-style restaurant that offers a wide variety of foods over a three-meal period. Restaurants now tend to specialize in specific foods such as steak, barbecue, seafood, health food, etc. Much of this specialization is seen in the fast-food restaurants. A big factor in the success of these types of restaurants is their ability to purchase competitively so that they can sell at competitive prices.

You can "stay ahead of the pack" if you watch for any sort of disruption to future supply of any of the food items on your menu. A very good example of this is produce, which fluctuates wildly in price due to long or short supplies. These overages or shortages can occur through changes in weather conditions—i.e., killing frost; long dry, hot spells; floods; etc.—or through such things as labor strife, insect infestation, or import/export law. Therefore, by watching for events that will affect supply/demand and price (either up or down), you will be able to feature the items that will be most profitable for you.

Where To Find Out About Important Legislative Changes

Your State and National Restaurant Association bulletins will keep you apprised of the latest legislative changes you will need to know about. So it is important that you belong to an association and receive its bulletin, and read what you receive.

In the last few years, the restaurant industry has absorbed some steep increases in the minimum wage, as well as increased costs from changes in work rules related to overtime hours. Another change that has occurred is the method by which tips to service personnel are reported. When changes such as these appear on the horizon, they usually mean that some adjustment—either to prices or to staff—may be necessary. Therefore, the sooner you know about them, the quicker you can formulate plans—and the smoother will be the result.

There is nothing more unsettling to most people than change. But since it is inevitable and occurring rapidly these days, your success as an entrepreneur could be related directly to your ability to handle it. One sure way is to stay alert and learn as much as possible about disturbing events before they occur.

HOW TO CASH IN ON CHANGES

Construction in your neighborhood can mean a boom in your business. When new buildings are under construction or when old buildings are being remodeled, there is always an influx of people into the area. These include the various construction trades and labor, as well as engineers, architects, administrators and inspectors. All of these people mean potential business for you. However, when opportunities present themselves they sometimes are accompanied by problems that have to be dealt with.

For example, in the case of construction, this can mean carpeting ruined by the muddy and dirty boots of the workers from the construction site. One way to handle this problem—while capitalizing on the opportunity for extra business—would be to take a tip from the New Orleans hotels. During Mardi Gras, they cover the lobby floors with plastic in order to protect the carpeting from any damage by revelers. There is no reason a restaurant couldn't do the same thing. Or you could let your imagination run wild and temporarily open "The Japan Room" with a checking arrangement for shoes and boots at the door. That might be fun, and could even bring you free coverage in the local news media. Once again, be alert to change so that you have time to plan, adapt, and execute for profit!

How Best To Deal With Changes That May Occur In Shopping Centers

Since there are many restaurants located in strip and major shopping centers, there are many events that may have an influence on them. A restaurant located in a strip center usually relies heavily on auto traffic for its business. And if street traffic patterns change, its business may experience beneficial or harmful effects.

For example, a strip center could be located on a major thoroughfare that carries a steady moving flow of traffic. As activity increases, the flow of cars could reach the point where a left turn to enter the center would become so difficult that people would pass by the restaurant. Thus, most of its business would come largely from one side of the street. Such a situation could be disastrous for a restaurant in that kind of location.

How do you deal with such a problem? You will need to work closely with the local business association to bring about additional control with traffic signal lights.

Major shopping mall restaurants present a somewhat different situation, in that they depend largely on foot traffic. When a mall adds stores, they often alter traffic patterns that could affect a restaurant. For instance, a "hot" location can become "cold" if new stores, more competitive than your immediate neighbors, move in at the other end of the mall. Such a problem might require a change in advertising technique, strategic placement of signs, or in a very extreme situation, actually moving to a new location.

Changes That Might Influence Your Business: A Checklist

- *A new hotel opens close by.* Be sure that the workers, auto valet, bellmen and front desk personnel know about your restaurant. You will want them to refer hotel guests to you. You may also be able to place advertising in the guest rooms.

- *A new factory with high employment opens within easy driving distance of your restaurant.* Pay a personal call to as many of the executive offices as possible. Also, be sure you introduce yourself to the secretaries. Ask them to remember your restaurant when they are making lunch or dinner reservations, or when booking special parties.

- *The city plans to build a new convention center.* This could well mean an increase in business for you. To make sure those who attend the convention will know about your restaurant, make contact with people in the convention bureau.

- *New senior citizen apartments are going up.* Gear your menus toward offering specials at reduced prices, and with smaller portions. Contact any formal social organizations for the elderly, and try to attract them as customers.

- *You notice a decline in the average check.* Do additional research to determine what specifically is causing the decline. Look toward a change in menu, addition of specials, increased advertising budget, or stepped-up sales training of your staff.

- *Fall off in liquor sales.* Find out why. Maybe it is part of a national trend related to drunk driving campaigns. If so, look toward picking up the lost sales with increased emphasis on your food sales. If it is a condition related only to your restaurant, look for a let down in service or pilferage.

- *An increase in theft of auto and auto accessories in your neighborhood.* Take on some sort of private security. Consider valet parking. Examine your parking areas for lighting and accessibility to your restaurant.

- *There is construction on the building housing your restaurant that has blocked your sign and has partly concealed your restaurant.* Try to have a temporary sign placed on the scaffolding that is responsible for screening your restaurant.

- *A new restaurant plans to open on your block.* Keep a close watch and be ready with promotional and sales planning in the event that it turns out to be strong competition.

- *There is a change in economic conditions, and a sudden surge in unemployment in your town.* This condition will hurt business whether the newly unemployed are your customers or not. During times such as these, everyone cuts back on spending. To help ease the cutbacks, you can run special promotions, especially tied to the family theme. Or you can offer reduced prices, all-you-can-eat deals, or coupons for discount. It is also very important to look for those areas where you can cut back on spending in order to be able to absorb the increases in food cost.

Remember, a change can mean new, fresh ideas that will open the way to expanded and original opportunities—even though they may be temporarily unsettling. You can profit from change if you look for the bright side. Be optimistic, and above all—keep that good old imagination working overtime!

10 How To Simplify Remodeling Or Expansion Plans

Table of Contents

10 How To Simplify Remodeling Or Expansion Plans

We all tend to equate success with size—the bigger, the better. While this is often true, it is not always the case. For some restaurant operators, expansion of present facilities or relocation has meant disaster. Your success, therefore, will depend largely on whether you have thoroughly examined and prepared yourself for this undertaking.

The following is a series of questions to ask yourself before you actually make the move toward expansion. The rest of this chapter deals with the steps you should take if "go and grow" is the right decision.

A Pre-Expansion Checklist

☐ Is my system for counting customers and tabulating sales accurate? Do I know when peak customer hours are? How many are served during those hours? Are the peak loads long enough and often enough to justify expansion?

☐ Is parking a problem that can only be solved by expansion? Are there other parking facilities available for lease or purchase? Have I looked around?

☐ Is the kitchen really worn out, or is it only in need of some overlooked repair? Will a larger kitchen produce more meals, or will it only require more labor for staffing, and, consequently, greater operating expense?

☐ Do I have the management expertise and/or capability to operate either a larger restaurant or additional restaurants? Have I worked up some preliminary financial plans relative to expansion?

☐ Will the expansion mean a sufficient increase in profits to justify the additional work that I will have to do?

☐ Do I really want to expand, or is it just an obsession to be bigger? Is the competition hurting me? Why? If I don't expand, will it hurt me more? Less?

☐ Has the market changed? Is it likely to change in the future?

Asking yourself the above questions will cause some deep soul searching for answers. In addition, each question will probably trigger another until you have fully investigated your reasons for expansion.

How To Sustain A Highly Successful Business Without Opening An Additional Restaurant: Two Case Histories

Some people feel that they want to develop chain operations, while others are happy tending and nurturing one restaurant. We see many examples of success on both sides. Companies like McDonald's and Shoney's have grown from very modest beginnings to dominant positions in their segment of the food service industry.

I have observed the success of restaurants such as Tony's and Pino's in Houston under the guiding hand of each of the owners. These two restaurants are both excellent examples of how dedicated, knowledgeable owners have developed and sustained highly successful businesses without opening additional restaurants. Each of these restaurants has an established long-time clientele. In addition, they are adding new customers all the time.

We all admire winners in our business, and here is how each of these owners has done it:

Tony's
1801 Post Oak Boulevard
Houston, Texas

Tony's is an expensive, world-class restaurant that features a French and Continental cuisine. It uses nothing frozen or canned, and has no equipment for reconstitution or even for warming. All food moves from stove to table. Tony's presents a formal yet warm and relaxing atmosphere.

Some of the awards the restaurant has won are:
—*Holiday Magazine Award* (12 consecutive years)
—*Playboy* (Top 25 American restaurants)
—*Dun and Bradstreet* (Top 10 in the U.S.)
—*Texas Monthly* (The Rolls Royce of Texas restaurants)
—*Cartier Award*
—*National Restaurant Association Hall of Fame*

Tony's is owned and operated by Mr. Tony Vallone. This gentleman started in the business as a young boy working in restaurant kitchens. At that time, he had a strong interest in food and utilized most of his time learning from various chefs and reading books on the subject.

Tony's first venture was a 100-seat medium-priced restaurant, featuring Italian food. As business grew, French items were gradually worked into the menu. In 1972, the restaurant was relocated to its present address. It was then that Mr. Vallone sensed the need for a fine French-Continental restaurant in the area. He felt that there was no competition in the field. And obviously, he was right. He has organized and sustained a truly outstanding restaurant. And although many others have tried to copy the restaurant, no one has come close to matching it.

How did he do it? How did Tony move from an established busy restaurant to a new location, and stay successful? Let Tony Vallone tell you—

"I have always considered that attention to detail and consistency of service and product are essential to success in this business. Although I do a small amount of advertising and promotion, I have relied mainly on word of mouth, and it has worked well for me.

"After I had started my first restaurant, I recognized the need for a high-quality establishment, and I worked toward providing one. You ask how I would advise others who are considering expansion on the building or additional restaurants: Study the move carefully and be certain you can handle the additional supervision that will be required. If you think you cannot keep up the same quality, don't make the move. Of course, you must also consider the numbers—they have to be positive.

"I would not consider opening any additional restaurants since I do not feel that I could give the kind of attention necessary to more than one. My customers and my staff are special to me, and I care for them in every possible way."

Mr. Vallone believes that all restaurants, regardless of price or menu, are basically the same. They all require a high degree of care and attention if they are to succeed.

*   *   *   *   *

**Pino's Restaurant
2711 Hillcroft
Houston, Texas**

Owners:

Mr. Giuseppi "Pino" Farinola

Mr. Adriano Farinola

This is a casual, candle-lit medium-priced restaurant that features Italian specialties. There is no cocktail lounge, but wine and beer are dispensed from a service bar. Pino started a 22-seat pizza restaurant near the University of Houston in 1960. His brother Adriano joined the business in 1963. And by 1970, the restaurant increased in size to 100 seats.

In 1970, due largely to a deteriorating change in their neighborhood during the late 60's, the brothers decided to move. So they purchased land and constructed their restaurant at its present location. The new location was considered by some to be too far "out in the country," and the general feeling was that they "wouldn't make it." The restaurant opened with 75 seats, and 90 days later it expanded to 85 seats. In 1974, they expanded again to 170 seats, which is its capacity at present. This is a very busy restaurant. It seems that there are always people standing in line waiting for tables.

How do they do it? In the words of these gentlemen:

> "We have always exercised close and continuous supervision over our food and service. In all the years that we have been in business, no one other than us has ever had a key to the door. One of us has always opened or closed the restaurant. We are 100% quality-minded. We personally check every delivery of food and supplies to be certain we receive what we have ordered. Because of this, our suppliers are very careful and send us only the best. We watch the details of the business very carefully. We supervise our staff, and we take great care to know our customers and see that they receive the best food and service that we can provide."

I asked them if they had considered such items as population, income, auto or pedestrian traffic or competition from other restaurants. Their answer was "no." Their main concern has only been for the quality of their offerings. And in their words, "there has been a line at the door since we opened." The brothers have reaped the rewards of their hard work over the years and can now enjoy the good life.

Stay On Top Of Changes

The need to be aware of changes is of utmost importance when considering expansion. For example, if you are located in a big city and you are weighing the probable success or failure of a lounge and restaurant in a downtown location, you must consider present and future energy costs, and their impact on individual driving habits.

An investment like this will rely mostly on the 4:00 P.M. to 7:00 P.M. cocktail-hour trade. Therefore, you must first determine what the market is. For instance, you may find out that the movement toward car and van pooling has "softened" the market. If this is the case, there may still be a strong and viable market available, but you may have to alter your thinking as to a restaurant concept in order to capture it.

DEVELOPING FINANCIAL DATA ON THE PROFITABILITY OF A NEW RESTAURANT

After asking yourself all of the questions in the "pre-expansion checklist," you must develop some financial data before going ahead to expand or remodel your restaurant, or open a second one. The data developed will eventually result in a pro forma statement, which will indicate to you whether or not the investment will be feasible.

This information will also indicate to your investor—a bank, individual, etc.—whether the plan is economically sound. Inasmuch as an investor will base its decision on the evidence you present in this statement, you would do well to consider having the document drawn up by a professional consultant. (The hiring of a consultant will be discussed in detail later in this chapter.)

The pro forma statement should contain both sales and expense projections. These figures will come from different record keeping sources. For example, if you are contemplating expansion of an *existing facility*, the past financial results of the business will be used. In addition, other economic data relating to increased sales potential must be assembled.

The following illustration shows how to use the information on these records to prepare a Pro Forma Statement.

How To Prepare A Pro Forma Statement

Let's say that ABC restaurant is five years old, and is located in an expanding area of a rapidly growing city. It is a table service restaurant with 100 seats for dining, and it offers a moderately priced menu. In addition to the dining room, it also has a small cocktail lounge with 15 seats. Although alcoholic beverage sales are good, most of the revenue is derived from the dining room rather than the lounge.

An examination of the operating statements for the past three years indicate that sales have risen as follows:

Year	Food Sales	Bev. Sales	Total
3	$450,000	$150,000	$600,000
	75%	25%	100%
4	$475,000	$160,000	$635,000
	75%	25%	100%
5	$510,000	$170,000	$680,000
	75%	25%	100%

(For simplification, all number amounts have been rounded off.)

Calculating percentage increases from year to year yields the following:

Year	Sales	$	% Increase
3	Food	450,000	
	Beverage	150,000	
	Total	600,000	
4	Food	475,000	5.6
	Beverage	160,000	6.7
	Total	635,000	5.8
5	Food	510,000	7.4
	Beverage	170,000	6.3
	Total	680,000	7.1

To simplify this example, let's assume that the increased sales were the result of menu price increases. Consequently, we can assume that, because ABC is considering expansion, the restaurant is operating at capacity. In other words, it is unable to accommodate any increase in patrons, and diners must regretfully be turned away at very busy times.

The next step is to break the sales down by seat. Because food is also served in the lounge, let's say that this restaurant has a total of 115 seats:

	$Sales	Per Seat
Year #3: Food	$510,000	$4,435
Beverage	170,000	1,480
Total	$680,000	$5,915

Assuming that there is space available for 30 additional seats with remodeling, and further assuming a 3% increase in dollar sales per seat to correct for expected price increases, we could project sales upon completion of the project as follows:

Food Sales:

145 seats $\times$ $4,568.05 = $662, 367

Beverage Sales:

145 seats $\times$ $1,524.40 = $221,038

Total Projected Sales: $883,405
Proof:

$5,915 $\times$ 3% increase = $177.45 per seat
$5,915 + 177.45 $\times$ 145 seats = $883,405

Obviously this is an oversimplification, but it is one way to arrive at the necessary financial data you will need. When you contemplate expansion, there are factors other than past history that you must also consider. Later in the chapter, you will see how to forecast sales using economic statistical data, which can be applied as a check on the accuracy of a forecast from historical data.

How To Forecast Costs And Expenses

Estimating these items, as shown in Figure 10-1, will require the use of a slightly different technique from the one outlined above. Here are some key points to keep in mind:

Cost Of Sales: These should remain constant with the addition of a new facility. For example, if food cost was 35% and beverage cost 22%, then you should be forecasting at the same percentage cost. In actuality, the costs may drop with the increase in volume. However, you would probably have a reasonable forecast by using the same ratios as before the remodeling.

Labor Cost: For the purpose of forecasting, many people would apply a similar percentage cost before remodeling to the in-

Typical Income and Expense Statement Before And After Renovation

Revenue:	Before	%	After	%
Food Sales	$510,000	75.0	$662,367	75.0
Beverage Sales	170,000	25.0	221,038	25.0
Total Revenue	$680,000	100.00	$883,405	100.0
Cost of Sales:				
Food	$178,500	35.0	$231,828	35.0
Beverage	37,400	22.0	48,627	22.0
Total COS	$215,900	31.7	$280,455	31.7
Operating Expense:				
Labor	$193,800	28.5	$238,520	27.0
Employee Benefits	27,200	4.0	35,335	4.0
Direct Op'n. Exp.	47,600	7.0	61,840	7.0
Entertainment	5,440	.8	7,065	.8
Adv. & Promotion	13,600	2.0	22,085	2.5
Utilities	20,400	3.0	26,500	3.0
Adm. & General	34,000	5.0	44,170	5.0
Rep. & Maint.	10,200	1.5	13,250	1.5
Total Op'n. Exp.	$352,240	51.8	$448,765	50.8
Profit from Op'ns.	$111,860	16.5	$154,185	17.5
Other Costs:				
Rent, Insurance	$ 34,000	5.0	$ 44,170	5.0
Depreciation	17,000	2.5	20,320	2.3
Interest	13,600	2.0	22,085	2.5
Restaurant Profit	$ 47,260	7.0	$ 67,610	7.7

Figure 10-1

creased sales volume. However, a more accurate way—and considering that the increased size may result in some unknowns—would be to analyze the labor requirement in the same manner as you would for any facility with which you have had little or no previous experience. (See Chapter 8.)

Other Operating Expenses: Here again, you can apply the same percentages of expenses that you have been experiencing before renovation to the increased sales figures. Employing this technique will probably yield an acceptable forecast for the expanded facility. However, this is a time of change, and it is an opportunity for you to examine closely each and every item in order to effect economies wherever possible.

For example, during remodeling, you may find that a new style broiler will allow for faster cooking at reduced energy cost. Further, you may feel the need to increase your advertising and promotion budget in order to realize the full potential of the new facility. Each of these items should then be adjusted accordingly. Keep in mind that a 1% savings in any cost or expense item in our example will yield an increase of $8,834 in profit before taxes. You, too, can have a similar pleasant experience in your own restaurant.

Multi-Unit Operations: We all look toward the day when we can consider ourselves "Captains of Industry." It fits nicely with our capitalistic system, and provides the often-needed incentive to "get out of bed and go to work." But like all dreams and goals, there is also a catch in this one.

Obviously, managing one restaurant is vastly different from managing two—as the complexities of running two restaurants often multiply at a rate much faster than the rate of growth. Business activities that are confined to one location can be supervised efficiently by one person. Multi-unit operations must also be organized in such a way to provide the same sound management and control on a *consistent* basis.

Therefore, if you are contemplating opening a second restaurant, there are certain important facts you should keep in mind. Consider the following:

1. Many diners will return to a restaurant because they enjoy the personal attention a manager or owner gives to them. There is an element of prestige or pride for patrons when recognized in front of their guests or companions by the "person in charge." You will want to continue this same personalized attention.

2. Diners want to feel confident that the food they are eating

has been properly handled by kitchen and service personnel. The presence of caring management conveys that message.

3. A major task that will confront you will be the problem of finding management people who will conscientiously watch your money for you. Once you have opened the new facility, you will find it necessary to spread yourself between the two. Since it is impossible to be in two places during the same meal-time hours, it follows that you will need some good and loyal people to assist you.

WHERE TO FIND GOOD MANAGEMENT PEOPLE TO STAFF AN ADDITIONAL RESTAURANT

Finding good management people can be a difficult job. However, there are many sources from which you can draw people—some of which may require you to spend some money for them. The following are a few of the sources available to you:

- *Executive Search Firms.* These companies specialize in finding people for their clients. Some of them specialize in certain industries, e.g., energy, manufacturing, etc. Other firms are more generalist in nature, and deal with a broad range of companies across industry lines.

  If you are considering retaining such a firm as an aid in your search for people, try to find one that has some contact with the food service industry. In addition, because these firms charge for their services, be sure you know what you are getting before you sign an agreement.

- *Colleges/Universities having courses in Hotel and Restaurant Management.* Some of the larger and better-known schools that offer these courses and that have placement services are: Michigan State University, Cornell University, University of Houston, Oklahoma State University, Florida International University and the University of Nevada at Las Vegas. There are also many smaller colleges and vocational schools that have programs in food service skills that can be drawn on.

  In order to reap the most benefit from these placement services, you should contact the person who is directly responsible for this job. In addition, prepare a well-organized and well-written presentation about the job or jobs that you are trying to fill. On it, include information about salary range, benefits and the reasons why working for your company would be beneficial.

- *The Open Market.* Through well-written newspaper advertisements and by "keeping an ear to the ground," you will be able to find many capable people for the job.

- *"Grow" Your Own Management.* A good organization, complete with advancement opportunity through training and exposure, will yield people who are ready to move "up the ladder." If you have developed such an organization in your present restaurant, you'll no doubt be able to select from a few likely candidates.

To sum up, the actual needs for your business will be determined by your organization plan and by the limits of your financial resources. The pro forma will give you a good indication of what you can afford. If you are honest with yourself during the process of projecting revenue and expense in the new business, you will have a guide that will warn you before over committing for an expense during pre-opening or in the early growth stages.

Your actual management needs will be largely determined by the following:

— The revenue volume in each of the restaurants

— The strength and quality of the production and service staffs

— The operating schedules in hours and days that will determine the amount of coverage needed

HOW TO SUCCEED AND EXPAND AS AN ABSENTEE OWNER

In order to establish controls for an absentee-owned business, you must be willing to delegate responsibility to those who will actually be running the restaurant on a day-to-day basis. Before the delegation is assigned, however, adequate control procedures in the form of overall supervision of operations, as well as fiscal accountability, must be established. As pointed out earlier in this Guide, internal control and accounting are two different functions—each one is necessary to the balance and control of the other. Consultants from firms such as our own, Gordon Associates, Inc., as well as many different public accounting firms, can assist you in these matters.

In order for a multi-unit operation to attain a high degree of success, it is necessary to develop and hold a competent and loyal management group. This can be accomplished in a number of ways, such as with monetary incentives in the form of bonuses, profit sharing plans, or by building a high standard of pride in the management group.

Every manager of a successful business, along with others on the staff, should have the opportunity to share in the proceeds derived from their efforts. Smart absentee owners know this. They also know that money paid out of profits works very much like seeding and fertilizing a garden—and just as a garden must be hoed and kept free of weeds, so too must a business be constantly tended and cared for.

To sum up, establishing control for absentee ownership is developed in three basic steps:

1. Establishing the management needs by development of concise organizational plans, including monetary needs.

2. Proving the ability of the business to provide the funds to support the plans.

3. Setting in place the operational and fiscal controls, including necessary incentives, to insure profitability of the business.

HOW TO GET STARTED ON AN ACTUAL EXPANSION PROGRAM

Before discussing the specific topic of site selection, it is necessary to define the difference between market research and site selection. For our purposes, the following definitions will suffice:

Market Research. The purpose of market research is to characterize a particular area or segment of the population with regard to such criteria as size, income, spending habits, etc. It is on this analysis that you base your decision as to the feasibility of making an investment, e.g., opening a restaurant.

Site Selection. Refers to the selection of a specific site or sites within a pretested market area. The site must conform to the parameters established as necessary to the success of the business.

When you research a market before deciding to invest in a restaurant, you will be able to obtain important information from the research findings from ongoing studies done by associations, agencies and governing bodies. These results are available in books, papers, and reports, and are found in office libraries and on newsstands. Additional information is also available from the professionals that did the original research.

If you retain a consultant to do the job for you, it may save you time and money in the long run. Consultants have the expertise to find the needed information quickly, and usually have extensive files containing necessary updated information. A consultant will be able to relate the economic potential of a market area in terms of population and spending habits to the intended project.

Selecting A Site

Once you identify a general market area, you can undertake the search for a site. The particular concept or theme you have in mind for your restaurant will dictate the needs for the site. The location of potential sites is a job for real estate people who should be given the necessary research data to make preliminary decisions. In turn, they will find and suggest to you a number of alternate locations, together with land or leasehold prices. Once this is done, you can evalute and select the best location. You can also decide whether leasing a facility or buying land and building is best for you.

Your decision regarding the potential value of a particular site requires verifying the economic value in terms of your need, as well as an acceptable location in the identified market area. In determining site value, many factors must be considered such as:

Sales Generators. These are activities carried out by people that bring about sales activity in a certain area. For example, a location surrounded by office buildings will surely generate a luncheon business. However, the same location may have nothing else in the area that will produce dinner or weekend business. Another similar location may have an office population as well as a nearby theatre district. This particular site may offer opportunities for both lunch and dinner business, as well as the much needed weekend activity.

Population. Simply because an area is heavily populated does not necessarily mean it is a good prospect. Much will depend on the restaurant concept plus the income level and spending habits of the area's residents. For example, an expensive restaurant may not survive in a low-income area any more than an inexpensive concept will make it in an affluent area. Age of the population is also a factor. To be successful, businesses must plan for the long run; thus ascertaining the ongoing trends is very important.

Traffic Volume. This poses a difficult dilemma since heavy automobile traffic can be a help or a hindrance. Much depends on the specific location and such factors as kind of street, i.e., two-lane, four-lane, boulevard, etc. You must know if the site is on the proper side of the street to make ingress and egress easily accessible. If, for example, you are on a four-lane street and dependent on an early cocktail hour business, your restaurant must be on the same side as the evening traffic flow. Traffic counts and patterns must be studied very carefully for direction at various times of the day and night, and for speed limits and total volume. Other considerations relate to curb cuts and growth trends within the city generally. Of course, the parking situation is of utmost importance.

Travel Distance. Depending on the type of restaurant, the prime market area is considered to be within a one to three mile radius. The secondary market may extend over a distance of five miles. Fast-food establishments generally cater to a market area of 1 to 2 miles, whereas a specialty dinner house attracts people from much greater distances. The fast-food restaurant will look at the potential in terms of volume at moderate and competitive price levels. The specialty house will offer much more in the way of service and menu, and necessarily charge much higher prices. The specialty house will require a wide market area, whereas the fast-food restaurant will operate in a rather narrow one.

Competition. You must survey the competition in any new area; you will see firsthand which kinds of restaurants are already there and, more importantly, which types are successful. You will also learn the price range being charged. This information will tell you whether or not your concept will be readily acceptable.

In order to present your request to a lending institution in the best possible light, it may be wise to consult a professional. In most—if not all—cases, lending institutions will require outside consulting reports with all loan requests. Obviously, this is because they don't want to make bad or questionable loans.

Many small businesses today, including restaurants, are facing greater difficulties in trying to qualify for loans. Hopefully, this situation will soften since the small business is a very important part of our economy. Nonetheless, you can help by being thoroughly prepared before requesting a loan. Thoroughly prepared means a complete package professionally prepared—whether you prepare it yourself or have a professional do it.

THE ADVANTAGES OF CONSULTING PROFESSIONALS

The importance of using competent consultants during the planning stage of a new business cannot be overemphasized. Such a person will either confirm or discount the opinion of an operator or potential investor regarding an intended new business.

Consultants are trained in research techniques and will search out and identify any positive or negative factors that may influence the business. In addition, a second opinion is particularly valuable because it is a neutral source outside the business.

The time when a person has become flushed with the success of one business and is casting about for a second can be a dangerous period. At a time such as this, people can become overwhelmed with their success and overlook the pitfalls in another venture. Good research, done by competent neutral consultants, may turn up information that is very valuable to the intended project. Investing in a new restaurant is a big step that can mean huge success or dismal failure. The money spent in planning and researching such a project is very little compared to the total investment—and could well be the wisest expenditure of all.

Finding Competent Assistance

There are many consultants and planners who list themselves as experts. Unfortunately, not all of them are competent. Consulting requires extensive experience in a particular field, a strong educational background, and the ability to communicate effectively both verbally and in writing. Further, the consultant must have an analytical mind and be able to translate findings into understandable, practical action plans for the client. Therefore, in order to avoid hiring the wrong person, you must do a thorough job of checking the references of the particular consultant (not just the firm he works for) you are considering.

Some consultants and consulting firms are listed in the Yellow Pages of your telephone book. You will find specialists in all phases of the business, including overall management assistance, personnel and facilities planning and design. There are also accounting firms that handle hotel and restaurant accounts, with two firms specializing in the hospitality industry:

— Laventhol and Horwath

— Pannell, Kerr and Forster

Both of these are large, international in scope, and have offices in most of the major cities. Another source of information is your local or state restaurant association. They generally maintain a file of people or firms who are reputable. You can also get help from the

Small Business Administration Office and possibly from your local Chamber of Commerce.

Once you choose a consultant, you must evaluate what you find. There are certain steps that should be taken in order to be sure that your project receives proper attention. First of all, you want to be sure that you have defined your plan. Before any consultant can work effectively with you, that person must have a full understanding of the task to be performed. Sometimes it is even wise to consult with someone in order to identify properly just what is to be done.

You should develop a program related to your needs and the needs of the project. It should take the form of an outline of just what you want to accomplish, and should include a time frame for completion. Nothing in this program will be "carved in stone," but it will provide a logical starting point for you.

Questions To Ask Before Hiring A Consultant

Once you develop your outline, you are ready to contact various consultants to assist you. Depending on your particular project, this can include architects, management, personnel, or kitchen planning experts. Once you have located the consultants, prepare a list of questions in order to establish credibility and expertise before proceeding beyond an initial interview. The following are examples of the kinds of questions you may want to ask prospective consultants. These questions should serve as a starting point for you:

- What is the particular speciality or specialities of your firm?

- Have you had practical experience in restaurant operation? Where? When? How long?

- Do you have a schedule of services offered? Do you have biographical sketches of yourself and your key people?

- If you are awarded a contract, who will do the work?

- Have you done this type of task before? Where? Who for?

- What is your fee arrangement? Do you write open-end (no limit) contracts, or will you guarantee a "not to exceed" price?

- Will you present a written proposal? Do you require a retainer?

- Can you provide a list of present or former clients who can be contacted for verification of your work?

- What is your educational background?

- What changes are occurring in this industry? How have you kept up with these changing events in the industry and in business generally?

You should then check the references that are submitted to you. In addition, it is very important for you to check with clients whose names *are not* submitted. You can identify them by perusing the consultant's client list. If such a list is not available, you might check with your restaurant association for information regarding other projects completed. Sometimes the association people are reluctant to endorse or criticize anyone, but you may be able to get names of persons with whom you can check further. Careful checking will insure that you do not spend money for services that may not satisfy your needs.

Getting Maximum Benefits From Consultants

Carefully read the proposals submitted on work to be done. In evaluating their content, be sure they cover your original outline, including any modifications you have made. In addition:

- Be certain that all of your work requirements are covered. A good proposal should have the total job broken down by phase, with estimates as to the time required for completion of each phase, as well as for the total job.

- The proposal should state clearly what is expected as a final result, i.e., a written report, hands-on assistance, complete drawings, including specifications, etc. Proposals for kitchen plans should be coordinated with your architect and construction group to assure that each person, including you, knows each other's specific responsibility.

- Starting and completion times should be indicated.

- Fee and expense structure should be spelled out clearly, along with an estimate of the total cost. Any necessary retainer amount should be specified.

- If the proposal has not been prepared so as to constitute a contract, then a separate document constituting a contract should be drawn with the proposal attached as an exhibit.

To summarize, the proposal should spell out each and every element of your deal; what work is to be done, how it is to be accomplished, how long it will take, who will do it and how much it will cost. If you expect a thorough proposal, then you must also accept the responsibility of communicating your desires to the consultant. That communication must be as complete as the proposal you hope to receive concerning the job that you want performed.

Competent Consultants Should Be Experienced Specialists

Those of us who have worked in the food service industry for any length of time are by nature "jacks of all trades." And that is as it should be, since the unusual nature of the restaurant business demands it. Every operator's day will be filled with a variety of tasks that include buying and receiving merchandise, actually preparing food or at least overseeing that preparation, checking yesterday's receipts, planning future menus, examining the last period's financial statements, fixing a malfunctioning dishwasher, interviewing prospective employees, etc.

Experienced consultants are familiar with these routine tasks, and are fully aware of the demands on the time of restaurant managers. Furthermore, they have taken the time and steps necessary to become specialists in certain specific areas of the business. There are two major areas in which consultants offer valuable services:

1. Management Services. This is a very broad category that includes several different but interrelated disciplines:

Financial Management And Control

☐ Design and implementation of internal control systems for proper management of expenses and income.

☐ Feasibility studies, including market research and site selection, to provide a basis for decision making regarding future investment in expansion or development for new business. Included would be the development of programs to be followed by designers and planners.

☐ Financial analysis of present business as related to realization of potential profits. Would probably include assistance in the area of financial projections and operating budgets.

☐ Business evaluation and appraisal of business value. This is a highly specialized area that requires far more than the application of a multiple to a few years of average earnings. This process also requires a detailed study of the industry, financial analysis of the particular restaurant, and a sound forecast of the potential earnings from accounting history and economic data.

☐ Complete analysis of all phases of restaurant operations, including menu evaluation or development, and the overall pricing structure for both food and beverage business. Food production and labor cost control to include purchasing, receiving, preparation, service and the analysis of those cost and expense items necessary to make it all work together for profit.

Personnel Administration

☐ Development of personnel policies and procedures, training manuals, and programs.

☐ Assistance in the development of organization and staffing plans.

☐ Development of policy and procedure manuals, standard recipe files, purchasing and receiving guides, sanitation manuals, and operating checklists.

2. Food Facilities Design Services. This relates to the design of the physical plant and includes several different but related activities:

☐ Development of preliminary plans to fit the food service program, as developed in keeping with proposed operating policies.

☐ Preparation of a budget estimate for food service equipment for use in line with the overall project cost estimate.

☐ Preparation of contract drawings, including selection of proper equipment. Interface with architects, engineers and owner in order to assure delivery of a totally acceptable project.

☐ Preparation of bid specifications for equipment and evaluation of bids as received.

☐ On-site supervision during and following installation in order to insure contractor compliance with all contracts as let.

☐ Table-top design, including china, glass and flatware. Consultation regarding type and necessary quantities of pots, pans and small utensils.

There is ample opportunity for a restaurant operator to secure assistance in any area where help is needed. Unfortunately, some people tend to view a consultant as someone who will look at a business and prepare a report that will never be used. While that may happen, it is usually not the fault of the consultant.

If you engage the services of a consultant, you should know precisely what you want done and exactly how you intend to follow up on the consultant's work. It is far less expensive to use a consultant for a given project than to carry one or more persons on the payroll for staff assignments. Further, if your business has no extra people for the staff work assignments, there is no way that these necessary tasks will ever be accomplished. When these conditions exist, you are very likely depriving yourself of much needed profits.

How To Make Advertising And Promotion Dollars Pay Off For You

Table of Contents

How To Make Advertising And Promotion Dollars Pay Off For You

It is virtually impossible to start a new restaurant operation in today's highly competitive world without advertising. And unless you are very lucky, you will also need some sort of sales promotion program in order to sustain a consistent flow of business. As with any other kind of business, the *successful* restaurant operator is the person who "makes things happen."

How Much Should You Budget For Pre-Opening Advertising?

If you are contemplating opening a new restaurant, you should include the cost of advertising in your pre-opening expense budget. One way to estimate your dollar needs is to rely on the average cost of advertising expense for all restaurants. This average is expressed as a ratio to sales and amount per seat, and can be found in Restaurant Industry Operations Report for the United States, published annually by the National Restaurant Association in cooperation with Laventhol and Horwath.

For example, in the 1981 study, it indicated that the average profitable restaurant serving *food* only spent $340 per seat, or 4.3% of net income on advertising and promotion during 1980. In the same year, the profitable restaurants serving both food and beverage spent an average of $97 per seat, or 2% of net income on advertising and promotion. (Average income and expense per category will vary in different parts of the country, and the study does not break down by city or state.)

To go back to the question of how much money is required for pre-opening advertising, we could start with the national averages as noted above. If the national average for food and beverage restaurants is 2%, and you are planning to open such a restaurant, you will probably need at least twice that much, or around 4% or 5% of the first year's estimated net income for advertising and promotion. The business will provide some of that expense from income, but there will be a *cash* need of at least one-half of that amount to cover pre-opening expense, as well as ongoing expense during those months when the business is new.

As an example, if you are opening a new place and forecasting $700,000 of net income in the first year, you should plan on spending $35,000 for advertising and promotion during that time. Your cash needs for those expenses before and shortly after you open will probably be about $20,000.

Too many people try to open restaurants on a "shoe string." If you want to give yourself every possible chance for success, then be sure you have sufficient capital to open and operate until your business becomes established.

HOW TO SELECT AN ADVERTISING AGENCY

There will be no problem finding an advertising agency. As a matter of fact, some—like all other purveyors of goods and services—will find you. As soon as the news regarding the impending opening of a new restaurant hits the street, the various suppliers start calling on the owners of the project. And some of them will be concerned with supplying promotional know-how, including advertising.

Advertising is usually quite expensive, but it is a necessary part of your success. Because of this, it is important for you to be very careful in your selection of an advertising agency.

Since you are advertising in order to attract customers to your restaurant, it becomes necessary to know your market population in terms of the best prospects for your business, and everything about them. For example:

- You will need to know their sex, age, educational level, where they live and work, what kind of work they do, what routes they use to drive to and from work, and how many of them use bus, train or van pools for transport.

- You will need to know, based on the foregoing, how best to reach these prospects, and which of the various media will do the best job. You have many choices of media to choose from, including television, radio, newspapers, direct mail, billboard advertising, as well as signs on taxis and buses.

The more information of this kind you have, the more intelligently you will be able to talk with and evaluate agencies and the services they sell. By now, it should be very clear to you that each of the chapters in this Guide fit together to make up one big picture. (If you have on hand some good market research data gathered during the planning stage, it will be just what you need at this time for planning your advertising campaigns.)

Some people will probably wonder why it is important to use an agency anyway. "We'll just write our own copy and contract directly with the media of our choice, and that will eliminate the middleman," they say "and we will save a whole lot of money in the process." Well, I say "maybe." Such a statement could be true if the person is skilled in advertising techniques. If not, the result could be just the opposite. Take, for example, the following:

- Consider a 30-second television spot on a local station that sells for some $2,000 to $4,000. If you buy a spot that is seen at the wrong time and on the wrong program, the major portion (or all) of the expenditure may be wasted.

- On the other hand, if you use an expert, he should be able to put the same ad in the proper place—creating enough business to pay for both the ad and his fee—and deliver solid profits for your restaurant.

When selecting an agency, find one that is active in the restaurant industry. It will be more aware of your special needs, and will be better able to tailor the program to reach your target market. Remember, it always pays to use a professional's help in something as critical as an advertising campaign.

How To Insure Success From Your Advertising Campaign

As mentioned, if you want to have a strong dollar return from your advertising outlay, you should first construct a budget. Furthermore, when contemplating the use of newspaper ads, remember that there will be an expense for the art work and layout plus the expense of setting the type.

Caution: Don't ever run a newspaper or magazine ad without first receiving a proof from the media. And read the proof very carefully to be sure that it says what you want it to say, and that it is free of spelling and punctuation errors. Also, if you can plan your advertising campaigns in advance for a given period of time, you will be less apt to find yourself in a hurry to meet a deadline and overall will reap far better results.

Here's a sample of what your budget should look like:

Newspaper Advertising Budget

Newspaper	Frequency of Ad
Circulation—250,000	2 times/week
Length of Promotion — 6 weeks	
Cost of Ad — $150	
Total cost of advertising:	
6 × 2 (twice/week) × $150 = = $1,800	
Coverage—6 × 2 × 250,000 (cir.) = 3,000,000 (persons)	

If you are using an agency, you will find that it will base its charge on an hourly rate, or as a percentage of the total ad cost. Measuring results against promises means knowing precisely what you contracted for, and the maintaining of a record of what you actually received. It is very easy to "lose" money on service contracts such as these. Therefore, good record keeping is a must.

Advertising Media—And How To Profit From Them

There are many other ways, besides newspapers and T.V., that you can use to advertise your restaurant:

- *Billboards and Posters*. Billboard ads can be a very effective means of advertising. You should make certain, however, that they are located on streets and highways traveled by people who are in your market area. Posters can be placed on buses, subways, taxis, etc. Both should be colorful and eye-catching. Also, they must be brief so as to be read quickly.

  In many areas, this kind of advertising can be quite expensive. In addition, in order to carry impact, these must be changed from time to time, and the cost of the artwork, paper, labor, etc. can become quite high.

- *Direct Mail*. This is a good form of advertising that can be planned to reach your specific market area. You can buy mailing lists from various sources such as list brokers, but the best lists should come from your own files. You should use it for the purpose of informing your steady customers of the various promotions you are planning to run.

- *Sample Menus.* It is a good idea to have an inexpensive mini-version of your regular menu available to give to your guests. Often diners will ask for a menu to take home, and the miniature is an excellent—and cheaper than handing out your regular menu—way to advertise. You don't have to wait for people to ask for one either. Offer one to each departing guest.

  You can also make personal calls on various office buildings, hospitals, plants and so on, to introduce yourself, invite people to visit your restaurant and leave a menu. With this method, you don't cover as much ground as a newspaper ad would, but you will be amazed at the response you'll get from the personal effort.

- *Radio.* Spot ads on radio will reach many people. Remember, though, that people listen to a particular station because it offers the kind of programming that suits their taste. For example, it might be all news, or country/western music, or talk shows, or a Dixieland band.

  Therefore, if you are placing an ad on the radio, be sure you are on a station that will reach your target market. Deciding on the "right" station as well as the "right" time will take considerable research or the advice of a pro—or it might even take both. The radio is a companion for many people at specific hours of the day—i.e., morning while getting ready for work, at the breakfast table, and in the car while spending a lot of time in rush hour traffic—so keep that in mind when using the radio as an advertising media.

HOW BEST TO PROMOTE YOUR RESTAURANT

When and how often should you promote your restaurant? The answer is "always!" There are two kinds of promotion. *First*, there is the unplanned or ongoing promotion that is constant. For example, you are promoting your restaurant when you serve good food in pleasant surroundings in a friendly and congenial manner. Your own personal affability and charisma will attract customers to your place.

In addition, all of the techniques and ideas espoused in this Guide are ways to promote your business! How? Through good and intelligent management. The kind that encourages and motivates every employee to work at producing top-quality food, drink and service, that in turn makes a *promoter* out of every happy diner who enters and leaves your restaurant. For a restaurant, there is nothing like a good reputation and "word of mouth" advertising.

Second, is planned or occasional promotion. Running promotions can be one of the real "fun" things the imaginative and creative operator can do. Also, there is a thrill to be realized from watching a successful promotion develop increased sales and profits for your restaurant. It is like what a salesman feels when he "closes a sale." It is the time when you can see the actual result of your creativity, imagination and hard work pay off. Of course, there is not much you can do about economic trends, massive changes in product cost, crippling legislation, or labor strife that affect your business. But you can make something happen in your own little corner with some well-thought-out promotion plans.

Reasons For Running Promotions

Running promotions is a must in today's heavily competitive marketplace. Here are a few reasons why they are so important:

1. They will let people know about your restaurant—and what it has to offer. One of the best ways to get business is to ask for it.

2. You can increase the sale of certain items by advertising "come ons." For instance, you may offer free hors d'oeuvres to increase your early evening cocktail business.

3. Your business may be local and you may want to reach out for some transient business in a market that you have failed to penetrate.

4. You may need to promote in order to compete favorably in your own market area.

5. They may help you pick up extra sales on slow days of the week.

SALES PROMOTION TECHNIQUES

Coupon Redemption

Coupon redemption is probably the biggest—and most widely used—promotional device in the country. There are billions distributed every year as promotions for all sorts of products. In the restaurant business, the usual forms of coupon promotions are either to offer something such as "a free chicken dinner when one is bought at the full price," or to offer something free such as "the first drink on the house."

Here's how they can pay off for you: You run an ad in the local paper with a coupon that entitles the bearer to one free Chicken dinner when one other dinner is purchased at the regular price of $9.95. Suppose the food cost to you on this dinner is 25%, or $2.49. Therefore, if you sell one and give one free, your total cost on the two dinners is still only 50%. And if you sell anything else such as a drink before dinner or a carafe of house wine (which is almost certain), your total cost will be reduced further. In the meantime, if the promotion is well received, you will be creating traffic and introducing new diners to your restaurant.

Complimentary first drinks in the cocktail lounge for all dinner guests is another traffic-builder designed to bring people to the restaurant.

Sampling

This technique consists of offering bite-size selections of items from the menu. For example, you might offer your patrons new items that you are introducing on the menu.

Complimentary Food And/Or Beverage

There are always times when it pays to "pick up the check," or to offer something complimentary like a bottle of wine with dinner when certain "important" people visit your place of business. "Important" could mean anything from persons in high places to a couple of your very good customers celebrating a wedding anniversary. Keeping an eye out for these kinds of situations and then doing something appropriate is always good for business. Therefore, it is beneficial to find out when your regular customers are celebrating birthdays, anniversaries, etc., and to keep this information in your promotion files for future use. "Fine," you may say, "but how do I go about getting this data?"

The best way to determine birthday and/or anniversary dates celebrated by your customers is to pay attention to those kinds of parties when held in your restaurant. At that time, you can get the necessary information from the guests and make the necessary notes in your suspense file. Then you will be ready for the next time that date rolls around. Furthermore, a card from you with a suggestion that they celebrate the occasion in your restaurant will be a big plus for you. If you think that "more is better," then you can offer a free bottle of wine or a cake when they dine with you. And, if possible, be sure you are in the restaurant and make the presentation personally, as it will have more impact and help your overall sales program.

Knowing your customers personally will often lead to learning about birthdays, anniversaries or other special occasions. When you are highly visible in your restaurant, and when you make the effort to meet and visit with your guests, you are bound to pick up plenty of information about their personal lives. Don't overdo it by spending too much time with any one guest, however. It is better if your contacts are friendly but brief. Just make sure you keep notes so that the information you get isn't lost or misplaced.

One more idea. Give out a free drink or other complimentary item for persons born under the current astrological sign. Stage this promotion each time the sign changes and enter the names, addresses and birth dates in your file for future use.

I know one restaurateur who keeps a card file in a rather inconspicuous place in the dining room. Each card tells him something about his customers. For example, if they have been traveling—where and when; information about birthdays, anniversaries, etc.; their hobbies or other particular interests; where they work and live; if they have children—whether they are at home, away at college, on a new job etc. He picks up the information through casual conversation from his guests when they visit his restaurant. And he never fails to make a note of any helpful information he can get. This is a great technique for opening a short conversation. It will greatly impress your guests with your apparent interest in them.

Gifts For The Ladies

There is one restaurant that I know of that when a couple leaves the restaurant, the host or hostess selects a rose from a bouquet on the Maitre d's station and presents it to the lady. While roses are not inexpensive, it is still a nice touch. And I will bet the cost is budgeted right along with the other expenses of the restaurant.

Happy Hours

Many cocktail lounges employ this promotion which generally consists of either discounting the price of drinks, or offering two drinks for the price of one. The hours for the promotion are specified, and are usually something like 4 p.m. to 7 p.m., Monday through Friday. To my knowledge, the most successful of the plans is the discounted price which seems to have considerably more customer appeal. The "two for one" promotion does not make a hit with those people who may not want the extra drink, but feel like they must take it since it has already been paid for.

* * * * *

The number and kinds of promotions you can try in your restaurant are endless. They are only limited by your own imagination and your flair for selling. So put on your thinking cap and try something new. Your customers will probably love you for trying to please them, and you will get great satisfaction along with extra dollars in profits from the increased sales that the promotions will create.

HOW TO MEASURE THE POTENTIAL OF YOUR PROMOTION PLANS

You should never enter into promotions without having a well-conceived plan. Your plan should contain all the elements, including: length of promotion (days, weeks, etc.), place (dining room, cocktail lounge, etc.), kind of advertising and cost, internal control, and the level of sales *before* the plan goes into effect.

Whatever the promotion is, you should keep very good records of the "freebies." For example, if you want to run the Chicken Dinner special, you will want to know what your average sales are without the promotion, and how many more you were able to sell during the promotional period. The cost of the promotion will include the food cost on the free dinner, as well as any advertising or promotional costs incurred.

CAUTION: You must always think these plans through very carefully. And here are a few rules to keep in mind while you do:

- Keep accurate records. You *must* know the financial results of any of these ad campaigns.

- Don't just think cost. While cost is certainly of prime importance, you must also consider volume and how increased sales affect your fixed expenses.

- Consider also what the long-term effect will be of introducing new diners to your restaurant.

- Be certain that your quality of food does not slip. Discount the *price*—not the *food*!

Again, the very best kind of advertising for a restaurant can be outlined in a simple form:

- Provide your guests with quality food and beverage.

- Serve the food and beverage in a smooth, efficient yet unhurried manner.

- Provide a pleasant, relaxing atmosphere for maximum enjoyment of your offerings.

- Spend as much time as possible personally watching out for your customers. Let them see that you care about them and appreciate the business they are bringing to you.

Do these things and you will greatly please and send forth a multitude of happy missionaries who won't be able to wait to tell all their friends and acquaintances about your fine restaurant. Run a restaurant in this fashion, and you will prosper!

ADDITIONAL PROMOTIONAL IDEAS THAT PAY OFF BIG

National Secretary Week

What To Do:

Think of a gift you can offer to the secretary being entertained. For example, it might be a flower or even a corsage.

The gift would be presented during the meal. Bosses should be encouraged to order the gift when making the reservation.

The promotion would be announced through the regular advertising source, i.e., newspaper, radio, etc.

A little fun could be added if all your service staff wore something like "We Love Secretaries" T-shirts that could be purchased in advance for the occasion.

Salute To The Good Customer

(For your regular customers.)

What To Do:

Inaugurate a coupon or dinner receipt program whereby customers can receive something "free" after a specified number of visits to your restaurant. For example, a free meal could be offered after a customer has been to the restaurant six times. Or, a complimentary bottle of wine could be offered to the diner who after three visits brings an additional guest or guests to the restaurant.

This kind of promotion can be announced internally in your restaurant by including it on table tents or in a promotional handout. Before starting such a program, be sure and give some serious thought to how you will control it.

Salute To Some Charity

(Those persons who make a certain stipulated contribution to the named charity.)

What To Do:

In cooperation with officials of the charity, devise a method whereby donors (certified by the charity) receive something complimentary at your restaurant. For instance, a complimentary carafe of wine could be offered with dinner for two when evidence of a stipulated donation amount is presented by the customer. If there are no legal barriers, you might even have your wine purveyor share in the cost (and the publicity)!

Support Your Local Sports Team

(Any local team, amateur or professional—football, baseball, basketball, hockey, soccer, etc.)

What To Do:

Offer a discount for selected dinner menu items to diners who present the ticket stub from one of the games you are promoting. These stubs could be valid only for the week (in the case of football) following the game, or for the entire season if you wish.

The promotion could be announced via newspaper, radio, posters, etc. Additional gain can be realized if you are active in such civic groups as the Chamber of Commerce, local Team Booster Club, etc., and do some personal promoting with those groups. In addition, you could ask for a place on one or more of the meeting agendas, and make the announcement at those times.

Saluting The Zodiac Sign Of The Month

(Those persons born under the sign that corresponds with the current month.)

What To Do:

Offer a free cocktail or after-dinner drink to those persons born under the current sign. Any form of identification such as driver's license can be shown. The main idea here is to create traffic and bring new customers to the restaurant.

Announcement can be made through newspaper or radio advertising, etc.

Be sure you record the names, addresses and birth dates in your birthday file. This is a good way to build up a list for later promotions. You can encourage new business by mailing out birthday cards to your customers.

12 Sure-Fire Ways To Increase Profits

Table of Contents

12 Sure-Fire Ways To Increase Profits

There are thousands of successful restaurants owned and operated by real pros. You, too, can have a restaurant that is as successful and profitable if you will use the practical working tools that are outlined throughout this Guide.

Here are some additional thoughts that may stimulate further ideas you can use to make those enormous profits you have been dreaming about.

HOW TO STAY AHEAD OF THE COMPETITION

- Every restaurant operator has his own ideas about how to sell food and drink. Therefore, it is a good idea to visit other operations, looking for unique ideas that you might adapt in your own restaurant. (In many cases, checking up on your competition is tax deductible. See Chapter 13 for more tax-saving ideas.)

- Be aware of happenings in your town. Visit with your banker, your insurance agent, and real estate people. These people are invaluable sources for information about neighborhood transition and longer-range changes that may affect your restaurant.

- Donate some of your time to some sort of community service. High visibility in the community will not only help to bring people to your restaurant, but you may also get free newspaper coverage for your business. In other words, show the community that you support it, and chances are the residents will help support you. (One owner I know sponsors a little league baseball team. He says that every family on the team has become a steady patron of his restaurant.)

- Another way to lend support to the community is to employ handicapped persons in suitable positions. Not only is it evidence of community support, but you may also find some loyal, dedicated long-term employees. (Bookkeeping and cashiering are just two positions where you may readily employ a handicapped person.)

- Establish contact with your Chamber of Commerce and with the Convention and Visitors Bureau. Both these groups act as evaluation committees that consider facilities for upcoming meetings and conventions. In addition to suggesting appropriate hotel and meeting facilities, these committees consider auxiliary amenities such as surface transportation, entertainment centers, shopping, and restaurants. Be sure to remain visible with these selection committees, so that you put yourself out in front of your competition for future business when the visiting associations choose your town for their convention.

- It may be profitable for you to become acquainted with:

  — hotel front office personnel,
  — taxi drivers,
  — tourist bureau people, since they constantly deal with transient people.

How To Make Certain That Your Guests Will Return

After you bring all this new business into your restaurant, you will, of course, want to be sure that your food and service are the very best that you can provide. Here are some suggestions for you to consider that will contribute to your success:

- Make certain your waiters remove soiled china and silver between courses. While there's some additional expense in doing this, treating your customers to a "touch of class" can be well worth it.

- Train, train, train your people. Work to make your employees function like a truly professional team. Graciousness and efficiency will encourage repeat business which is, of course, the foundation of your restaurant.

- Keep your restaurant lively and interesting for your guests, i.e., live flowers on each table, place mats for the children. Friendly, caring employees will also help to make it so.

- Background music can be complementary to gracious dining. However, be sure it is appropriate to your particular type of clientele. Remember, there is a difference between loud music and noisy music. The former is right in some places and actually helps sales. Noisy music can be irritating and may even drive business away.

    Recently I took a friend to dinner at a new restaurant that was catering to a properly attired middle-class, middle-aged dinner crowd. The help were young and bright looking. However, the music being piped in was obviously chosen to please the employees, not the guests. It was so annoying to me that I left. Other nearby guests also commented on the unsuitable music.

- Sales incentive plans for servers will help to keep things moving.

- Visiting and conversing with guests indicate your interest in them. However, it can be overdone and become a negative factor in your business. For instance, servers and managers can become boring when they don't know when to quit talking. This can also mean that if you or your service people are spending too much time at any one table, other guests are probably being ignored.

    Managers and servers must know how to "hit and run." In other words, the real restaurant pros know how to carry on a conversation with each and every customer who feels like talking. They do it without actually letting it interfere with the job of providing equal service to every guest.

- Sanitation and neatness are an important part of good service. Even though your restaurant is basically clean, it can still look messy. So, keep tabs on this. In addition, clean, crisp uniforms on smiling well-groomed servers will surely bring guests back to your restaurant.

- Work for consistency in your menu offerings. Guests often return to a restaurant because they like one particular item. Be sure your offerings remain consistently good day after day.

How To Provide An Atmosphere That Says "Welcome—We Want Your Business"

- Fit the price to the service or vice versa. While French service and table-side cooking is lovely to observe and experience, you can't have it with cheese sandwich prices. You must know your market thoroughly and work it carefully.

For example, if you were to offer three specials for $6.95, one each of chicken, veal or shrimp scampi, most people who dine out regularly will know that at $6.95, the only intelligent choice is the chicken. The shrimp would probably be too small, and the veal a less-than-quality cut or grade.

- Don't be so rigid that you can't make exceptions to the menu or provide special items on request. Although requests of this kind are sometimes disruptive, you should do everything you can to please your guests. And don't be afraid to charge for extra or special service if the charge is warranted.

- Remember, there are a lot of people who can't function in the morning before they have three or four cups of coffee. These people are also in a hurry to get each one of those cups. If you serve breakfast, put the coffee on the table in insulated serving containers. It's a nice touch and will allow your servers to handle more orders, instead of running around the dining room filling coffee cups.

It is now possible to provide brewed decaffeinated coffee. The difference in taste is remarkable compared to instant packets—and your patrons will appreciate it. Many people are requesting decaf especially at luncheon and dinner meals. And if necessary, charge extra for it. Your guests know from shopping that it is more expensive than regular coffee.

- Other products that should be offered include one or more diet soft drink selections, along with at least one brand of light beer. If you want to find out about additional eating trends, spend some time in the grocery or convenience stores and see what is new.

IN-HOUSE SELLING: THE WAY TO FAME AND FORTUNE

- If your service staff presents the menu—or even just the special or specials of the day—orally, be certain they know what they are talking about. Servers should know as much as possible regarding the items, including ingredients used, method of cooking and style of service. Even if your offerings are described only on a written menu, the servers should be thoroughly familiar with preparation so they can answer questions intelligently.

- When seating a party, diplomatically inquire who will be paying the check. It will often save embarrassment later on.

- Some restaurants publish a daily complimentary synopsis of local and national news, with sporting event scores of the season and stock market quotations. It is usually placed on a table or counter in the morning and at noon. This is especially effective if you have a large white-collar business clientele.

- The use of clip-ons or tip-ups on the menu for advertising specials can be an aid to sales. There is no denying the fact that they are used successfully in many restaurants. For example, I recently dined in a famous Detroit restaurant that uses so many clip-ons that one must hunt for the menu. Evidently they work, since this restaurant has been in business for over 35 years.

- Another sales tool is the special dessert and after-dinner drink menu that is presented following the completion of the entire course.

- Depending on your type of establishment, and if you use place mats, have something of interest to your guests imprinted on the face. It's a good way to advertise your restaurant, town, state, resort, etc. Games and puzzles aren't a bad idea either. They will frequently occupy children, as well as adults.

- Funny sayings and unusual descriptions on the menu go very well in some kinds of restaurants. As a rule, they should fit in with the overall theme and decor of the restaurant.

How To Hold On To Those Hard-Earned Dollars

- Do forecast your sales, and budget your cost and expense. Also, be realistic to set attainable goals on cost and expense, and work to make them. However, it's important to put a little "reach" in your sales goals.

- Watch the details of the business with diligence. For example:

  — Weigh the meat
  — Don't buy ice at the price of fish or shrimp
  — Inspect the produce, and check all invoices for everything you buy

- Employee theft can be another factor in your profit picture. Mr. Richard Ward, Vice President, SAGA Corporation, has studied the in-house pilferage and theft in business. According to him, all businesses lose some 2.5% to 3.0% of total sales through theft. Therefore, showing up in unexpected parts of your restaurant—and at different times—may save thousands of dollars for you.

- If a specialized task confronts you, consult an expert. In the long run, you will probably realize a savings—plus you will save yourself a great deal of worry and frustration.

- Don't start a restaurant if it is to be under-capitalized. The days of starting a business on a shoestring are long gone. Present interest rates, plus commodity prices and customer resistance all make for a difficult situation even in established restaurants. For new restaurants, they add up to a situation that is almost guaranteed to insure failure.

How To Build A Responsible Staff

Smooth and efficient running of your restaurant stems from your staff. Building such a staff depends on:

- A good training program.

- Your selection of dedicated and responsible employees. A good source of labor is the retired person. Some of these people are perfect for particular positions. Even though they may be limited as to earnings, you can still use them on a part-time basis.

- Showing your appreciation by rewarding your employees for good service. This will insure that the good ones will stay. Don't forget to compliment your people on a job well done, everyday.

ECONOMIC AND SOCIAL CHANGES THAT CAN MEAN OPPORTUNITIES FOR YOU

The following facts are a part of today's society. In order to be successful, you must take advantage of them:

- Fast-food restaurants now account for over 35% of the total restaurant business in the U.S. In fact, *The Detroit Free Press* recently stated in an article that the first McDonald's restaurant, opened in Des Plaines, Illinois in 1955, may be purchased and moved to the Henry Ford Museum in Detroit. "You cannot address popular eating habits today without a nod to McDonald's," says Peter Logan, manager of Media Relations for the museum. Today's lifestyle requires people to look for quick meals and food that they can carry off the premises.

- The senior citizen population is increasing, and these retired people like to travel. That means more tours and group business. It also opens up an opportunity for box-lunch-type meals for people on the go.

- Catering in homes and for such events as picnics has always provided good opportunities for additional business. The need for this service will increase as people continue to enjoy more leisure time, and as more and more women work.

- For those operators who have established a good reputation in the business, there are many opportunities to manage restaurants under contract or by leasehold. While the opportunity is vast, there are a couple of words of caution in order here:

    — Be sure you negotiate a deal you can live with and that won't hurt your reputation or your pocketbook.

    — Good management is essential to every business. Don't stretch yourself or your management staff too thin. It is very easy to get greedy and suffer losses in the process.

13

How To Get Top Benefit From Tax Savings And Shelters, And Build Financial Security

Table of Contents

13 How To Get Top Benefit From Tax Savings And Shelters, And Build Financial Security

There are numerous smart, legal ways that you can use to protect your profits and build personal wealth. Unfortunately, many restaurants don't take advantage of them and get into serious financial difficulties as a result. Of course, not all of these strategies are well known. In order to help you, we have included a small sampling of the benefits restaurant owners can legally help themselves to.

IMPORTANT: Some of the ideas given in this chapter involve legal and tax areas that are best discussed and implemented with the help of a professional adviser.

By special arrangement with the publisher, the following material has been excerpted from Executive Reports Corporation "Restaurant Owner's Tax Letter." If you write to Executive Reports Corporation, Attention: Audrey Walker, Dept. RMG, 210 Sylvan Avenue, Englewood Cliffs, New Jersey 07632 and mention my name, you may receive a full year's subscription to the Restaurant Owner's Tax Letter at a $24.00 savings from the regular annual price of $155.40. "ROTL" is published 26 times a year and provides continuing important and timely advice—the kind you'll want to act on immediately to increase profits, cut taxes and generally rest easier about your financial and legal affairs.

HOW YOUR RESTAURANT MAY BE ABLE TO PAY YOUR LIVING EXPENSES—TAX-FREE

You may be able to set things up so your restaurant business pays your everyday household expenses—rent, mortgage payments, utilities, repair costs and so forth. Basically all that's required is that:

1. Your restaurant operation be incorporated;

2. The household be located on the premises;

3. You need to be close by at *all* times for the smooth running of the restaurant; and

4. The corporation makes it a formal requirement of your employment that you live on the premises.

The big tax payoff is that if these conditions are met, what your restaurant corporation pays for your living expenses is fully deductible by your corporation and tax free to you. This could be the equivalent of a tax-free salary increase of many thousands of dollars.

If any of this sounds familiar, it's because this tax break for living expenses is the same break that allows your corporation to provide you and your employees with tax-free meals. Of course, you can be sure the Revenue Service will take a tougher position on tax-free household expenses than it does with meals—many more revenue dollars are at stake. Nevertheless, taxpayers can and do prevail. For example:

> John and Mike Harrison and their wives incorporated their business. Both families lived on the premises so that they could be reached quickly when problems arose. A typical workday for the Harrisons began at 5:30 in the morning and ended at 6:30 or later at night. The Harrisons and some of their employees ate their meals on the business premises, and the corporation picked up the tab. In addition, the corporation paid the gas and electric bills for the Harrisons' residence.

The Tax Court ruled that the corporation's payments for the meals and utilities were deductible by the corporation and tax free to the Harrisons. *Reason:* The nature of the business required that the Harrisons eat and live on the premises [Harrison, TC Memo 1981-211].

What was the Harrisons' business? Dairy farming. And what does a dairy farm have to do with a restaurant? A lot, we think. They are both demanding operations: Like a farmer, you may have to get up early to accept and check deliveries, and closely supervise every aspect of the operation (usually until late at night). In addition, it certainly helps if you are available around the clock for security reasons and for any emergency that may arise.

Will the Government permit you to take advantage of this tax-free break for living expenses? Only the Government itself knows the answer. Much depends on the facts and circumstances of your own individual situation—and you and your professional adviser are the ones best suited to make that judgment.

HOW TO SET THINGS UP SO THE RESTAURANT PAYS PERSONAL MEDICAL BILLS

Owners of incorporated restaurants are in an especially strong tax position. *Reason:* Besides being restaurant owners, they are also *employees* of their restaurant corporations. And corporations can give fringe benefits to employees. This means that the corporation can pick up the tab for many of the owner's everyday family expenses—either tax free or tax deferred. (Self-employed restaurant owners may get similar breaks; see the next section.) Here's a prime example of tax-free medical payments:

> Smith's restaurant corporation sets up a health plan. The corporation contributes to the plan by paying health insurance premiums on a policy covering Smith and other employees. The premiums are fully deductible by the corporation as a business expense and tax free to Smith. Benefits paid by the policy are also tax free to him. In effect, the plan turns money Smith might ordinarily receive as fully taxable salary into tax-free medical payments.

EXAMPLE: If you have $2,500 of unreimbursed medical expenses in 1982 and an adjusted gross income of $50,000, you would not be entitled to a medical deduction. *Reason:* You can only deduct your out-of-pocket medical expenses, including health insurance premiums, that exceed 5% of your adjusted gross income. And here there is no excess (5% of $50,000 equals $2,500). So you would be out of pocket the entire $2,500 paid for medical expenses.

But there is a way around this problem.

> *Idea In Action:* You have your corporation set up a health insurance plan that reimburses you for all your medical expenses. You are not out of pocket one thin dime for your medical expenses. And your corporation?

It pays $2,000 a year in premiums. Your corporation deducts the $2,000 as a business expense. Assuming it is in the 30% corporate tax bracket, your corporation saves $600 in taxes.

Payoff: You get, in effect, $2,500 tax free at an after-tax cost to the corporation of only $1,400 ($2,000 less $600). To get the same $2,500 after taxes, the corporation may have to give you a salary increase of as much as $5,000 (if you're in the top 50% tax bracket) at an after-tax cost to the corporation of $3,500.

The icing on the cake is that your corporation can be selective about who is covered by the plan. It can set up a plan that covers only its most important employee—you. In other words, when it comes to a health plan funded by commercial insurance, your corporation can discriminate in favor of its key people.

How to Cash In On A Tax-Free Health Plan Even Without Incorporation

You may be able to get the benefits of a "corporate" health plan without incorporating. What's required: Your spouse must be an employee of your restaurant.

Generally speaking, self-employed restaurant owners can't take advantage of medical reimbursement plans. The tax law limits tax-free coverage to employees—and self-employeds are not considered employees. On the other hand, a self-employed restaurant owner is free to set up a health plan for his or her employees. Here's what to do:

(1) Make your spouse a formal employee. In other words, pay your spouse a salary for work done at the restaurant. Then, (2) transfer your family health insurance policy to your spouse. And finally, (3) set up an employee health plan for one or more of your employees—*including your spouse*—and reimburse them for their insurance premium payments.

Payoff: The premiums are (1) fully deductible by you as a business expense, and (2) tax-free to your spouse and any other covered employees. Benefits paid are also tax-free. Furthermore, since your spouse's medical policy also covers you and your children, you have managed to set up a health plan for yourself, the self-employed restaurant owner.

How A Restaurant Can Pay The Owner's Life Insurance Premiums

Every restaurant owner would like to get top insurance protection at an affordable cost. A traditional winner here has been split-dollar insurance.

The typical split-dollar setup works as follows: Your restaurant takes out cash value life insurance on your life. Each year it pays the portion of the premium equal to the increase in the policy's cash value for that year. You pay the remainder of each year's premium costs—if any. And you get to name the beneficiaries and reap the following benefits:

1. After a few years, your annual premium costs are little or nothing. For example, your average yearly cost of insurance protection can be much less than comparable term coverage.

2. The policy really doesn't cost your restaurant anything. *Reason:* The policy's cash value belongs to the restaurant. So it eventually gets back every penny it lays out from the policy's proceeds. Meanwhile, you are, in effect, receiving an *interest-free* loan from your restaurant.

Tax result: Your restaurant gets no deduction for the premiums it pays. But you must pay tax on the value of the insurance protection you receive, less your share (if any) of the premium. But, even after taking taxes into account, your cost for this kind of insurance protection is extremely low when compared to other life insurance setups.

But some owners take their basic split-dollar setup one step further. They turn the low premiums into no premiums by using a variation called the bonus split-dollar plan.

In this setup, your company pays the *entire* premium. You don't pay anything at all. The portion of the premium that you would ordinarily pay is charged to you as compensation. Because it's compensation, the restaurant gets a deduction for it. (Although you have to pay tax on this, as explained below, it should be much less than the premium you'd otherwise pay.) And your restaurant still gets the cash value. This raises the following question and answer.

Question. But that's the problem. Because the restaurant is paid the cash value, won't my family be receiving a lot less insurance protection?

Answer. True, your actual insurance coverage is always less than the face value of the policy. As the cash value of the policy goes up, so does your restaurant's portion of the proceeds. *Result:* Your insurance protection goes down gradually as the years pass. This may be acceptable if your need for such protection will also diminish. But if not, here's what to do. Have the policy pay the dividends. Use these dividends to buy additional insurance up to the amount of the policy's cash value. Any excess dividends can be used to lower the premium payments by the restaurant. (Whether used to pay premiums or buy additional insurance, the dividends are taxable to you.)

Result: Your restaurant still recovers its loan—but now an amount equal to 100% of the face value of the policy is available to your family. And by using bonus split-dollar, you not only get additional coverage, but you also get it at a lower cost. Your restaurant is paying your part of the premium as well as its own. Of course, the additional payment by your restaurant is taxed to you, just as if you had received a bonus. But if you had made your portion of the premium payment yourself, you'd probably be out-of-pocket more than twice as much. Let's look at the next example:

> Your portion of the premium is $500 and you're in the 40% tax bracket. If you pay the premium yourself, you are out-of-pocket $500. But let's say your restaurant pays the $500 premium and charges it to you as compensation. You're out-of-pocket $200, the tax on $500. *Result:* You've saved more than half the cost of having your restaurant pay your portion of the premium.

Another benefit: Unlike some other compensation plans, it is not necessary to get Government approval of your split-dollar setup. Here's what to do: If you are interested in split-dollar insurance, see your insurance and tax advisers. Split-dollar does not require a special type of policy; ordinary life insurance is almost always used. But there are all sorts of variations to the way you and your restaurant share the insurance costs. Your advisers can help you decide which method would be best in your situation.

HOW YOU CAN CUT YOUR FAMILY TAX BILL BY GIVING YOUR CHILD A SHARE OF THE BUSINESS

Let's say your son or daughter works for your incorporated restaurant. So you can no longer take a dependency deduction for your child on your tax return. But he or she can still be very useful to you taxwise by helping you nail down some substantial family and company tax savings.

Typical situation: You own a corporation that operates two restaurants. Your son is in charge of one of these and has been doing a fine job. You decide it's time to give him a share of the action—you're going to give him some stock in your corporation. Besides being the right thing to do from a family standpoint, the gift of stock also has some—

Tax advantages: When your corporation distributes dividends, the dividends on your son's stock are taxed to him—not to you. Since your son is in a lower tax bracket than you, splitting dividend income with him results in a lower overall tax bite. Let's look at the following situation.

> Set up a new corporation to take over the restaurant your son is managing. Then give him at least a 50% interest in the new corporation. Result: Giving this stock to your son also cuts the corporate income tax. *Reason:* With two corporations, you get a double benefit from the lower tax rates on the first $100,000 of corporate income.

How much are the tax savings? It depends. Let's say your present restaurant corporation has a taxable income that runs around $250,000. This gives your corporation an annual tax bill of $94,750. You decide to spin off your new corporation. It has a taxable income of $100,000, leaving your old corporation with $150,000. *Result:* The combined corporate tax is $74,500 ($48,750 for the old corporation, $25,750 for the new one). So, by getting the double benefit from the lower corporate rates, you save more than $20,000 a year, year in and year out.

Furthermore, there are also these extra advantages: (1) Like your old restaurant corporation, your new one is entitled to a 10% investment credit on up to $125,000 ($150,000 beginning in 1988) of used equipment purchases each year. (2) Each corporation can annually expense (currently deduct) up to $5,000 in machinery and equipment through 1987 (up to $7,500 in 1988 and 1989, and up to $10,000 for 1990 and thereafter).

Let's say the new corporation idea sounds okay to you. You may still wonder why it's necessary to bring your son into the picture—why you couldn't get the tax benefits of a new corporation on your own. The reason is that the setup simply wouldn't work if you tried it solo.

Here's why: The Government has an ace up its sleeve. While it cannot ignore the whole setup, the tax law does permit the Government to deny you the benefits of the lower tax rates if just one of the reasons behind the spin-off is tax savings. It's pretty hard for you to prove that you didn't have tax-savings in mind—unless you can show that some outside factor forced you into the deal (such as having to incorporate in another state to get a local franchise). So, when the Revenue Service plays this ace (Sec. 1551 of the tax law), it's usually a winner. However, there's a way out. If your son owns 50% or more of the stock of the new corporation, you can trump the Government's ace. *Result:* The corporation will get the full benefit of the lower tax rates.

If this sounds like what you've been looking for, go ahead. But note:

1. Your child must be over 21;

2. he cannot own stock in your present company;

3. your professional adviser should help you every step of the way.

HOW A SPECIAL TAX LAW PROVISION CAN EASE THE BURDEN OF ESTATE TAXES ON A FAMILY-RUN RESTAURANT

Many restaurant owners worry that estate taxes will force their families to sell the restaurant. True, estate tax liberalizations have reduced the chances of paying a Federal estate tax. But for some restaurant owners, even a modest estate tax bill can be painful. They simply may not have the cash available to pay it.

Fortunately, the tax law does provide some relief for their families. They may be able to postpone estate taxes. When a family inherits a restaurant or any other closely held business, it can elect to pay no estate taxes on the restaurant for five years. Then the estate can pay off the bill in equal installments over the following ten years. This, in effect, permits a family to stretch out the payment of estate taxes over 15 years. Contrast this to most other estates: The full estate tax is due nine months after the decedent's death.

In return for tax deferral, the law says that interest must be paid each year on the unpaid portion of the tax. However, there is a special break here too. The estate pays a low rate of 4% on the tax attributable to the first $1 million of closely held business property (the 4% rate is fixed; it does not change with the prime rate). The regular interest rate on tax underpayments is much higher and applies to the estate tax due on the excess.

Which estates qualify for tax deferral? The restaurant must constitute 35% of the adjusted gross estate (gross estate less expenses, debts and losses) for the estate to qualify. In addition, the restaurant owner must have operated the restaurant as either (1) a sole proprietor, (2) a partner owning 20% or more of the capital interest in a partnership or owning an interest in a partnership with 15 or fewer partners, or (3) a shareholder owning 20% or more of the voting stock in a corporation or owning stock in a corporation with 15 or fewer shareholders. Each restaurant operation in which the decedent held a qualified interest may be combined for purposes of the 35% test *if* the decedent owned at least a 20% interest.

Moreover, an additional extension may be available to you. The Government can, at its discretion, grant an extension of up to 12 months after the last installment is due to pay the remaining estate tax. To get this additional extension, the estate must show reasonable cause why the estate tax cannot be paid on time.

Caution: The 15-year tax deferral can be lost. The Government can require a family to pay all of the deferred tax if a payment is more than six months late. The family must also pay all of the deferred tax outstanding if 50% of the restaurant business is disposed of. A family can elect tax deferral by attaching a notice of election to a timely filed estate tax return. The notice must contain:

1. the amount of tax to be paid in installments,

2. the date chosen for making the first installment (no more than five years after the decedent's death),

3. the number of annual installments (no more than 10),

4. the properties shown on the estate tax return that make up the qualified business interests, and

5. the reasons why the estate is eligible for installment payments.

What To Do Now To Keep A Restaurant In The Family—And Pay No Estate Tax

An owner whose restaurant's business is growing steadily might have an estate tax problem. The biggest asset in the owner's estate will probably be the stock of the restaurant corporation. And if the restaurant corporation continues to grow, an overly large share of the owner's estate will go to the Government in estate taxes.

The owner needs something that, *for estate tax purposes only,* will freeze the value of the restaurant's stock at its current value. This can be accomplished by using a tax-free transfer. An owner can impose an estate tax freeze by issuing new stock in the restaurant corporation. Done properly, this "recapitalization" allows the owner to:

1. impose a cap on the value of the restaurant stock that's included in his taxable estate,

2. make a tax-free gift to his children of the future growth of the company stock, and

3. keep control of the restaurant.

Background: Anything left to a spouse is exempt from estate tax. Starting in 1987, up to $600,000 in assets can be left to children estate tax free. (In 1985, it's only $400,000.) By combining these two estate tax breaks, a restaurant owner and his spouse can ultimately leave $1.2 million to their children. But considering the increasing values of property, an owner's estate may well exceed that figure. Let's look at the following tax-saving idea:

> Mr. Nolan owns 1,000 shares of Restaurant Corp. voting common stock. The current value of the shares is $500,000. Nolan sets up a recapitalization plan for Restaurant Corp. The corporation issues two new types of stock: 1,000 shares of non-voting common and 1,000 shares of voting preferred stock. Nolan exchanges his common stock for the voting preferred. The voting preferred has a fixed value of $500,000 and pays an annual dividend of 8%. Nolan gives his children the new non-voting common stock.

Result: The value of the new common will rise as the value of the restaurant business rises, so all future increases in the value of the corporation go to the children. On the other hand, the value of Nolan's preferred stock stays fixed at the current $500,000 value. And through his voting rights, Nolan stays in complete control of the restaurant. He also has a right to the first $40,000 (8% of $500,000) of the restaurant's profits each year. And there's also an estate tax shelter: Nolan won't have to worry about the value of his taxable interest in the corporation being any larger than what can be sheltered from estate tax. If he dies first, he can leave the preferred stock to Mrs. Nolan estate tax free. Mrs. Nolan will be entitled to $40,000 a year for life. She can pass on the $500,000 of stock to the children tax free. If Mrs. Nolan dies first, Mr. Nolan can leave the $500,000 of stock directly to the children without any estate tax problems.

How about income taxes? A recapitalization has no income tax consequences—either to the owner or the corporation—as long as there is a business purpose behind it. The Government says that estate planning—the desire to prevent the corporation from being liquidated to pay estate taxes—qualifies as a valid business purpose

[Ltr. Rul. 8035014]. And giving children a stake in the growth of the restaurant increases their incentive to do all they can to see that the business continues to prosper.

How about gift taxes? The Revenue Service may say that the new common stock has some current value. In that case, there may be a taxable gift to the children in the form of the new common they receive. But to the extent the common stock has value, the preferred has less value. So the owner's estate tax will be reduced.

Caution: Taxpayers who have received preferred stock in a recapitalization may be subject to tax at ordinary income rates if they sell the stock [Internal Revenue Code Section 306]. But this is not a problem in Mr. Nolan's case. Reason: He does not intend to sell his preferred stock. He wants it eventually to pass to his children.

If you are interested in the benefits of freezing your estate by recapitalizing your restaurant, talk things over with your professional adviser. A recapitalization is a sophisticated move. And while the tax-saving potential may be large, there are too many things that can go wrong if you try to handle it yourself.

HOW TO GET A BIG TAX BREAK FOR SUPPORTING YOUR PARENTS—EVEN THOUGH THEY'RE NOT YOUR DEPENDENTS

A successful restaurant operation is often a family affair, with some or all of Father, Mother and the older children doing their part. But then who looks after the little ones while the rest of the family is working? Frequently, it's Grandma and Grandpa, or other relatives.

While you may not give these older relatives any cash for all the help they provide, you may still give them a financial boost by taking care of some of their bills.

Even though this help may add up to a tidy sum over the course of a year, you still may not be able to claim your older relatives— let's say your parents, for example—as tax dependents. *Reason:* Each parent has more than $1,000 of gross income and that disqualifies them as dependents. However, a slight change in the way you and your parents handle things may put you in line for a different— but still substantial—tax break.

Surprise tax winner: If you switch over to direct cash payments to your parents—instead of paying their bills—you may qualify for a valuable "child care" tax credit. (This is the credit available to working people for what they pay someone to look after their under-age-15 children.) In other words, just a single change in the way you help your parents can convert non-deductible payments toward their support into tax-saving child care payments. Here's what to do: Pay your parents a regular hourly wage for their babysitting services. *Result:* The money is still used for your parents' support, but now some of it qualifies for the child care credit.

And, for your parents, it's tax-free income. If both your parents are at least 65 years old, they owe no tax if their gross income subject to tax is less than $7,400. If one is under 65, no tax is owed if their gross income subject to tax is less than $6,400; if both are, it's $5,400.

Note: The tax-free amounts above are based on 1984 figures. The figures are scheduled to change in 1985 due to indexing, a new system that pegs the personal exemption, zero bracket amounts, and tax rate brackets, to increases in the Consumer Price Index.

And although the payments are considered earnings, chances are your age 65-to-70 parents won't lose any Social Security benefits. *Reason:* A Social Security recipient between those ages is allowed to earn money without losing benefits. In 1984, a recipient between those ages could have earned $6,960.

HOW PUTTING YOUR SPOUSE ON THE PAYROLL CAN PAY OFF IN THOUSANDS OF DOLLARS IN EXTRA DEDUCTIONS

The owners of many family-run restaurants may be missing out needlessly on tax deductions. With a simple change in their payroll setup, they may be able to pick up $4,000 or more in extra deductions. Here's a typical example:

> Mr. Brown owns a restaurant and Mrs. Brown works at home. But two or three times a week she comes in to the restaurant to help with the bookkeeping. She also fills in when anybody on the staff is out sick or on vacation.

Mr. Brown has never paid Mrs. Brown a salary for the work she's done. He figures there is nothing to gain by paying her a salary. The money simply goes from his pocket to hers. Nor does he pick up any tax advantages. They file a joint tax return. So half of his income is taxed to her—and vice versa—regardless of who earns it.

Mr. Brown is right about the joint return, but that's only part of the tax story. However, there's a basic tax strategy. Mr. Brown should put Mrs. Brown on the restaurant payroll as a restaurant employee. That way, the Browns can claim two new deductions on their joint return that they are not entitled to now. *Result:* A lower taxable income on the Browns' joint return.

Deduction #1: Individual Retirement Account. Mr. Brown has an existing IRA. But as long as Mrs. Brown is a "non-working" spouse, the most Brown can contribute and deduct for himself and Mrs. Brown is $2,250 annually. Let's look at the following.

> *Idea In Action:* When Mr. Brown puts his wife on the payroll, Mrs. Brown is able to set up and contribute to her own IRA. They can deduct up to $2,000 *each* to an IRA. Total annual deduction: $4,000—$1,750 more than before.

If you're self-employed, making your wife a bona fide employee costs nothing extra. Wages paid to your spouse are exempt from Social Security tax. And although your wife's wages are taxable to her, you get an offsetting business deduction for the wages paid. So her salary stays in the family, and her IRA money goes toward retirement.

If your restaurant is incorporated, wages paid to your spouse are subject to Social Security tax and other local payroll taxes. If your wages are now fully subject to Social Security tax (under $37,800 in 1984), the added expense will be small. But if some of your salary is exempt from Social Security tax, you will end up paying higher Social Security taxes. However, you will also be in line for—

Deduction #2: Marriage penalty deduction. A working couple is entitled to a special deduction to offset something called the "marriage penalty." The joint income of a working couple is taxed more heavily if they are married than if they are not. However, married couples are allowed a deduction of 10% of the lower earning spouse's income, up to a maximum deduction of $3,000. Of course, as a non-working spouse, Mrs. Brown has no earnings and the Browns have no marriage penalty deduction.

> *Idea In Action:* If Brown's restaurant is incorporated, the Browns are in line for a marriage penalty deduction when Mrs. Brown goes on the payroll. For example, let's say the restaurant pays Mrs. Brown $20,000 over the course of the year (and correspondingly decreases Mr. Brown's salary). Result: The Browns are entitled to a $2,000 marriage penalty deduction.

Important point: If Brown's restaurant is run as a sole proprietorship, the Browns can't get a marriage penalty deduction; the tax law denies the deduction for amounts paid by a self-employed taxpayer to his working spouse. Here's a dollars-and-cents payoff. Let's say the Brown's taxable income has been running around $60,000 a year. With Mrs. Brown on the payroll, the Browns pick up $3,750 in extra deductions ($1,750 plus $2,000).

HOW TO NAIL DOWN TOP TAX DEDUCTIONS WHEN YOU TAKE YOUR SPOUSE ALONG ON A CONVENTION OR BUSINESS TRIP

Let's say you and your spouse are going to attend a restaurant convention or trade show. As long as your primary reason for the trip is restaurant business, you are entitled to tax breaks—even though you take a vacation side trip.

Your expenses: You can deduct your cost of getting to and from the convention site. In addition, you are entitled to deduct your meals and lodging while at the convention. The cost of any vacation side trip is, of course, a nondeductible personal expense.

Your spouse's expenses: Her expenses are also deductible if she's your partner in the restaurant business. Reason: The tax rule is that a spouse's expenses are deductible if "the wife's presence on the trip has a bona fide business purpose" [Reg. §1.162-2(c)]. But if your spouse is not involved in the restaurant and she's just coming along to keep you company and do some vacationing, her expenses are not deductible. Nevertheless, you are still entitled to these government tax-cutters. Despite the tough general rule, the Government allows you to deduct some or all of the cost of your spouse's transportation, meals and lodging.

Getting there and back: Let's say you and your spouse are flying to a convention. If you travel by air and get a bargain rate for two travelers, you can still deduct what it would have cost you to go alone.

And it's even better if you drive to the convention. Then, the entire cost of your transportation is deductible. Reason: You would have spent the same amount whether or not your spouse accompanied you.

Meals and lodging: As with your air fare, you can deduct the cost of a single room even though one-half the cost of a double room is less. As a general rule, however, your spouse's meals are not deductible. However, there is a tax-saving exception. You may be able to deduct your spouse's meal when she comes with you to a business lunch or dinner. It can be strictly a social affair. The Government requires that the atmosphere be quiet and conducive to business— it's not necessary that business actually be discussed.

THIRTEEN DOLLAR-SAVING TAX CREDITS RESTAURANT OWNERS COMMONLY OVERLOOK

Most restaurant owners know that the tax law, in effect, gives them a big price discount on kitchen equipment and other big-ticket items they purchase for their restaurants. This discount comes by way of the so-called 10% investment credit. This credit is a dollar-for-dollar reduction in an owner's tax bill, equal to 10% of the cost of equipment purchased during the year. So, at tax return time, the owner receives his price discount in the form of tax savings. And there's another tax surprise.

What restaurant owners may not be aware of is that some of the smaller items they buy for their restaurants also qualify for the investment credit. And while the credit for each of the items may be much smaller than the one for say, a convection oven for their kitchen, all those credits can add up to big tax savings.

Here are thirteen of the most common—and most commonly overlooked—tax-savers that are generally available to restaurant owners the first year that the property is put into use:

1. The investment credit is available for booths for customer seating [Senate Finance Committee Report No. 95-1263].

2. Wall-to-wall carpeting is generally ineligible for the credit, but it is eligible when the carpeting is fastened to wood strips that are nailed along the wall [Rev. Rul. 67-349, 1967-2 CB 48].

3. Movable wall partitions qualify for the credit if they are not made a permanent part of the building [Rev. Rul. 75-178, 1975-1 CB 9].

4. Wall panel inserts designed to hold condiments and beverage bars may both be eligible [Senate Finance Committee Report No. 95-1263].

5. The cost of updating or redecorating a restaurant's dining room and kitchen may qualify for the investment credit [Senate Finance Committee Report No. 95-1263].

6. Special electrical or plumbing connections qualify if they are necessary for and used directly with specific items of equipment (e.g., freezers) [Rev. Rul. 66-299, 1966-2 CB 14].

7. Vending machines, such as those that dispense cigarettes, are eligible for the credit [Reg. 1.48-1(c)].

8. Outside restaurant ornamentation, like false balconies,

qualifies. The ornamentation must be nonessential to the operation or maintenance of the building [Senate Finance Committee Report No. 95-1263].

9. Display racks and shelves are eligible for the 10% investment credit [Reg. 1.48-1(c)].

10. Leased new equipment, a water softener unit, for instance, qualifies for the credit, if the lessor agrees to pass the credit through to the restaurant owner [I.R.C. 48(d)]. (Note: The credit cannot be obtained for leased property that was used beforehand.)

11. Lighting used to illuminate the exterior of the restaurant (though not the parking lot), qualifies [Senate Finance Committee Report No. 95-1263].

12. Floor tiles applied with adhesives qualify for the investment credit [Senate Finance Committee Report No. 95-1263].

13. Other items that are used in connection with the restaurant business, like a stereo system, intercom system, fire extinguisher and the like, qualify for the same reasons kitchen equipment does.

The 10% investment credit is also available for *used* property. However, only $125,000 ($150,000 beginning in 1988) of the cost of such property is eligible for the credit. (There is no dollar limit on the cost of new property eligible for the credit.)

Important: This is not a complete list of restaurant purchases that can qualify for the investment credit. There are many more. So where there's a question about a particular item, be sure to check with the restaurant's tax adviser.

WHY LEASING PROPERTY TO YOUR RESTAURANT MAY BE A GOOD WAY TO NAIL DOWN TAX-SHELTERED PROFITS

Restaurant earnings paid out as dividends are taxed twice—once at the corporate level and again at the individual. They are not deductible on the restaurant's return. That's why the owner of a corporation wants to grab each and every opportunity to pay out corporate earnings that the corporation can deduct. For instance, a bonus that is tied into restaurant earnings is deductible as a reasonable business expense. Here's what to do:

If your restaurant corporation is about to buy a building or piece of equipment, maybe it should think about leasing instead—from you. If the lease is based partly on restaurant revenue, the rents paid to you are, in effect, deductible earnings. The following is a typical situation.

> Country Kitchen, Inc. needs a banquet facility. Instead of Country Kitchen buying the building, the restaurant's shareholders, Mr. and Mrs. Polk, buy the lot, build the new banquet hall and then lease it to the restaurant.
>
> Under the terms of the long-term lease, Country Kitchen, Inc. pays the Polks an annual rent of $30,000 plus a percentage of the restaurant's annual gross revenue. And the restaurant takes a deduction for the full amount—fixed payment plus percentage. (Over the course of the lease, the gross revenues of the restaurant should grow, and the percentage payments should grow along with it.)

Will this kind of lease arrangement be tagged a disguised dividend by the Government? Not as long as certain guidelines are followed. For example, there must be a legitimate business purpose behind the leasing arrangement (e.g., the restaurant cannot secure reasonable finance terms on its own). And the lease terms must be reasonable. Percentage leases are common in commercial real estate, but you can't go overboard. You must deal with your corporation at arms length. That means the rent terms must be comparable to what you would be able to negotiate with an outside tenant.

Ask your adviser: To get an idea of what the guidelines are in these types of lease arrangements, your tax adviser may want to take a look at a recent case, *Roman Systems, Ltd.*, that's the subject of the following article.

Creative Lease Setup Leads To Bigger Deductions

It's not uncommon for a restaurant corporation to have trouble obtaining a lease on its own. Landlords often want the restaurant's shareholders to assume personal liability for the lease. One restaurant figured out how to bypass the problem in a way that allowed the restaurant to pass earnings to its shareholders free of corporate income taxes.

> **Recent case:** Roman Systems, Ltd., a restaurant corporation, was unable to enter into a lease. Reason: Roman Systems' credit was not good enough, and four of its six shareholders were unwilling to guarantee payment of rent.

Plan of attack: The two willing shareholders formed a partnership—

Two Romans—and entered into the lease with the landlord. Roman Systems then sublet the restaurant from Two Romans for a higher rental than the partnership paid to the landlord.

Result: The partners were personally liable to the lessor. But in exchange for assuming this risk, they received extra rent from Roman Systems. Ltd.

The corporation took a deduction for the higher lease payments to Two Romans. But the Revenue Service argued that the rent paid to Two Romans did not reflect the fair market value of the leased building. According to the Revenue Service, the fair rental value—determined by arms length bargaining between strangers—was the amount that Two Romans paid the lessor. So the excess rental was not really rent. It was a way to siphon off the corporation's profits to the two risk-assuming partners. Result: No deduction for the excess. But the Tax Court said the rent was fully deductible since:

> The fair rental value of the building is not determined solely by the rent paid by Two Romans. *Reason:* The lessor undoubtedly would have charged the corporation a higher rent since it was a higher credit risk. What's more, the rent charged Roman Systems by Two Romans was in line with the rent paid by other restaurants. Since the sublease had a legitimate business purpose and the amount of the rent was reasonable, Roman systems can deduct the full amount of rent paid [Roman Systems, Ltd., TC memo 1981-273].

HOW YOU CAN GET A TAX-FREE, INTEREST-FREE LOAN FROM AN UNEXPECTED SOURCE

You can, in effect, borrow money from your Individual Retirement Account—and do it tax free and interest free. That may come as a surprise: As a general rule, the tax law prohibits borrowing from an IRA. Loans are treated as "premature distributions," subject to a 10% penalty tax, as well as the regular income tax on distributions.

However, in two situations, the tax law does permit you to have access to your IRA funds on a tax-free, short-term basis. Technically speaking, these are not considered loans, so they don't violate the prohibition against borrowing. But the bottom line is that you do get temporary use of your money.

Loan Strategy #1.
You can roll over part or all of the funds from one IRA into another IRA. The key here is that you have 60 days to complete the

rollover. In the meanwhile, you can put the funds to any use you want. For example:

> Smith, age 40, has an IRA of $5,000. Smith gets hit with a $5,000 medical emergency and does not have the cash at hand to pay the bill. Smith has a $10,000 Government bond maturing in 45 days, but he can't wait that long.
>
> Therefore, Smith makes a withdrawal from the IRA and pays the medical bill. Within 60 days, he receives the bond proceeds and deposits an amount equal to his original IRA withdrawal into an IRA at his bank.

Result: Smith gets the cash from his IRA to pay a pressing bill. And because Smith rolled his IRA withdrawal over into another IRA within 60 days, it's tax free. There is no penalty tax and no regular income tax. (Note: Rollovers from one IRA to another generally are permitted only once in a one-year period and, of course, there is no deduction for the rollover.)

Loan Strategy #2.

An IRA withdrawal is "premature" only if you are under 59½. If you are 59½ or older, there is no penalty tax. The withdrawal is, of course, subject to the regular income tax. However, if the withdrawal doesn't exceed $2,000, you can redeposit the money by the tax return due date for the year of the withdrawal and get a standard IRA deduction that offsets your taxable distribution (assuming you are still working and eligible to make IRA contributions). *Net result:* The tax-free use of your money for much longer than 60 days.

> *Example:* Jones, age 60, promised his son a home computer as a graduation present but is short of cash. So, Jones withdraws $2,000 (or any lesser amount) from his IRA on July 1 and uses it to pay for the home computer. Then on or before April 15, 1985, he puts the money back in his IRA.

Result: Since Jones is over age 59½, there is no penalty tax on the IRA withdrawal. But he does have to report the $2,000 withdrawal on his tax return for that year as a regular IRA distribution.

However, Jones has also made an IRA contribution—even though the "contribution" was merely a redeposit of the funds withdrawn earlier. And, because he made this contribution before the due date of his tax return for the year, he can claim a $2,000 deduction for the contribution on his return (of course he cannot make any other IRA contributions for that year). So the deduction will wash out the taxable income he has on the July withdrawal—making it effectively tax free. (Jones can, of course, withdraw more than $2,000, but he won't be able to shelter the amount in excess of $2,000 with an IRA deduction.)

HOW TO PUT MONEY INTO YOUR RESTAURANT NOW SO YOU CAN GET A TAX-FREE REPAYMENT LATER

Your incorporated restaurant may need some cash. It could get the money from a bank—but the interest rates would be too high. So instead, you loan the necessary money to the restaurant and benefit from a tax-savings. If the transaction is a bona fide loan—and you handle things right—you'll pay no tax on the restaurant's repayment. (You will owe tax on interest you receive.) Otherwise, the Government may say your "loan" is really a capital contribution. That would make the repayment a fully taxable dividend. Let's look at the following example of a winning case:

> Mr. C, the president and sole owner of C, Inc., loaned his company money and charged interest. The company used the advance to buy inventory in quantity at bargain prices. The company's debt was evidenced by a demand note, which made C a general creditor of the company. The company made repayments of the principal and also paid interest on the loan. He reported the interest as interest income on his return and the company deducted the interest on its income tax return.

The Government said the transaction was a contribution to capital, so the repayments were taxable dividends to C. This was a taxpayer victory since a Federal District Court said that the advance was a loan, not a capital contribution. The company had a valid business purpose for borrowing from C instead of a bank—he charged lower interest. And C was not putting his money at risk. He was a general creditor of the company (the company was considered a good credit risk by the banks). Granted, there was no fixed period for repayment and no collateral. But those facts are not that important. C controlled the company and he knew he would be repaid [Culbersons, Inc., 45 AFTR2d 80-313].

How To Avoid A Government Hassle

When you set up the loan to your restaurant corporation, keep an eye on the following points. They are the factors the courts say work in your favor—they are characteristics of a debt and help you to nail down loan tax treatment.

1. Instrument's name and treatment are common to bond-like securities;

2. Non-subordination to claims of other creditors;

3. Fixed maturity date in reasonable future;

4. Non-convertibility into stock;

5. No voting rights;

6. Valid business purpose (not tax avoidance); and a

7. Reasonable ratio of debt securities to stock.

This leads us to the question of: What's a reasonable ratio? Three-to-one is usually considered safe. But this is only a rule of thumb—and the same is true of the other factors. There's no absolute guarantee that the presence (or absence) of any of these factors will decide the issue. So you'll want to get expert advice before making a loan to your company.

How The Tax Law Can Help You Get The Money You Need To Open Another Restaurant

The tax law contains a special provision—Section 1244—that can help restaurant owners get the capital they need for expansion. Section 1244 allows a restaurant corporation to issue stock with built-in protection. You can offer potential backers stock that carries a kind of tax insurance. And you can make this offer at no cost to your restaurant. Uncle Sam picks up the tab.

To see how restaurants and investors alike can profit from Sec. 1244, let's check out a typical situation:

> Halfpenny Restaurant, Inc. wants to open another restaurant. It must issue more stock to raise capital. Halfpenny has already lined up a number of possible investors. Brown, for example, is considering putting up $75,000. He sees Halfpenny as having plenty of long-term potential, but he's still reluctant to give the deal the go-ahead.

Here's where Sec. 1244 comes in. Halfpenny issues stock that qualifies under Sec. 1244 and informs Brown of that fact. This one move may be just the edge that swings Brown in the restaurant's favor because, with Sec. 1244, Brown has tax insurance: (1) If Brown sells his stock a few years down the road at a profit, he gets low-taxed long-term capital gain treatment. But (2) if the worst happens and the investment doesn't pan out, Brown can write off his loss as a dollar-for-dollar deduction against ordinary income. He doesn't have to settle for a limited capital loss deduction. Brown can write off his full $75,000 investment if the stock becomes worthless. (The deduction limit is $100,000 for joint filers, $50,000 for singles.)

Without Sec. 1244, the loss story is completely different. In any one year, Brown must use $6,000 of his long-term capital loss on the stock to get a maximum deduction of $3,000 against ordinary income. The rest has to be carried over to future years. And if the loss is offset against ordinary income, it will take Brown thirteen years to recover his investment. That doesn't help him when he needs help the most—at the time he suffers the loss.

Obviously, Sec. 1244 puts Brown in a much better tax position. And it's exactly the kind of tax sweetener that can win investors for your restaurant.

The key question is how can my restaurant issue stock that qualifies under Sec. 1244? There is very little you have to do. It's practically automatic. There's really only one major requirement. Your stock issue under Sec. 1244 cannot exceed $1,000,000, less the amount of stock that's already outstanding. This dollar figure is based on the amount of property and money received for the stock, plus contributions to capital and paid-in surplus.

That's it! Your restaurant doesn't have to file anything with the Government or adopt any sort of formal Sec. 1244 plan. Of course, considering what's at stake, you'll want to talk things over with your professional adviser before you go ahead and issue the new stock.

How You Can Write Off The Cost Of Checking Up On Your Competition

You may be thinking of making major changes in your menu. Or maybe you are redecorating the place. Or perhaps you are looking for a new chef for your kitchen or new entertainers for your cocktail lounge.

What do these situations have in common? Simply this: Before making any decision on these matters, you may want to check out what your competitors are doing. And the cost of checking out your competition may be a deductible travel expense. You can write off the cost of travel that qualifies as an "ordinary and necessary business expense." This should, of course, include your automobile costs in checking up on Sam's Bar and Grill across town or Chez Pierre out in the suburbs. It may also cover your travel costs (including meals and lodging) when you go out of town overnight. For example, here's what actually happened in a recent case.

Mr. Russo was the manager of Garden Square Bowling Lanes. Garden Square consisted of a cocktail lounge, restaurant, coffee shop, banquet facilities and bowling lanes. One of Russo's duties was to sign up entertainers for the cocktail lounge. He spent 35 Saturday evenings in one year visiting other lounges in search of talent. He also paid monthly visits to other bowling centers to check out their business operations. And Russo made trips to San Diego and Las Vegas to view bowling tournaments [Russo, TC Memo 1982-248].

Russo's travel costs were fully deductible. The Tax Court said that the costs were an ordinary and necessary business expense for Russo since the trips had a sufficient connection with his responsibilities as manager of Garden Square.

Important: You must keep adequate records to back up your travel deductions in case of an audit. This means a contemporaneous diary of where you travel, when, for what business purpose and the amount of the expense, supported by receipts for your lodging and any other expense over $25.

HOW A RESTAURANT MAY BE ABLE TO GIVE EMPLOYEES BIGGER PAYCHECKS AT NO EXTRA COST

Would you like to be able to give your lower-paid employees—dishwashers and kitchen helpers, for example—more take-home pay at no cost to you? Of course, you would. And that's exactly what you can do, thanks to a special tax break. The tax law gives an income tax credit—called the earned income credit—to low-income workers (those earning less than $10,000) who have dependent children living with them. Your accountant (or whoever does the books) can give them the credit in advance via reduced withholding. The workers don't have to wait until they file their tax return. The result is more take-home pay without your raising their pay. Even more remarkable: If the credit exceeds what's withheld for income taxes, the worker gets an advance payment of the credit in each paycheck from the restaurant.

"That's fine for them" you might say, "but what about the restaurant? How does it get reimbursed for paying the advance?"

Again, it doesn't cost the restaurant anything. Any advance credit it pays out is used to offset its payroll tax liability. The payments offset other income tax withholding, the employees' share of Social Security tax, and the restaurant's share of Social Security tax, in that order. If the advances exceed the restaurant's total payroll tax bill, it may either (1) uniformly reduce advance payments to all employees, or (2) treat the excess as an advance payment of its own income tax bill.

How to handle it:

Your employees who qualify for advance payments file a completed Form W-5 with the restaurant. It's a simple form. Your accountant figures the amount of each employee's advance from the Government's Advanced Earned Income Credit Payment Table and adds the proper amount to the employee's pay. Your accountant then notes on payroll tax Form 941 that your restaurant has made advanced earned income credit payments and deduct the advances from the payroll tax due. (Note: An advance doesn't count as wages, so there's no payroll tax on it.)

You will want to keep the following questions and answers in mind:

Question. What if the advance earned income credit payments turn out to be bigger than the actual credit the employee is entitled to on his return?

Answer. That's the employee's problem. Your restaurant shows the total amount of advance payments it makes during the year on the employee's Form W-2. The employee is liable for any excess when he files his tax return.

Question. I pay my waiters and waitresses minimum wage too. Will they qualify for this break?

Answer. Probably not, if they receive tips. But if their wages and tips come to less than $10,000 for the year, they can qualify just like anyone else.

Remember: If an employee files a Form W-5 with your restaurant, you *must* make advance payments. But it is up to the employee to file the form each year. You are not obligated to take any action until the employee does file. Of course, you may want to let your employees know about this tax break. If so, the easiest thing to do is distribute Form W-5 to the employees. It will let them know if they qualify for the credit.

Why Refresher Courses Have Built-In Tax Savings

If you're one of the many restaurant owners who each summer mix a little pleasure with brushing up on trends in the restaurant business, don't overlook the tax savings inherent in taking a refresher course. You can deduct the cost of education that's undertaken to maintain or improve your business skills. A restaurant management course is an example.

Exactly what expenses are deductible? First, you can deduct your direct costs, including books, tuition and the like. In addition, you can deduct the cost of transportation plus—if you must travel away from home overnight—the cost of meals and lodging away from home. The following situations may influence some of your decisions regarding travel.

Your restaurant is located in Chicago. The courses you want to take are being given in Chicago and Philadelphia. If you go to Philadelphia to take the courses, will you forfeit your deduction for travel, meals and lodging?

Answer: No. You can pick and choose the education center that you prefer.

How about sightseeing? While you're in Philadelphia, you expect to do some sightseeing and some visiting—you have a lot of friends and business acquaintances in the area. How will this affect your deduction?

Answer: As long as your primary reason for going is to take the courses, your deductions won't suffer. However, the actual cost of visiting and sightseeing comes out of your own pocket—it's not deductible. On the other hand, if your primary reason for going to Philadelphia is sightseeing and visiting, with a refresher course thrown in on the side, you can deduct only the actual cost of attending the course. Everything else, i.e., travel, meals, and lodging, is nondeductible.

> Mr. Smith, a salesman, enrolled in a university-sponsored continuing education travel program. The objective of the program was to promote interpersonal effectiveness in business and professional settings. It was not geared to any particular occupation. The program held three hours of workshops and lectures each day. And participants were free to choose which sessions they'd attend. Smith took his wife and children on the trip and spent two hours per day at the sessions, leaving the remainder of the time for recreational and sightseeing activities.

Tax result: Smith's trip was essentially for recreation. He spent most of his time on personal pursuits and his family accompanied him. Therefore, his travel, meals and lodging are not deductible. However, the expenditures directly allocable to education—the tuition, books and so forth—are deductible [Rev. Rul. 84-55, IRB 1984-16].

In addition to keeping a close eye on the time spent on business versus pleasure, you'll also want to keep a detailed record of all your education expenses. While a good memory may help you pass the courses you are taking, it—without proof—won't nail down your deductions if your return is audited.

HOW TO MAKE SURE THE RESTAURANT GETS THE BENEFITS OF A CORPORATE SETUP

A restaurant owner usually incorporates to protect himself from restaurant debts and to get the tax breaks that go with the corporate form. So it would be a shame if, after going to all the trouble of incorporating, the owner ends up with none of these benefits. But it happens practically every day and can mean disaster for owners. Moreover, all it takes is a few slipups and a court will rule that the corporation is invalid. *Result:* The owner is stuck with the corporation's debts and owes a big bill for back taxes. Let's see what can occur:

> Mr. Everett incorporated his retail business. Everett engaged James G. Smith to do advertising for his business. When the contract with Smith was drawn up, Everett did not mention that the business was incorporated. In fact, he personally paid the first bill. Then, Everett, Inc. had financial difficulties. The second bill went unpaid. When Smith sued, Everett claimed that he was protected from personal liability because his corporation had contracted for the advertising.
>
> Everett did not inform Smith that he was acting on behalf of his corporation when he signed the contract. Therefore, said the Court, he is personally liable for the fees—even though Everett had incorporated and Smith's services were valid corporate expenditures [James G. Smith & Associates, Inc. v. Everett (App. Ct. Ohio 1982) 439NE2d 932].

Don't let it happen to you: Make sure you don't end up holding the corporate bag: If you want the benefits of a restaurant corporation, make sure you look, act and sound like a corporation. For the most part, this is merely a matter of formalities—making sure all the i's are dotted and the t's are crossed. As we've seen, failure to comply with these formalities can prove very costly.

Here is a list of some of the more important things a restaurant owner can do to make sure his corporation is treated like one.

Organizing A Restaurant Corporation

- See that Articles of Incorporation are properly drafted, signed and filed with the appropriate state agency;

- If a partnership existed prior to the incorporation, file a formal notice of partnership dissolution and notify the partnership's creditors;

- Hold a shareholders' meeting and elect a Board of Directors;

- The Board of Directors should hold an organizational meeting and elect officers, adopt by-laws, issue stock and adopt the corporate seal;

- Change letterheads and other printed forms and stationery to reflect the corporate name;

- Open a bank account in the corporate name and deposit all sums received on and after the day of incorporation in that account;

- Revise the restaurant's listings in business and telephone directories to reflect the corporate name;

- All insurance, such as fire and public liability, should be assigned or reissued to the corporation;

- All contracts and leases should be modified to indicate that the corporation is now the contracting party (i.e., that the restaurant owner is only acting as agent for the corporation); and

- Apply to the Government for a Federal employer's identification number for the corporation.

How To Operate As A Corporation

- Make sure all major transactions of the corporation are included in the corporate minutes;

- Hold annual stockholders meetings to elect directors for the following year and approve acts of the directors for the previous year;

- Keep the accounting records of the corporation separate and apart from the records of the shareholders and directors;

- Keep the stock register up to date and complete with all stock certificates signed and distributed;

- Maintain proper documentation for all of the corporation's employee benefit plans, buy-sell agreements, and the like.

Important: Some people say incorporation can be a do-it-yourself affair; there are kits you can buy that are designed to help you incorporate your business. *This is not recommended.* The laws are too complicated and the stakes are too high. Get a reputable attorney and accountant and follow their advice.

HOW TO USE A WELL-DRAWN CORPORATE MINUTE BOOK TO ELIMINATE RISKS IN THE INCORPORATED POCKETBOOK

The minute book may be one of the most important—and often overlooked—records kept by an incorporated restaurant. It contains the minutes of the Board of Directors' and stockholders' meetings. As an owner of your restaurant corporation, the corporate minutes are within your control. Carefully drawn and recorded, they can back the restaurant up when settling differences with the Revenue Service.

Here are some of the areas which are particularly susceptible to investigation by the Government. Your corporate minute book can help make the difference.

Restaurant-owner's compensation: Is it reasonable? The minutes can state that the salary paid to an owner-employee of the restaurant corporation is based on both his ability to run the day-to-day business of the restaurant, and on the responsibilities he assumes. Minutes can also justify salary increases by spelling out increased productivity and exceptional managerial skills.

Corporate leases: To help nail down the restaurant's deductions for rent, a corporate resolution formally approving the terms of the lease should appear in the minutes, together with a copy of the lease.

Accumulation of earnings: Are they unreasonable? Generally speaking, many restaurants don't have this concern. Reason: A restaurant can accumulate $250,000 of earnings without being hit with a penalty tax. But a larger restaurant operation may be faced with the problem *unless* it can show a valid business purpose for the over $250,000 accumulation. The minutes can set out the precise reasons why the accumulations were necessary (e.g., restaurant expansion, working capital, or to protect the business during slow periods).

Retirement plans: Including your restaurant corporation's qualified profit-sharing or pension plan in the minutes provides an examining agent with all the first-hand proof he or she needs to see how the plan is set up and operating. The minutes can indicate that the plan is for the benefit of all the restaurant's employees and doesn't discriminate in favor of the restaurant owner.

These are just some of the situations where well-drawn minutes can play a vital role. There are many others. For instance, the minute book can reflect the basis of the corporation's group-term insurance plan, and any deferred compensation plans for the restaurant owner. Minutes can specify what and who are covered by the restaurant's medical reimbursement plan, and the justifications of any buy-sell agreement covering retirement, death or disability of an owner-employee of the restaurant. And minutes are particularly useful in establishing the arm's length character of business transactions between, let's say, your restaurant corporation and a shareholder.

However, minutes won't come to the rescue of a corporation that says one thing in the minutes and does exactly the opposite. The Revenue Service will look through form to the substance of corporate activity when it challenges a deduction. In order to avoid problems, draw your minutes accurately and precisely. Let your tax adviser look them over before they are recorded to make sure their language squares with the corporate and tax results you want—or are required—to attain. And make sure they are not just paid lip service.

Index